QUALITY:
THE REFERENCE BOOK FOR GOVERNMENT CONTRACTS

by
Robert E. Schomberg

BOOK PUBLISHERS, INC.
P.O. BOX 21492
TAMPA, FLORIDA 33622

Typesetting: Presentation Graphics

Printed in the United States of America

Library of Congress Cataloging-in-Publication Data

Schomberg, Robert E., 1937-
Quality: the reference book for government contracts.

Includes index.
1. Public contracts--United States.
I. Title.
KF849.S36 1988 346.73'023 88-30430
ISBN 0-931541-13-1 347.30623

CONTENTS

PREFACE

The goal of this book is to present a comprehensive study of the quality requirements and specifications of government contracts. The following programs form the quality portions of all government (military) contracts.

1. MIL-Q-9858A - Military Specification - Quality Program Requirements.
2. MIL-HDBK-H50 - Handbook - Evaluation of a Contractor's Quality Program.
3. MIL-I-45208A - Military Specification - Inspection System Requirements.
4. MIL-HDBK-H51 - Handbook - Evaluation of a Contractor's Inspection System.
5. MIL-STD-45662A - Military Standard - Calibration Systems Requirements.
6. MIL-HDBK-H52A - Military Handbook - Evaluation of a Contractor's Calibration System.
7. AQAP-1 - NATO Requirements for an Industrial Quality Control System.
8. AQAP-4 - NATO Inspection System Requirements for Industry.
9. AQAP-6 - NATO Measurement and Calibration Systems Requirements for Industry.
10. AQAP-9 - NATO Basic Inspection Requirements for Industry.
11. NASA (National Aeronautics and Space Administration).
    a. NHB 5300.4(1B) - Equivalent to MIL-Q-985A.
    b. NHB 5300.4(1C) - Equivalent to MIL-I-45208A.
    c. NHB 5300.4(1D-2) - Space Shuttle Program.

Many defense contractors and contractors' personnel have expressed their concern as to the alleged ambiguity of the above quality programs and the requirements of those programs. In this book we provide a step-by-step study of the requirements, and show the inter-relationship of these requirements.

At present, there is no contractual requirement for the implementation of the military handbooks that supplement the programs. Contractors should obtain copies of these handbooks to understand how the government assures itself that the products and services it is purchasing, meet the requirements and specifications of a government contract.

References to DLAM 8200.1, the Defense In-Plant Quality Program, are made in this book. This Department of Defense (DoD) manual was prepared by the Defense Logistics Agency (DLA), and is distributed to all government personnel performing Contract Quality Assurance (CQA) at all government contractor facilities. This manual was created to help all government personnel understand the quality requirements of the Federal Acquisition Regulation (FAR). This manual should be required reading for all contractors' personnel and for companies who would like to obtain government contracts.

The beginning chapters of this book will give a brief history of the government contracting system, the contract, the acquisition process, how to obtain bidding lists, how to obtain government publications and specifications, the reason for the need for a documented and approved quality system, the FAR, and finally, the formatting of a quality manual that will meet the requirements of a contract.

The terms *quality/inspection manual,* and *quality and/or inspection* as used in this book refer to the requirements of MIL-Q-9858A, MIL-I-45208A, NASA and NATO quality inspection system programs. In Table 1, page 29, a conversion chart of quality requirements depicts the relationship of the various quality programs and inspection systems that make up the quality requirements of government contracts.

HISTORY OF GOVERNMENT CONTRACTING

A brief history of the government (civilian and military) acquisition system is presented here, to give the reader insight into the reason why many people consider the government acquisition (purchasing) system a morass of bureaucratic red tape.

The government purchasing system is an elaborate operation, which in its present form is the product of an evolutionary development spanning a period of over two hundred years. During this period, the acquisition system has acquired a sophistication unparalleled in history. This development did not happen overnight, suddenly, or without opposition.

During the American Revolutionary War, the acquisition of supplies and material in support of the young American Military Forces (Militia), was frequently accomplished by local requisitions. For example, a paper (script) was given to a merchant or farmer promising to pay for the goods or services so requisitioned. This method of acquiring the needed goods and supplies was derived principally from the ingenuity of the individual field commander and his troops. This included bartering for, or finding food, clothing and shelter.

In 1789, Congress established the Department of War for the administration of military (ground and sea) affairs. In the same year, Congress established the Treasury Department in order to purchase supplies and negotiate contracts for the Continental Army.

With the enactment of the Purveyor of Public Supplies Act in 1798, the Treasury Department became the government's first recognized purchasing agent. Within this grant of authority was the responsibility to procure all of the necessary arms needed to support the new nations, armed military forces, and all supplies needed for the general service use (GSA) of the United States of America.

By 1798, Congress recognized the growing importance of the naval forces and established a separate Department of the Navy. Congress then decreed, that from that time on, all purchases and contracts for supplies and services for the military would be made by, or under the direction of, the chief officers of the respective departments of the Army and Navy. The Treasury Department no longer served as the sole purchasing agent for the government of the United States. The new role of the Treasury Department was to provide the means for the purchasing of the stores and supplies required by the military services.

The fact that the Secretaries of the Army and Navy and their respective staffs were now in a position to procure stores and supplies directly for their respective branches of the armed services, gave these people and special interest groups a tremendous amount of power. This power was due to the ability of these groups to disperse vast sums of public funds. This led to such widespread abuse that by 1808 Congress enacted legislation that forbade any member of the government, which included the Executive and Legislative branches, from deriving any benefits from the purchasing of supplies and services, civilian and military.

In 1809, Congress imposed an additional restriction, whereby, *formal advertising* would be required in the acquisition of supplies and services for any branch of the United States Government.

This was the first of many acts Congress enacted in order to effectively control the expenditure of public funds. This particular statute required all purchases and contracts made by, or at the direction of, the Secretaries of the Army and Navy, to be made by open purchase order or by formal advertisement. The purpose of this statute was to prevent the granting of special consideration to any individual or group of individuals.

In the years to follow, Congress periodically enacted additional legislation for the purpose of protecting the government and the people of the United States from the evils of corruption. The problem did not attain major proportions during the period from the Revolutionary War to 1861, as the nation's armed forces were so small, that acquisition requirements were insignificant. However, this was not the case within the civilian sector of the government, where misuse was growing rampant.

When it became certain that those states that was to comprise the Confederacy, were going to secede from the Union, prior to, and during the outbreak of the Civil War hostilities, military procurement assumed major proportions. For the first time in our history, military procurement became big business. Congress, in order to establish a fundamental procedure for military procurement, on the 2nd of March 1861, enacted the *Civil Sundry Appropriation Act*. This Act remained in force until the 19th of February, 1948, when Congress enacted the *Armed Services Procurement Act* (ASPR). During this period, all government procurement policies including those of the military establishment, were of prime concern to both Executive and Congressional commissions that were established in order to investigate and recommend new methods for controlling, effectively, the procurement of supplies and services for the federal government. Many different recommendations were made to improve the government acquisition system. There prevailed a general consensus within these commissions that a higher degree of centralized procurement was required. Formal advertising, for bids, was the general consensus of these commissions. In 1874 and again in 1878, Congress passed several important amendments to the Civil Sundry Appropriation Act of 1861. Congress redesignated it as Section 3709 of the Revised Statutes of the United States. In 1910, Congress enacted another amendment to the Revised Statute 3709. Formal advertising remained the prevalent method for the purchasing of all government supplies and services.

During World War II the general consensus was that the armed forces of the United States has displayed judicious management and sound judgment in the use of their extensive purchasing powers. Based on this premise, a proposal was made for Congress to enact legislation whereby the armed forces would continue to comply with the restrictions of formal advertising, but expand the armed forces authority to employ, where circumstances would warrant, the principle of *Procurement by Negotiation.* After considerable debate, Congress enacted the *Armed Services Procurement Act* of 1947, which became effective when signed into law by President Truman, on the 19th of February 1948. This Act was arranged systematically as Chapter 137, Title 10, *United States Code* (USC) by the 84th Congress in 1956. All the laws and regulations which govern military acquisitions are derived from the Constitution of the United States which cites Article I, Section 8, Clause 12, and states, "Congress shall have the power to raise and support armies" and Clause 13 states, "To provide and maintain a Navy." As the constitution did not mention the air force, the United States Attorney, in 1948, issued an edict that it was an army within the meaning of Clause 12. In 1962, the newly organized *Defense Supply Agency* (DSA) was recognized as an integral part of the Department of Defense, with authority to support its transactions and operations in accordance with the prevailing laws and regulations.

The following chapters are based on the *Federal Acquisition Regulations* (FAR), which regulates the manner in which the federal government purchases supplies and services, and how the DLA administers government contracts and verifies the control of product quality.

CHAPTER ONE

The Contract

DEFINITION OF A CONTRACT

A contract is an agreement between the buyer of supplies, services, product (the government is the direct buyer in cases of prime contracts), and the seller (the contractor), for certain considerations and exchange of values (most often monetary values). The use of purchase orders is another method used for the buying of supplies, services and products. The government will generally use the purchase order method if the total value of the purchased goods is less than ten thousand dollars, or, as calls on a *Basic Ordering Agreement* (BOA). Purchase orders, are also the instruments of buying when other national governments have needs to fulfill.

CONTENTS OF A CONTRACT

A government contract will contain all the terms and conditions of the contract. The contract terms and conditions define the rights and obligations of the buyer (government) and the seller (contractor).

It is recommended that contractors obtain a copy of Title 48 - *Federal Acquisition and Regulations System* (FAR), effective April 1, 1984, and the Department of Defense (DoD) - *Federal Acquisition Regulation Supplement* (FARS). The FAR is issued by each of the following offices:

1. The Department of Defense
2. General Services Administration.
3. National Aeronautics and Space Administration.

The clauses in the FAR are the common acquisition policies, procedures, contract clauses and forms as used by governmental agencies who are responsible for procurements. The FAR is arranged systematically in Chapter 1, Title 48 of the Code of Federal Regulations. Contractors should be well versed in the contents of the Federal Acquisition Regulations. These regulations are the legal and binding contract terms the contractor has agreed to upon signing of, and the subsequent award of, the government contract.

HIGHER LEVEL QUALITY REQUIREMENTS

There is a limited exception to the above FAR guidance. This exception is when the FAR clause 52.246-11, Higher Level Contract Quality Requirement (government specification), is invoked in a contract. If the FAR 52.246-11 requirement is invoked in a contract, the contract has to specify what the higher level of quality requirement is. The higher level requirement will be either MIL-Q-9858A or MIL-I-45208A. If the higher level of requirement has been omitted from the contract, the contractor should notify the local DCAS quality assurance representative or the appropriate administration and contracting officer at the DCASMA. If there is no local DCAS office, notify the contracting officer at the buying facility. This problem should be resolved as soon as possible. Failure to remedy this omission promptly could be costly for the contractor.

THE ACQUISITION PROCESS

All government purchases have their origin in a particular government agency need for a service or product. This need for a service or product sets into motion a sequence of events that begins with the submission of a *purchase directive* (request) by the requisitioning agency and ends with the delivery of that service or product.

The term purchase request is normally used to describe the form which is employed by the agency (civilian or military) to initiate the contracting cycle (see page 12, The Defense System Acquisition Cycle). There is no standard Department of Defense (DoD) form prescribed for this purpose, as each department has for many years been using a distinctive format pertinent to its individual activity.

The purchase process begins when a DoD activity needs a particular product or service which it describes in a purchase directive, and which it submits to the purchasing or contracting activity of that agency. The requiring activity is responsible for all applicable specifications, plans, or drawings, or, if such are not available, for providing a description which adequately specifies all the essential features of the supplies or services. In addition, the purchase directive must include the quantity, time and location of delivery, fund citation (needed for payment), and all the essential information needed to form a descriptive and precise requirement for purchase.

In the course of processing the purchase request, the contracting officer must ascertain if the description is sufficiently precise to afford maximum competition by a prospective bidder of such service or product. A determination must be made as to whether or not the delivery schedule appears realistic; if not, the contracting officer may challenge it, as delivery and performance schedules which are unrealistic tend to prevent full competition by the prospective bidders for the contract. Furthermore, unrealistic delivery or performance schedules usually result in higher contract prices, and thereby, involve unnecessary and excessive expense to the government.

The contracting officer must determine if the contractors who answered the *Invitation For Bid* (IFB), *Request For Proposal* (RFP), or *Solicitation and Offer* (see page 13), are responsible in-so-far as conforming with the financial and technical requirements as prescribed by the Federal Acquisition Regulation. Other considerations such as responsiveness (in formal advertising), responsibility, conformance to delivery schedules, quantity, eligibility (meeting the requirements of congressional enactments as they relate to the prescribed standards of a manufacturer, regular dealer, agent, and/or assembler), plant facilities, equipment, personnel, integrity, record of past performance, and if appropriate, review of the debarred/suspended/ineligible list to ascertain if any of the contractors under consideration appear on it. The evaluation then proceeds to consideration of conformance with all the clauses which are incorporated in the solicitation. Moreover, the contracting officer must determine, depending upon the nature and the size of the requirement, if the bids or offers meet the minimal, general, additional, and/or special standards as required by the Federal Acquisition Regulation. Finally, the contracting officer must compare the offerings of the various contractors with respect to price, discounts, transportation, and any other factors which had a direct or indirect bearing on the final price of the acquisition prior to making the award.

After considering all the factors inherent within the evaluation phase and by comparing the offerings of those contractors who remain in competition after the elimination process. The contracting officer will finally award the contract to the contractor whose offer is in the best interest of the government, price and all other factors considered. On page 14, is a sample Award/Contract form used by the government procurement offices.

The acquisition process does not end with the award of the contract. This phase is followed by the extremely important function of administering the contract. To insure the successful implementation of this responsibility, it is the policy of the DoD to require purchasing offices to use to the fullest possible extent, the assistance provided by the *Defense Contract Administration Services* (DCAS). In compliance with this policy, the FAR states, "Except as otherwise prescribed in this regulation, contracts shall be assigned performance of all contract administration functions." Each military department must limit the retention in the purchasing office of the contract administration functions and then only in those functions where the benefits derived therefrom are clearly evident. Even in those exceptional instances where administration functions are retained in the purchasing office, approval at a level higher than the contracting officer is required. Usually, this is the *Head of the Contracting Activity* (HCA). DCAS is a major component of DLA, and is composed of several regions which are established in strategic geographical locations across the United States. Each of the *Defense Contract Administration Services Regions* (DCASR) provides contract administration services in support of the several military departments and other DoD components. These services include contract management, government property management, quality assurance, payments to defense contractors, support to small business, and surveillance of defense contractor progress to ensure timely delivery of the supplies and/or services.

The acquisition process begins with the receipt of the purchase directive at the purchasing office. From that point it continues in a progressive, methodical manner towards the fulfillment of the services or supplies set forth in the directive. In the process, it requires the personal attention of the contracting officer to ensure the entire operation conforms to all of the restrictions imposed by the FAR. The process normally ends with the inspection, acceptance, and delivery of the product or services as originally described in the purchase directive. Other requirements in the contract such as warranties, liability inclusions, etc., extend the contract administration functions beyond the delivery of the product and/or services.

THE DEFENSE SYSTEM ACQUISITION CYCLE

RDT&E PROGRAM STRUCTURE	6.1 RESEARCH	6.2 EXPLORATORY DEVELOPMENT	6.3 ADVANCED DEVELOPMENT	6.4 FULL-SCALE ENGINEERING DEVELOPMENT	6.6 PRODUCTION/ DEPLOYMENT
PROGRAM PHASES DODINST 5000.1		PROGRAM INITIATION	DEMONSTRATION AND VALIDATION	FULL-SCALE ENGINEERING DEVELOPMENT	PRODUCTION/ DEPLOYMENT
BASIC ACQUISITION ACTIVITIES	• TECHNOLOGY BASE DEVELOPMENT •ANALYSIS OF MISSION RECONCILED WITH OVERALL CAPABILITIES, PRIORITIES, AND RESOURCES	• THREAT ANALYSIS • OPERATIONAL NEED • CONCEPT ANALYSIS •TECH/ECONOMIC FEASIBILITY • RISK IDENTIFICATION • ALTERNATIVES • COST ANALYSIS • PRELIMINARY DESIGN FACTORS • INITIAL CHARACTERIZATIONS/ SYSTEM SPECIFICATION	• UPDATE OPERATIONAL NEED • ADVANCED ANALYSIS • TECH/ECONOMIC CONFIDENCE • RISK RESOLUTION • BEST ALTERNATIVES • DEVELOPMENT OF PRELIMINARY LIFE CYCLE COSTS • ASSESSMENT • DEVELOPMENT PROGRAM PLAN (TECHNICAL, COST, LOGISTICS, SCHEDULE) • ADVANCED DESIGNS	• UPDATE OPERATIONAL NEED • ENGINEERING DEVELOPMENT • PROJECTED PRODUCTION CAPABILITY • DEVELOPMENT TEST AND EVALUATION • OPERATIONAL SUITABILITY • LIFE CYCLE COSTS • PRODUCTION DELIVERY SCHEDULE • PRODUCTION AND LOGISTICS SUPPORT PLAN	• PRODUCTION OF OPERATIONAL MATERIAL • OPERATIONAL EMPLOYMENT • IMPLEMENT LOGISTICS/ MAINTENANCE PLANS • PRODUCIBILITY/PRODUCT IMPROVEMENTS • STOCKPILE MANAGEMENT SURVEILLANCE
OBJECTIVES	TECHNOLOGY RESEARCH	PAPER STUDIES	CRITICAL ISSUES EVALUATED	ENGINEERING EVALUATION DT&E AND OT&E	OPERATIONAL HARDWARE
DOD PROGRAM MILESTONES DODINST 5000.1 DODINST 5000.2		▲ MILESTONE O (MENS) APPROVAL OF MISSION NEED AND PROGRAM INITIATION	▲ MILESTONE I (DSARC I) APPROVAL TO DEMONSTRATE SELECTED ALTERNATIVES	▲ MILESTONE II (DSARC II) APPROVAL FOR FULL-SCALE ENGINEERING DEVELOPMENT AND LIMITED PRODUCTION FOR OT&E	▲ MILESTONE III (DSARC III) PRODUCTION RELEASE APPROVAL FOR SERVICE USE (ASU)

SOLICITATION, OFFER AND AWARD

1. THIS CONTRACT IS A RATED ORDER UNDER DPAS (15 CFR 350) ▶ RATING | PAGE OF PAGES

2. CONTRACT NO. | 3. SOLICITATION NO. | 4. TYPE OF SOLICITATION ☐ SEALED BID (IFB) ☐ NEGOTIATED (RFP) | 5. DATE ISSUED | 6. REQUISITION/PURCHASE NO.

7. ISSUED BY CODE | 8. ADDRESS OFFER TO *(If other than Item 7)*

NOTE: In sealed bid solicitations "offer" and "offeror" mean "bid" and "bidder".

SOLICITATION

9. Sealed offers in original and ________ copies for furnishing the supplies or services in the Schedule will be received at the place specified in Item 8, or if handcarried, in the depository located in ________ until ________ *(Hour)* local time ________ *(Date)*

CAUTION – LATE Submissions, Modifications, and Withdrawals: See Section L, Provision No. 52.214-7 or 52.215-10. All offers are subject to all terms and conditions contained in this solicitation.

10. FOR INFORMATION CALL: ▶ A. NAME | B. TELEPHONE NO. *(Include area code) (NO COLLECT CALLS)*

11. TABLE OF CONTENTS

(√)	SEC.	DESCRIPTION	PAGE(S)	(√)	SEC.	DESCRIPTION	PAGE(S)
		PART I – THE SCHEDULE				PART II – CONTRACT CLAUSES	
	A	SOLICITATION/CONTRACT FORM			I	CONTRACT CLAUSES	
	B	SUPPLIES OR SERVICES AND PRICES/COSTS				PART III – LIST OF DOCUMENTS, EXHIBITS AND OTHER ATTACH.	
	C	DESCRIPTION/SPECS./WORK STATEMENT			J	LIST OF ATTACHMENTS	
	D	PACKAGING AND MARKING				PART IV – REPRESENTATIONS AND INSTRUCTIONS	
	E	INSPECTION AND ACCEPTANCE			K	REPRESENTATIONS, CERTIFICATIONS AND OTHER STATEMENTS OF OFFERORS	
	F	DELIVERIES OR PERFORMANCE					
	G	CONTRACT ADMINISTRATION DATA			L	INSTRS., CONDS., AND NOTICES TO OFFERORS	
	H	SPECIAL CONTRACT REQUIREMENTS			M	EVALUATION FACTORS FOR AWARD	

OFFER *(Must be fully completed by offeror)*

NOTE: Item 12 does not apply if the solicitation includes the provisions at 52.214-16, Minimum Bid Acceptance Period.

12. In compliance with the above, the undersigned agrees, if this offer is accepted within ________ calendar days *(60 calendar days unless a different period is inserted by the offeror)* from the date for receipt of offers specified above, to furnish any or all items upon which prices are offered at the price set opposite each item, delivered at the designated point(s), within the time specified in the schedule.

13. DISCOUNT FOR PROMPT PAYMENT *(See Section I, Clause No. 52-232-8)* ▶	10 CALENDAR DAYS	20 CALENDAR DAYS	30 CALENDAR DAYS	CALENDAR DAYS
	%	%	%	%

14. ACKNOWLEDGMENT OF AMENDMENTS *(The offeror acknowledges receipt of amendments to the SOLICITATION for offerors and related documents numbered and dated:*	AMENDMENT NO.	DATE	AMENDMENT NO.	DATE

15A. NAME AND ADDRESS OF OFFEROR | CODE | FACILITY | 16. NAME AND TITLE OF PERSON AUTHORIZED TO SIGN OFFER *(Type or print)*

15B. TELEPHONE NO. *(Include area code)* | 15C. CHECK IF REMITTANCE ADDRESS ☐ IS DIFFERENT FROM ABOVE - ENTER SUCH ADDRESS IN SCHEDULE. | 17. SIGNATURE | 18. OFFER DATE

AWARD *(To be completed by Government)*

19. ACCEPTED AS TO ITEMS NUMBERED | 20. AMOUNT | 21. ACCOUNTING AND APPROPRIATION

22. AUTHORITY FOR USING OTHER THAN FULL AND OPEN COMPETITION:

☐ 10 U.S.C. 2304(c)(   ) ☐ 41 U.S.C. 253(c)(   )

23. SUBMIT INVOICES TO ADDRESS SHOWN IN *(4 copies unless otherwise specified)* ▶ ITEM

24. ADMINISTERED BY *(If other than Item 7)* CODE | 25. PAYMENT WILL BE MADE BY CODE

26. NAME OF CONTRACTING OFFICER *(Type or print)* | 27. UNITED STATES OF AMERICA *(Signature of Contracting Officer)* | 28. AWARD DATE

IMPORTANT – Award will be made on this Form, or on Standard Form 26, or by other authorized official written notice.

NSN 7540-01-152-8064
PREVIOUS EDITION NOT USABLE

33-1 . .

STANDARD FORM 33 (REV. 4-85)
Prescribed by GSA
FAR (48 CFR) 53.214(c)

☆ GPO : 1985 O - 461-275 (20004)

AWARD/CONTRACT

1. THIS CONTRACT IS A RATED ORDER UNDER DPAS (15 CFR 350) ▶ RATING | PAGE OF PAGES

2. CONTRACT *(Proc. Inst. Ident.)* NO.

3. EFFECTIVE DATE

4. REQUISITION/PURCHASE REQUEST/PROJECT NO.

5. ISSUED BY CODE

6. ADMINISTERED BY *(If other than Item 5)* CODE

7. NAME AND ADDRESS OF CONTRACTOR *(No., street, city, county, State and ZIP Code)*

CODE | FACILITY CODE

8. DELIVERY

☐ FOB ORIGIN ☐ OTHER *(See below)*

9. DISCOUNT FOR PROMPT PAYMENT

10. SUBMIT INVOICES *(4 copies unless otherwise specified)* TO THE ADDRESS SHOWN IN: ▶ ITEM

11. SHIP TO/MARK FOR CODE

12. PAYMENT WILL BE MADE BY CODE

13. AUTHORITY FOR USING OTHER THAN FULL AND OPEN COMPETITION:

☐ 10 U.S.C. 2304(c)( ) ☐ 41 U.S.C. 253(c)( )

14. ACCOUNTING AND APPROPRIATION DATA

15A. ITEM NO.	15B. SUPPLIES/SERVICES	15C. QUANTITY	15D. UNIT	15E. UNIT PRICE	15F. AMOUNT

15G. TOTAL AMOUNT OF CONTRACT ▶ $

16. TABLE OF CONTENTS

(✓)	SEC.	DESCRIPTION	PAGE(S)	(✓)	SEC.	DESCRIPTION	PAGE(S)
		PART I — THE SCHEDULE				PART II — CONTRACT CLAUSES	
	A	SOLICITATION/CONTRACT FORM			I	CONTRACT CLAUSES	
	B	SUPPLIES OR SERVICES AND PRICES/COSTS				PART III — LIST OF DOCUMENTS, EXHIBITS AND OTHER ATTACH.	
	C	DESCRIPTION/SPECS./WORK STATEMENT			J	LIST OF ATTACHMENTS	
	D	PACKAGING AND MARKING				PART IV — REPRESENTATIONS AND INSTRUCTIONS	
	E	INSPECTION AND ACCEPTANCE			K	REPRESENTATIONS, CERTIFICATIONS AND OTHER STATEMENTS OF OFFERORS	
	F	DELIVERIES OR PERFORMANCE					
	G	CONTRACT ADMINISTRATION DATA			L	INSTRS., CONDS., AND NOTICES TO OFFERORS	
	H	SPECIAL CONTRACT REQUIREMENTS			M	EVALUATION FACTORS FOR AWARD	

CONTRACTING OFFICER WILL COMPLETE ITEM 17 OR 18 AS APPLICABLE

17. ☐ CONTRACTOR'S NEGOTIATED AGREEMENT *(Contractor is required to sign this document and return ________ copies to issuing office.)* Contractor agrees to furnish and deliver all items or perform all the services set forth or otherwise identified above and on any continuation sheets for the consideration stated herein. The rights and obligations of the parties to this contract shall be subject to and governed by the following documents: (a) this award/contract, (b) the solicitation, if any, and (c) such provisions, representations, certifications, and specifications, as are attached or incorporated by reference herein. *(Attachments are listed herein.)*

18. ☐ AWARD *(Contractor is not required to sign this document.)* Your offer on Solicitation Number ________________, including the additions or changes made by you which additions or changes are set forth in full above, is hereby accepted as to the items listed above and on any continuation sheets. This award consummates the contract which consists of the following documents: (a) the Government's solicitation and your offer, and (b) this award/contract. No further contractual document is necessary.

19A. NAME AND TITLE OF SIGNER *(Type or print)*

20A. NAME OF CONTRACTING OFFICER

19B. NAME OF CONTRACTOR

BY ____________________
(Signature of person authorized to sign)

19C. DATE SIGNED

20B. UNITED STATES OF AMERICA

BY ____________________
(Signature of Contracting Officer)

20C. DATE SIGNED

NSN 7540-01-152-8069
PREVIOUS EDITION UNUSABLE

26-107

STANDARD FORM 26 (REV. 4-85)
Prescribed by GSA
FAR (48 CFR) 53.214(a)

☆ GPO : 1985 O - 461-275 (20005)

CHAPTER TWO

The Contractor

THE CONTRACTOR

The contractor is a supplier of materials, services and products to the government. The contractor is also a buyer of such materials, services and products that are to be integrated into a finished product. Most contractors fit into both categories. The contractor will most likely be selling needed materials, services and products to other national governments in order to fulfill their basic needs.

It is to be noted that the United States Government, other national governments, and contractors are steadily switching from sole source purchasing, to multi-source. Sole source means that there is only one source where needed services, materials and products can be obtained. Multi-source purchasing is used to gain the benefits of increased competition, up-to-date advanced technology, lower costs, and more advantageous delivery schedules and shipping costs.

HOW TO OBTAIN CONTRACT BIDDING LISTS

The Commerce Business Daily, is a newsletter-sized daily publication of the United States Commerce Department. In this newsletter the federal government announces its needs and bidding opportunities to all interested parties in the form of synopses, with information on where and how to request the entire solicitation package.

Other information in the publication includes notices of award of contract, amendments to solicitations, and how to request Standard Form 129 - Bidders Mailing List Application.

Many agencies of the federal government such as, the Army, Navy, Air Force, Department of Agriculture, Public Health Service, U.S. Fish and Wildlife Service, NASA, U.S. Department of Commerce, and the U.S. Congress, list their procurement in the *Commerce Business Daily.*

Many agencies of the federal government, such as the Army, Navy, Air Force and others, maintain purchasing offices where current solicitation lists are maintained and open to view for prospective contractors and vendors. These solicitation lists are also available upon request.

The Commerce Business Daily costs $243 a year for first class mailing, $173 a year for second class mailing, $122 for a six month trial subscription and $87 for a second class mailing. The foreign subscription rate is $216.25 a year and $108 for 6 months, plus air mail rates. A two year subscription is available at the above yearly rates also. Subscriptions expire one year from the date of the first issue, and one expiration notice is mailed approximately 90 days prior to the expiration date of the subscription. Following is the address where the Commerce Business Daily may be purchased:

Superintendent of Documents
Government Printing Office
Washington, DC 20402-9371
Telephone Number: (202) 783-3238
Check or money orders are to be made out to:
Superintendent of Documents

Another excellent source of information concerning government solicitations (for military and NASA contracts) is the nearest office of the Small Business Administration that is usually part of the local Defense Contracts Administration Service office, located in a contractor's area. If it is not listed in the local directory, contact the nearest Army, Navy or Air Force base to find the location of the nearest DCAS office. The personnel at these offices are well versed in the methods of obtaining the necessary information.

Following is a list of toll-free 800 numbers for the various Defense Logistics Agency small and disadvantaged offices.

AGENCY	TELEPHONE NUMBER	AREAS OF RESPONSIBILITY (BY STATE)
DCASR Atlanta	1-800-551-7801	GA
	1-800-331-6415	TN,SC, AL, LA, FL
DCASR Boston	1-800-321-1861	NY, RI, CN, MA, NH, VT, ME
DCASR Chicago	1-800-826-1041	IL
	1-800-637-3848	WI, IN
DCASR Cleveland	1-800-551-2785	OH, MI, KY
DCASR Dallas	1-800-225-8574	AZ, AK, LA, OK, NM, TX
DCASR Los Angeles	1-800-251-5285	CA
	1-800-624-7372	HA, ID, MN, NV, OR, WA
DCASR New York	1-800-807-3000	NY, NJ, CN, Overseas
DCASR Philadelphia	1-800-843-7694	PA
	1-800-253-9503	DE, MD, NJ, VA, WV, DC
DCASR St. Louis	1-800-325-3419	CO, IL, KA, ND, SD, UT, WY

The telephone numbers of the Defense Logistics Agency supply centers where purchasing information can be obtained are:

- Defense Construction Supply Center - Columbus, OH
  1-800-263-3272
- Defense Electronics Supply Center - Dayton, OH
  1-800-225-9771
- Defense Fuel Supply Center - Alexandria, VA
  1-800-648-8893
- Defense Industrial Supply Center - Philadelphia, PA
  1-800-831-1110
- Defense Personal Support Center - Philadelphia, PA
  1-800-523-0705
- All Other Centers
  1-800-523-2601

HOW TO OBTAIN GOVERNMENT PUBLICATIONS AND SPECIFICATIONS

Government publications, specifications and standards are obtained by submitting the NPFC 4120/6 Specifications and Standards Requisition Form (see page 21) to:

Naval Publications and Forms Center
5801 Tabor Avenue
Philadelphia, PA 19120-5099

Telex: 834295 Western Union: (710) 670-1685
Telephone Number: (215) 697-3321
Inquiry Number: (215) 697-4834
(Inquiry number is not to be used for ordering)
Operators available Monday thru Friday
8:30am to 4:00pm (Eastern Standard Time)

Telephone Requests are serviced by a telephone answering machine 24 hours a day, 7 days a week. Calls are limited to five line items only. Emergency requests are processed as priorities. Abuse of this system results in delays and the system becomes ineffective.

Helpful Ordering Information:

1. All amendments and revisions will be automatically issued with the basic specifications, unless specified otherwise by the requestor.
2. Only the latest edition of the specification requested will be issued. Documents referenced within a specification must be requested separately.
3. Slash sheets, for example: MIL-E-1/306B must be individually requested by document number. Slash sheets will not be issued as a set.
4. Industry standards are ordered from the preparing technical societies, not NPFC Philadelphia.
5. NPFC Philadelphia stock only current specifications and standards listed in the DODISS.
6. Superseded/cancelled specifications are not stocked at NPFC.

A copy of the preceding items may be obtained from:

Director
Navy Publications and Printing Service Office
Building 4, Section D
700 Robbins Avenue
Philadelphia, PA 19111-5094

Requests must be submitted via your procurement/contracting officer for certification of need.

All types of requests should be submitted in the following way utilizing 4120/6 Form NPFC (see page 21).

Block Number 1. CAGE, UIC or System Assigned number.

Block Number 2. Give complete mailing address, including zip code.

Block Number 3. Your internal control number. Fill out if necessary.

Block Number 4. The number of the documents you are ordering.

Documents are to be listed in the following order. In each category, list the document numbers in numerical order.

a. Military Specifications.
b. Military Standards
c. Federal Specifications.
d. Federal Standards
e. Qualified Products Lists.
f. Others.

Block Number 5. Quantity of documents being ordered (five or fewer).

Block Number 6. Title of the specification or standard. From the DoD index of Specifications and Standards.

Block Number 7. Signature of the requestor.

Block Number 8. Date this form is filled out and mailed.

Block Number 9. If this order form is due to a Request for Quotation or Request for Proposal, insert closing date of such.

(1) Your CAGE, UIC or System Assigned number goes here.

(2) Print or type

Attn:

Your address goes here

If your address has changed please check the box. ☐

(3) Your internal control number goes here
Fill out if necessary

SPECIFICATIONS AND STANDARDS REQUISITION

Please print or type all information. Documents ordered must appear in the DoD Index of Specifications and Standards. Requests submitted on this form will speed service. Reorder forms will be enclosed with each shipment.

FORWARD REQUEST TO:
Naval Publications and Forms Center, Code NPODS
5801 Tabor Avenue, Philadelphia, PA 19120-5099

STANDARDIZATION DOCUMENT NUMBER	QUANTITY	TITLE *(From DoD Index of Specifications and Standards)*
(4)	(5)	(6)

IMPORTANT NOTES

- *Requests For Official Use Only Documents must be submitted via cognizant DoD Inspection Office or Contract Administrator for certification of "need to know."*
- *Non Government standardization documents will not be furnished to commercial concerns. Copies may be purchased from the appropriate Non Government Association.*
- *Questions concerning documents not listed in the Department of Defense Index of Specifications and Standards (DODISS) should be directed to NPFC Attn: Code 105 or Call (215) 697-2667.*

Please enter your CAGE (formerly FSCM) or UIC number at top of this form. It will expedite your order.

5. SIGNATURE OF REQUESTER	6. DATE PREPARED	7. CLOSING DATE *(IFB RFQ or RFP)*
(7)	(8)	(9)

NPFC 4120/6 (3-86)

CHAPTER THREE

A Documented System

THE NEED FOR A DOCUMENTED AND APPROVED QUALITY SYSTEM

Prior to, and after receiving an award of contract, pre-award and post-award surveys will be held at the contractors plant by the government to determine the following:

1. Does the contractor have the capability of performing the contract?
2. Has the contractor planned for all aspects of the contract?
3. Does the contractor understand all of the specifications and requirements of the contract?
4. Is there mutual agreement between the contractor and the government as to the interpretations of all specifications and requirements of the contract?
5. Does the contractor understand that the government quality assurance representative is acting on behalf of the government at all times?
6. Have all government and contractor differences been resolved prior to the start of production?

Many factors will be used by the government in determining whether or not a post-award conference will be held at a contractor's plant, and, in determining if all deficiencies found during the pre-award survey have been cleared up. Following are some of the factors used to determine whether or not a post-award will be held:

1. Pre-award survey findings and recommendations.
2. Results (if applicable) of previous post-award conferences.
3. Criticality and complexity of the supplies/services being purchased.
4. Any adverse quality history?
5. Is the contractor new to the government purchasing system?
6. Have there been any internal changes in the contractor's plant that could affect product quality or delivery schedules, such as, new personnel, new or extensively repaired production machinery or test equipment?

7. What extent of subcontracting will the contractor do?
8. Will all or part of the finished product be subcontracted out?

Contractors are solely responsible for the control of product quality. Following are some questions contractors should address:

1. Is the contractor confident that the products and/or services being offered to the government for acceptance meet and conform to all of the contract requirements and specifications?
2. Is the contractor controlling the purchasing of services, goods, and materials that will eventually be integrated into the finished product?
3. Does the contractor have written and approved procedures that control the purchasing of the required materials, services, and goods?
4. Does the contractor have procedures for verifying that the raw materials being purchased to specific requirements and specifications actually contain the physical and/or chemical properties required?
5. Does the contractor have procedures and instructions for the qualification and re-qualification of subcontractors/suppliers?
6. What feedback does the contractor get from its receiving department or other departments as to the quality of the supplies, parts, sub-assemblies, assemblies or services being purchased?
7. Have all of the requirements and specifications of the contract been reviewed?
8. Have provisions for special controls, processes, test equipment, fixtures, tooling and skills required been planned for?
9. Have the necessary procedures and instructions been written and approved prior to the start of production?

These are some of the questions that need to be answered in the form of written procedures and instructions. Without written and approved procedures and instructions, can the contractor assure itself, the government, and other customers of the repeated quality of product or service being offered for sale?

Prior to each Quality Control Publication (QCP) in this book, the quality program requirement for that publication is stated and discussed. The relationship of MIL-Q-9858A and MIL-I-45208A to the various other quality programs is shown in these discussions. A chart comparing each requirement of

MIL-Q-9858A to MIL-I-45208A and the NATO and NASA requirements is depicted on pages 29-30 of this book.

In Chapter Four is a sample table of contents for a quality manual. Each chapter in this table of contents follows the alpha designators of the DLAM 8200.1 manual. The publications for organization and planning have been presented first in this table of contents. They are the topics that have to be addressed first in the contract cycle. All other alpha designators will follow the sequence of the DLAM 8200.1.

QUALITY ASSURANCE UNDER A SINGLE STANDARD

DLAM 8200.1, Page 102, Part II, Paragraph 9-1104 - Quality Assurance Under A Single Standard states, "Where a single standard system is established, Government QA requirements apply to the entire contractor's operations and all supplies produced hereunder...A contractor desiring to operate under a single standard of quality control will direct his request to the Chief of the QA element of the CAO through the QAR at his facility." The QAR at the contractor's facility will make a statement as to the merits of the request, and the Chief of the QA element will make the decision based on the contractor's previous quality history and the thoroughness of the contractor's quality system. Approval to operate under a single standard quality system is not easily or usually obtained.

PREAWARD SURVEY OF PROSPECTIVE CONTRACTOR QUALITY ASSURANCE	*If more space is required, continue on the back in Section IV or attach continuation sheets.*	FORM APPROVED OMB NO. **3090-0110** SERIAL NO. *(For surveying activity use)*

SECTION I – GENERAL

1. PROSPECTIVE CONTRACTOR	2. LOCATION

SECTION II – COMPANY AND SOLICITATION DATA

1. QUALITY ASSURANCE ORGANIZATION *(Describe briefly and attach organization chart.)*

2. QUALITY ASSURANCE OFFICIALS CONTACTED *(Names, titles, and years of quality assurance experience)*

3. QUALITY RELIABILITY, MAINTAINABILITY REQUIREMENTS WHICH APPLY	☐ MIL-I-45208	☐ MIL-C-45662	☐ OTHER *(Specify)*
	☐ MIL-I-45007	☐ MIL-STD-785	
	☐ MIL-Q-9555	☐ MIL-STD-470	

4. IDENTICAL OR SIMILAR ITEMS HAVE BEEN ☐ PRODUCED ☐ SERVICED BY PROSPECTIVE CONTRACTOR.

SECTION III – EVALUATION CHECKLIST

STATEMENTS		YES	NO
1. AS PERTAINS TO THE CONTRACT, THESE ITEMS ARE UNDERSTOOD BY THE CONTRACTOR	a. Exhibits, technical data, drawings, specifications, and approval requirements.		
	b. Preservation, packaging, packing, and marking requirements.		
	c. OTHER *(Specify)*		
2. Records available indicate that the prospective contractor has a satisfactory quality performance record during the past twelve (12) months for similar items.			
3. Used or reconditioned material and former Government surplus material will be furnished by the prospective contractor. *(If Yes, explain in Section IV, on the back of this form.)*			
4. Prospective contractor will require unusual assistance from the Government.			
5. Did prospective contractor fulfill commitments to correct deficiencies, as proposed on previous surveys, when awarded that contract?			
6. Quality control, inspection, and test personnel.	NUMBER SKILLED / NUMBER SEMI-SKILLED		
7. Inspection to production personnel ratio.	RATIO :		
The following are available and adequate. (If not applicable, show "N/A" in "Yes" column.)			
8. Inspection and test equipment, guages, and instruments for first article and production (including solicitation specified equipment).			
9. Calibration/metrology program.			
10. Written procedures and instructions for inspections, tests, process controls, and other requirements; conformance thereto; in conjunction with other planning control functions.			
11. Control of specifications, drawings, changes and modifications, work/process instructions.			
12. Quality assurance/control organizational structure.			
13. System for determining inspection, test, and measurement requirements.			
14. Controls for selecting qualified supplies and assuring the quality of purchased materials.			
15. Material control: identification, segregation, maintenance, preservation, and correction of defects.			
16. Government furnished property controls.			

NSN 7540-01-140-5527 1406-101 **STANDARD FORM 1406** (10-83) Prescribed by GSA, FAR (48 CFR) 53.209-1(d)

SECTION III – EVALUATION CHECKLIST – STATEMENTS, Continued	YES	NO
17. In-process inspection controls.		
18. System for timely identification and correction of deficiencies to prevent recurrence.		
19. Preservation, packaging, packing, marking controls.		
20. Quality control records (such as, inspection, test, corrective actions, calibration, etc.		
21. Controls for investigation of customer complaints and correction of deficiencies.		
22. Reliability and/or maintainability program.		

SECTION IV – QUALITY ASSURANCE RECOMMENDATIONS

1. RECOMMEND ☐ AWARD ☐ NO AWARD *(Provide full substantiation for recommendation)*

If more space is needed, use plain paper, identify continued item(s), and attach to this form.

NO. OF PAGES ATTACHED, IF ANY ☐

2. SURVEY MADE BY *(Include signature, typed/printed name, and office)*	3. TELEPHONE NO. *(Include area code)*	4. DATE SUBMITTED

5. REVIEWING/APPROVING OFFICIAL *(Include signature, typed/printed name, and office)*	6. DATE APPROVED	7. NEXT HIGHER AUTHORITY *(Code/title)*

STANDARD FORM 1406 BACK (10-83)

CONVERSION CHART FOR QUALITY REQUIREMENTS					
PROCEDURE TITLE	ALPHA DESIGNATOR DLAM 8200.1	PARA. MIL-Q-9858 A	PARA. MIL-I-45208 A	REQ. NO. AQAP-1 NATO	REQ. NO. AQAP-4 NATO
ADV. METROLOGY REQ.	A	4.5		209	
BAILED PROPERTY	B	7.2.3		212	
COMP. ITEM INSP. & TEST	C	6.3	3.2.1	213	211
CORRECTIVE ACTION	D	3.5	3.2.3	206	213
COSTS RELATED TO QUAL.	E	3.6			
DRAWINGS, DOCU., CHG.	F	4.1	3.2.4	200	203
GOVT. FURNISHED MATL.	G	7.2.1	3.6	212	
GOV'T. INSP. AT SUBCON. FAC.	H	7.1	3.11	210d	205d
HANDLING, STOR. & DEL.	I	6.4		217	212
INDICATION OF INSP. STAT.	J	6.7	3.5	216	203b
MATL & MATLS. CONTROL	K	6.1		211	303
MEASURING & TEST EQUIP.	L	4.2	3.3	209	204
NONCONFORMING MATL.	M	6.5	3.7	215	210
ORGANIZATION	N	3.1		202	
PLANNING	O	3.2		203	202
PROCESS CONTROL	P	6.2	3.4	211	206
PROD. TOOL. USED AS A MEDIA IN.	Q	4.3	3.3	209	204
PROD. PROCESS & FABR.	R	6.2		211	206
PURCHASING DATA	S	5.2	3.11.3	210	205
RECORDS	T	3.4	3.2.2	205	203
RESP. FOR CONTROL OF PURC.	U	5.1		210	205
STATIST QC & SAMPL. PRO.	V	6.6	3.9	214	209
USE OF CONT. INSP. EQUIP.	W	4.4	3.3		
WORK INST/INSP. & TEST DOC.	X	3.3	3.2.1	205	203
RECEIVING INSPECTION	Y	6.1	3.12	210	205
SPECIALIZED SAFETY (WHEN SPECIFIED IN CONTRACT-SEE DLAM 8200.1-PART 2-PARA. 4-200 AND B3.	Z	1.4			
DESIGN CONTROL				207	
ACCOMODATION & ASSIST.				210	215
NOTES:					
TABLE 1					

QUALITY REQUIREMENTS CONVERSION CHART - NASA AND SPACE SHUTTLE			
ALPHA DESIGNATOR FROM DLAM 8200.1 CONTRACT QUALITY REQUIREMENTS	NASA NHB 5300.4 (1B) EQUIVALENT TO MIL-Q-9858A PARAGRAPH	NASA NHB 5300.1 (1C) EQUIVALENT TO MIL-I-45208A PARAGRAPH	NASA NHB 5300.4 (1D-2) SPACE SHUTTLE PROGRAM PARAGRAPH
A			
B	1B 1300, 1301	1C 204	1D 511
C	1B 704, 705	1C 304	1D 505
D	1B 802	1C 302	1D 506, 507
E			
F	1B 302, 706	1C 202, 302	1D 502, 503
G	1B 1300	1C 204	1D 511
H	1B 503, 504	1C 301, 302	1D 503
I	1B 1100, 1101	1C 203, 302	1D 503, 509
J	1B 706	1C 304	1D 502
K	1B 601	1C 203, 303	1D 505
L	1B 603, 900, 905	1C 310	1D 507
M	1B 510, 800, 801, 803 804, 806, 810	1C 303, 502	1D 506
N	1B 200, 201, 203, 204, 206	1C 201	1D 500
O	1B 202, 205, 300, 301, 701, 1000		1D 200, 300, 400, 401, 500, 501
P	1B 206, 603		1D 504
Q			
R	1B 600, 602, 603, 604		1D 504
S	1B 502, 506	1C 302	1D 502
T	1B 506, 706	1C 302, 305	1D 502
U	1B 500, 510, 800	1C 300, 302	1D 503
V	1B 1200, 1201	1C 311	1D 510
W			
X	1B 701, 702, 703, 705, 707	1C 302, 304	1D 505, 507
Y	1B 505	1C 304	1D 503
Z			1D 202, 203, 200
IDENTIFICATION & DATA RETRIEVAL			1D 502
MAINTAINABILITY			1D 400, 401
HUMAN ENGINEERING			1D 201
QUALIFIED PRODUCTS	1B 705		
TABLE 1 (CONTINUED)			

CHAPTER FOUR

The Quality Manual

THE QUALITY MANUAL

Quality manuals have been developed by government contractors to envelop a formal quality system and procedures that are required by the FAR clauses of a government contract. The quality manual, as developed, contains an Introduction to the contractors quality system explaining the way in which the company adheres to the quality requirements of a contract, a *Cover Page* for the manual that shows compliance to the documentation requirement, a *Scope* statement that states the quality controls imposed on the system, a *Statement of Policy* that describes the company's commitment to quality, how the company amends and revises its system and procedures, and finally, the *Table of Contents* that describes the order in which the quality publications appear.

COVER PAGE

Page 37 depicts a sample coverpage a company may use to fulfill the documentation requirement of a quality manual. It should include the information that appears in the lower right hand section of the sample cover page. The information is as follows:

1. *Manual Serial Number*: A serial number shall be assigned to each manual distributed, and in the possession of the user.
2. *Manual Distribution*: A record of whom each manual was distributed to shall be kept by the QA department. When an addition, revision or deletion to the manual is made, copies will be distributed to the individuals on the list.
3. *Date Reviewed*: The date the quality manual was last reviewed. The quality manual has to be reviewed on an annual basis or when changes to the manual have been made.
4. *Approved by*: The signatures of the chief officer (or representative) of the plant, and the signature of the quality assurance director/manager of the plant/facility.
5. *Reviewed by*: The signature of the government quality assurance representative or other authorized government personnel assigned to the plant/facility.

INTRODUCTION TO A QUALITY MANUAL

The following is a sample introduction to a company's quality manual:

This quality manual is published and maintained by the quality assurance department of (Company's Name), and distributed under the direction of the quality assurance department, by the publications department. The quality manuals purpose is to set forth understandable, documented, and approved procedures for the writing and use of all work instructions. This includes:

1. All production, inspection, test, process instructions and the documentation thereof.
2. Procedures related to the purchasing of supplies, services and their control.
3. Procedures for the setting up of a calibration system and the maintenance of such a system.
4. All other procedures as specified in MIL-Q-9858A, MIL-I-45208A or the NASA and NATO quality programs (as applicable).

The quality publications in this manual cover all aspects of the way in which the (Company's Name) does its business. From the establishment of the planning cycle, to the packaging and shipment of the finished product.

This quality manual is distributed and maintained on a controlled-copy basis, with all quality manual holders receiving copies of new or revised procedures/publications, and will remove and destroy all obsolete procedures/publications. When revised, quality procedures/publications are issued, they are to be inserted into the quality manual according to the Quality Control Publication (QCP) number. Periodically, notices will be issued to all holders of the quality manual. These notices will contain instructions to delete from the manual, publications/procedures that are no longer valid or are obsolete.

SCOPE

Adequate controls throughout all of the contracts performance must be established. This includes the manuals introduction, scope, statement of policy, and the company's policy of amendments and revisions, which relates directly to section 2.0 of MIL-Q-9858A. The sections of the manual should include a format as to the various ways in which the company will control the following:

1. The planning stage.
2. The identification of all special processes.
3. Inspection and testing.
4. Certifications.
5. Records.
6. Audits.
7. Purchasing - Subcontractor, supplier and vendor material controls.
8. Work instructions.
9. Preservation, packaging and shipping controls (this includes handling controls).
10. The reporting of nonconforming materials and corrective actions required.
11. Quality cost reporting.
12. Engineering controls.

In the *Allied Quality Assurance Publication* AQAP-1, paragraph 102 - Scope states, "This document establishes requirements for quality control system elements to be designated, established, and maintained by the contractor for the purpose of ensuring that material and services conform to requirements and for the furnishing of objective evidence." As required in MIL-Q-9858A, the furnishing of objective evidence as to the quality of products and services is also specified in AQAP-1, and the NASA programs. Is there objective evidence that the products and services offered to the government for acceptance will not contain nonconforming material?

STATEMENT OF POLICY

A well written statement of policy to a quality manual will be beneficial to a company's image. It is a statement of commitment by a company to produce products and supply services that meet the highest quality standards available. This is a major task for any company, large or small, to achieve. The success or failure of an enterprise may very well be determined by a company's ability to achieve this "Quality Goal". Only a company's integrity will justify its policy statement. Following is a sample statement of policy.

(Company's Name) Statement of Policy

(Company's Name) commitment to a policy of producing a quality product that meets or exceeds the requirements of MIL-Q-9858A or (MIL-I-45208A, NASA, NATO-*As is the case may be) and the requirements and specifications of the contract as specified in our quality manual, will make it clear to our customers, that product quality is here to stay. Quality is built into our system from top management to every member of our team; from concept to the finished product.*

Adherence to the procedures of the quality manual is mandatory for every member of the (Company's Name) team. This is necessary in order to achieve our goal of quality products and competitive pricing.

Company's Name
Title of Approving Official
Name of Approving Official

AMENDMENTS AND REVISIONS

MIL-Q-9858A, paragraph 2.2, Amendments and Revisions, states, "Whenever this specification is amended or revised subsequent to its contractually effective date, the contractor may follow or authorize his subcontractors to follow the amended or revised document provided no increase in price or fee is required." This statement is interpreted to mean; if the date of the amendment or revision to MIL-Q-9858A is after the date of the contract, the contractor does not have to conform the amendment or revision unless the contractor does so voluntarily with no increase in cost to the government. "The contractor shall not be required to follow the amended or revised document except as a change in contract." This means, the contractor does not have to follow the amended or revised document unless there is a change (modification) to the contract. If there is a modification to the contract and the contractor has determined that this amendment or revision makes the performance to the contract more costly, the contractor could then ask for monetary relief. If a contractor elects to follow the amendment or revision, the contractor must follow the amendment or revision in full.

1.2

QUALITY ASSURANCE MANUAL

PREPARED AND MAINTAINED BY

(NAME OF COMPANY)

QUALITY ASSURANCE DEPARTMENT

TELEPHONE NUMBER

MANUAL SERIAL NO. ________

ISSUED TO ________________

DATE REVIEWED ____________

APPROVED BY ______________

APPROVED BY ______________

REVIEWED BY ______________

SAMPLE COVER PAGE

SAMPLE QUALITY MANUAL TABLE OF CONTENTS

1.2 Contractual Intent

Paragraph 1.2 - Contractual Intent

1.1 Cover Page of Manual
1.2 Introduction to Manual
1.3 Scope of System
1.4 Statement of Policy
1.5 Quality Control Publications
1.6 Interim Quality Control Publications
1.6 Identification Stamps, QCP
1.7 Quality Audits - Contractor
1.8 Quality Audits - Subcontractor
1.9 Quality Workshops
1.10 Training and Certification

3.0 Quality Program Management

Paragraph 3.1 - Organization - Alpha Designator N

3.1 Company Organizational Structure
3.2 Quality Assurance Organizational Structure
3.3 Quality Assurance of the Contract Cycle
3.4 Inspection and Testing Locations

Paragraph 3.2 - Initial Quality Planning - Alpha Designator 0

3.5 Contract Quality Requirement Analysis
3.6 Inspection Planning
3.7 Reliability Planning

6.0 Manufacturing Control

Paragraph 6.3 - Completed Item Inspection and Test - Alpha Designator C

6.1 Final Inspection
6.2 Final Acceptance Testing
6.3 Deliverable Documentation Review
6.4 Final Acceptance Processing, Documentation and Finished Product

3.0 Quality Program Management

Paragraph 3.5 - Corrective Action - Alpha Designator D

3.8 In-House Corrective Action
3.9 Supplier/Vendor Corrective Action

Paragraph 3.6 - Costs Related To Quality - Alpha Designator E

3.10 Costs Related to Quality

4.0 Facilities and Standards

Paragraph 4.1 - Drawings, Documentation and Change - Alpha Designator F

4.1 Engineering Documentation and Change
4.2 Request for Deviation/Change

7.0 Coordinated Government/Contractor Actions

Paragraph 7.2.1 - Government Furnished Material - Alpha Designator G

7.1 Government Furnished Material and Property

Paragraph 7.1 - Government Inspection at Subcontractor/Vendor Facility - Alpha Designator H

7.2 Government Inspection at Subcontractor/Vendor Facility

6.0 Manufacturing Control

Paragraph 6.4 - Handling, Storage and Delivery - Alpha Designator I

6.5 Handling, Storage and Delivery

Paragraph 6.7 - Indication of Inspection Status - Alpha Designator J

6.6 Indication of Inspection Status

4.0 Facilities and Standards

Paragraph 4.2 - Measuring and Test Equipment - Alpha Designator L

4.3 Calibration Definitions and System Responsibilities
4.4 Calibration Control and Recall
4.5 Calibration Specifications and Instructions
4.6 Certification and Control of Dimensional Instruments

4.7 Subcontracting of Calibration and Repair Work
4.8 Employee-Owned Measuring Equipment

Paragraph 4.3 - Production Tooling Used as a Media of Inspection - Alpha Designator Q

4.9 Production Tooling Used as a Media of Inspection

Paragraph 4.4 - Government Use of Contractors Inspection Equipment Alpha Designator W

4.10 Government Use of Contractor's Inspection Equipment

6.0 Manufacturing Control

Paragraph 6.5 - Nonconforming Material - Alpha Designator M

6.7 Failure Reporting
6.8 Material Review Process
6.9 Material Review Board
6.10 Material Review Board Documentation
6.11 Scrap Control

Paragraph 6.2 - Process Control and Production Processing and Fabrication - Alpha Designators P, R

6.12 Process Control
6.13 Soldering
6.14 Welding

5.0 Control of Purchases

Paragraph 5.1 and 5.2 - Responsibility for the Control of Purchases and Purchasing Data - Alpha Designators S, U

5.1 Request for Supplier/Vendor Quality Evaluation
5.2 Quality Survey of New Supplier/Vendor
5.3 Supplier/Vendor Quality Evaluation Report
5.4 Supplier/Vendor Process Certification
5.5 Procurement Quality Assurance Review
5.6 Supplier Quality Rating
5.7 Supplier/Vendor Parts Qualification
5.8 Source Inspection at Subcontractor/Vendor Facility

3.0 Quality Program Management

Paragraph 3.3 - Work Instructions/Inspection and Test Documentation - Alpha Designator X

3.11 Work Instructions and Inspection/Testing Documentation
3.12 Automated Test Equipment
3.13 Inspection and Test Reporting

6.0 Manufacturing Control

Paragraph 6.1 - Receiving Inspection - Alpha Designators K, Y

6.15 Receiving and Raw Material Inspection
6.16 Material Purge

CHAPTER FIVE

Contractual Intent

QUALITY PUBLICATIONS

MIL-Q-9858A states, "The contractor shall provide and maintain a quality program acceptable to the Government for supplies and services covered by the contract. The quality program shall be in accordance with MIL-Q-9858A." Paragraph 1.2 - Contractual Intent states, "The quality program, including procedures, processes and product shall be documented and shall be subject to review by the Government Representative...The individual instructions and records for preparing instructions and records do not document a program." Government contractors are required to write a quality manual that describes their quality program and its intent to conform to the requirements of the contract. The quality procedures in a quality manual must be traceable to all documented and approved manufacturing, production, inspection and testing instructions that are used throughout the complete contract planning and production cycle. Quality Control Publications 2.1.1 and 2.1.2 are sample procedures that contractors may use to address the topic of quality manual publications control when writing a quality manual.

The NASA requirements are particularly specific in relation to quality program plans. NHB 5300.4(1B), paragraph 1B206 states, "The contractor shall prepare, maintain, and implement a Quality Program Plan which describes how the contractor will ensure compliance with cited quality requirements. The Quality Program Plan shall be submitted as required by the Request for Proposal or contract. The Plan format shall be readily identified with each cited requirement. The Plan shall cover all quality program activities for the time period or phase authorized, be updated periodically, and resubmitted, as specified in the contract, and serve as the master planning and control document."

For an inspection system, NHB 5300.1(1C), paragraph 1C201 states, "An Inspection System Plan shall be prepared and submitted as required by the contract. The Plan shall cover activities for the contract period and shall include:

1. An organizational chart showing each element of the quality organization and its relation to the entire organization.

2. A narrative description of the contractor's existing system for implementing quality provisions, including proposed changes to the existing system needed to meet cited provisions and the time schedule for implementing such changes. The plan should be arranged in the publication or the plan should contain a cross-reference to applicable sections thereof.

3. Reference to contractor quality documents to be utilized in meeting inspection system provisions."

NHB 5300.4(1D-2), Safety, Reliability, Maintainability and Quality Provisions for the Space Shuttle Program, chapter 5, 1D5000, paragraph 3 states, "The contractor shall prepare, maintain, and implement a Quality Plan which describes how he will ensure compliance with the requirements set forth herein. The Plan content shall be readily identified with each cited requirement and shall cover all quality activities for the contract."

The above NASA requirements have been dealt with in an extensive manner here. This was done to show how NASA approaches the requirement for a quality plan/manual. The NASA specification expands, clearly, on the similar requirements of MIL-Q-9858A as it pertains to a documented and approved quality program and procedures.

QUALITY CONTROL PUBLICATION	QCP NO. 2.1.1
	PAGE NO. 1 OF 4
	ISSUE DATE:
TITLE: CONTROL OF QUALITY CONTROL PUBLICATIONS	APPROVED BY:
	REVISION NO:
	REVISION DATE:

1.0 PURPOSE

The purpose of this quality control publication is to provide a set of instructions for the preparation of all quality control publications. This includes the proper method for securing the necessary approvals and distribution of the published copies.

2.0 INTENT

The intent of this QCP is to instruct personnel assigned to prepare, revise, authorize, and distribute quality control publications, in the method of their preparation, revision, and distribution.

3.0 DEFINITIONS

3.1 Quality control publications are the directives issued by the quality assurance department that establishes the methods and procedures required to administer and control the quality of the product and services the company offers for sale. Quality control publications provide for the basic information that is required for describing the control that is necessary to protect product quality. Additional controls and instructions are addressed in the individual instructions.

4.0 APPLICABLE FORMS AND PUBLICATIONS

4.1 Quality Publications Status Log, Form 2.1.1-1

4.2 Quality Control Publications, Form 2.1.1-2

4.3 Quality Publication Initiation/Change, Form 2.1.1-3

4.4 Inspection/Test Instructions, QCP 3.3.1

QUALITY CONTROL PUBLICATION	QCP NO. 2.1.1
	PAGE NO. 2 OF 4
	ISSUE DATE:
TITLE: CONTROL OF QUALITY CONTROL PUBLICATIONS	APPROVED BY:
	REVISION NO:
	REVISION DATE:

5.0 PROCEDURE

5.1 New quality control publications may be requested by supervisory personnel. A rough draft should be prepared using Form 2.1.1-3, outlining the purpose of the quality control publication.

5.2 Revisions to existing QCP's may be requested by any supervisory personnel. Form 2.1.1-3 will be used to describe the proposed change completely using references to the original QCP to explain the reasons for the proposed change. Form 2.1.1-3 when filled out, will then be submitted to the quality assurance department for review, approval, writing and publication.

5.3 The quality assurance department will assign a QCP number to new publications consistent with the number of the section headings of MIL-Q-9858A.

5.4 A record of work in process will be maintained on the Form 2.1.1-1. Form 2.1.1-1 illustrates the *Quality Publication Status Log* that is used for recording the data relative to initiating the QCP.

5.5 Quality control publications will be typewritten on the form illustrated in Form 2.1.1-2. This form will be filled out as follows:

Block 1 - For recording the name and address of the company, the telephone number, and the publications specific title that refers to it's content.

Block 2 - For recording the assigned QCP numbers.

Block 3 - For recording page numbers.

Block 4 - For recording the date when the publication is to take effect.

Block 5 - For approval signature (director of quality assurance department or authorized representative).

Block 6 - For recording the latest revision designation of the publication.

QUALITY CONTROL PUBLICATION	QCP NO. 2.1.1
	PAGE NO. 3 OF 4
	ISSUE DATE:
TITLE: CONTROL OF QUALITY CONTROL PUBLICATIONS	APPROVED BY:
	REVISION NO:
	REVISION DATE:

Block 7 - For recording the latest date of revision.

Block 8 - For typing in the body of the publication. A sample body for all publications is pictured in this QCP.

5.6 The format for all QCP's is as follows:

a. Purpose
b. Intent
c. Definitions (if applicable)
d. Applicable forms and publications
e. Procedure

Under Purpose
A clear statement as to the publications purpose. (example - see 1.0 of this publication.)

Under Intent
A clear description of departments, functions or items affected by the publication.

Under Definitions
Clear definitions of the meaning of unique or special words or items appropriate to the publication.

Under Applicable Forms and Publications
Listing of forms and quality publications applicable to the Quality Control publication (QCP).

5.7 When drafts and final revised publications have been completed, they are to be distributed to the departments affected, for coordination and approval. Each draft of the publication is distributed using the Quality Publication Initiation/Change, Form 2.1.1-3. After review, and if necessary, with corrections made to the proposed initiation or change, the appropriate supervisory personnel are to sign the form indicating approval of the initiation/change.

QUALITY CONTROL PUBLICATION	QCP NO. 2.1.1
	PAGE NO. 4 OF 4
	ISSUE DATE:
TITLE: CONTROL OF QUALITY CONTROL PUBLICATIONS	APPROVED BY:
	REVISION NO:
	REVISION DATE:

5.8 After all supervisory personnel have approved the initiation/change, the form is to be submitted to the director of quality assurance or an authorized representative for approval. The approval signatures are to be placed in blocks 7 and 10 of the form.

5.9 Approved and published QCP's are to be distributed to authorized quality manual holders.

5.10 All quality publications are to be reviewed annually by the quality assurance department to ensure continued correctness, proper revision levels, and applicability to current procedures and instructions used

QUALITY PUBLICATIONS STATUS LOG

PUBLICATION TITLE	QCP NUMBER	INITIATOR	DATE BEGUN	DATE COMPL.	APPROVAL	DATE APPROVED

FORM 2.1.1-1

NAME AND ADDRESS OF YOUR COMPANY ① TELEPHONE NO. QUALITY CONTROL PUBLICATION TITLE:	QCP NO. ②
	PAGE NO. OF ③
	ISSUE DATE: ④
	APPROVED BY: ⑤
	REVISION NO: ⑥
	REVISION DATE: ⑦

⑧

FORM 2.1.1-2

QUALITY PUBLICATION INITIATION/CHANGE FORM

PUBLICATION NAME ①		QCP NUMBER ②
STATUS (CHECK ONE) ③	DRAFT ☐	FINAL FORMAT ☐
DEPARTMENT INITIATING: ④		NAME OF INITIATOR ⑤

IF CHANGES OR CORRECTIONS ARE REQUIRED, WRITE COMMENTS HERE:

⑥

DEPARTMENT SUPERVISORS APPROVAL

NAME/TITLE ⑦	DEPARTMENT ⑧	DATE ⑨

APPROVAL/QC DIRECTOR ⑩

NAME ⑪	DATE ⑫

FORM 2.1.1-3

QUALITY CONTROL PUBLICATION	QCP NO. 2.1.2
	PAGE NO. 1 OF 2
	ISSUE DATE:
TITLE: INTERIM QUALITY CONTROL PUBLICATIONS	APPROVED BY:
	REVISION NO: 0
	REVISION DATE:

1.0 PURPOSE

The purpose of this quality control publication is to describe the preparation and distribution of *interim* quality control publications.

2.0 INTENT

2.1 Interim quality publications are used to provide:

a. Emergency changes to existing quality publications.

b. Expedite the application of interim publications, pending the publications final approval and incorporation into the quality manual.

c. The one-time or limited use of the publication until it has been incorporated into the quality manual.

3.0 APPLICABLE FORMS AND PUBLICATIONS

3.1 Interim Quality Publications, Form 2.1.2-1

4.0 PROCEDURE

4.1 Requests

4.1.1 Requests for the initiation or use of interim quality publications will be submitted to the quality assurance department for approval prior to the initiation or dissemination of the interim publications.

4.2 Distribution

4.2.1 If distribution is required by other than holders of the quality manual, a distribution list will be submitted by the supervisor of the requesting department to the quality assurance department for approval and distribution.

4.3 Preparation of

4.3.1 The interim quality publication, Form 2.1.2-1, is to be filled out as follows:

QUALITY CONTROL PUBLICATION	QCP NO. 2.1.2
	PAGE NO. 2 OF 2
	ISSUE DATE:
TITLE: INTERIM QUALITY CONTROL PUBLICATIONS	APPROVED BY:
	REVISION NO: 0
	REVISION DATE:

1. Name, title, department of the requestor.
2. The control number of the interim publication. The control number will follow the same numbering system as used for the QCP numbers as described in QCP 2.1.1, except that a -1 will follow the number.
3. The publications release date.
4. The page number of the publication, starting with 1. If the interim publication supersedes a previously issued bulletin, the appropriate page numbers shall be cited.
5. The QCP number of the superseded publication.
6. The release date of the superseded publication.
7. The specific title of the publication.
8. The complete text of the interim publication.
9. This block will be checkmarked relative to any of the four statements as follows:
   a. Retain this publication until further notice.
   b. This publication is invalid after (date)
   c. This bulletin will be incorporated into Quality Publication No. ——— by (date) ————
10. Approval signature of the director of quality assurance after review. If the interim publications instructions are applicable to other departments, signatures of the applicable supervision will be required.

4.4 Distribution

4.4.1 When the interim quality publication has been accepted and all necessary signatures have been obtained, it is to be reproduced and the required distribution be made. Distribution is to be made to all quality manual holders, and if required, any additional names on the distribution list (see paragraph 4.2.1) are to receive copies.

INTERIM QUALITY PUBLICATION

NAME OF INITIATOR (1)	TITLE	DEPT
TITLE (7)	NUMBER OF INTERIM QCP: (2) DATE: (3) PAGE NUMBER (4) QCP SUPERSEDED: (5) DATE SUPERSEDED: (6)	

TEXT

(8)

(10)

DIRECTOR OF QUALITY ASSURANCE

(9)

RETAIN THIS INTERIM PUBLICATION UNTIL FURTHER NOTICE: ☐

THIS INTERIM PUBLICATION WILL BE INVALID AFTER (DATE) ☐

THIS INTERIM PUBLICATION WILL BE INCORPORATED INTO QUALITY CONTROL PUBLICATION NO. ______ BY (DATE)__________ ☐

FORM 2.1.2-1

QUALITY STAMPS

Several quotations from MIL-HDBK-H50, NHB 5300.41B, NHB 5300.4(1C), and NHB 5300.4(1D-2) are used in this section to show the relationship between the MIL-Q-9858A, MIL-I-45208A, NASA programs and the following quality control publication, QCP 2.2.1. This and other similar discussions throughout this book will help in the understanding of the linguistics of government quality program specifications.

Paragraph 3.4 of MIL-HDBK-H50 states, "The contractor is responsible for controlling and assuring quality and for providing objective evidence that this control and assurance do, in fact, exist." Paragraph 6.2 states, "Means for identifying approved and rejected product shall be provided." Paragraph 6.7 states, "The contractor shall maintain a positive system for identifying the inspection status of products. Identification may be accomplished by means of stamps, tags, routing cards, move tickets, tote box cards or other normal control devices." MIL-Q-9858A permits contractors to select any method for indicating inspection status, provided only that it cannot be mistaken for government identification (This means, do not copy the government stamps). The use of stamps is one of the ways in which contractors are able to identify the inspection status of materials, and products, at any stage of the contract cycle. QCP 2.2.1. is a sample of a quality control publication that may be used to help format a procedure that will best fit a contractors needs.

NASA's, Quality Program Provisions, NHB 5300.4(1B), paragraph 1B1000, Stamp Control System, states, "The contractor shall establish and maintain a documented stamp control system including written procedures, which provide for the following:

1. Stamps, decals, seals, torque wax, paints, signatures, etc., shall identify that articles and materials have undergone source and receiving inspection, in-process fabrication, end-item testing, storage, and shipment.

2. Stamps shall be traceable to each individual responsible for their use and records shall be maintained to identify individuals with specific stamps. Fabrication and inspection stamps shall be of different design."

Paragraph 1B1001, Stamp Restriction, states, "Contractor's stamps shall not contain the designation NASA." NHB 5300.4(1C), paragraph 1C306, states, "Controls shall be maintained for continuously indicating the inspection status of articles and materials by using identifications distinctly different from

Government inspection identification. This shall be accomplished by means of stamps, seals, or decals on individual articles and materials; or tags, routing cards, etc...Contractor stamps having the same shape as NASA stamps are permissible providing the contractor stamp does not include the designation "NASA". NHB 5300.4(1D-2), Safety, Reliability, Maintainability and Quality Provisions for the Space Shuttle Program, paragraph 1D508, states "The contractor shall establish and maintain a documented stamp control technique, including written procedures, that provides for the following:

a. Stamps, decals, seals, torque wax, paints, signatures, etc., shall identify that articles and materials have undergone source and receiving inspection, in-process fabrication and inspection, end item fabrication and inspection, end-item testing, storage and shipment.

b. Stamps shall be traceable to individuals responsible for their use and records shall be maintained to identify individuals for their use and records shall be maintained to identify individuals with specific stamps. Unissued stamps shall be kept secure to prevent unauthorized use.

QUALITY CONTROL PUBLICATION	QCP NO. 2.2.1
	PAGE NO. 1 OF 4
	ISSUE DATE:
TITLE: QUALITY STAMPS	APPROVED BY:
	REVISION NO: 0
	REVISION DATE:

1.0 PURPOSE

This quality control publication establishes the procedures for the issuing, using and controlling the quality inspection identification stamps that are required for identifying the inspection status of products.

2.0 INTENT

This QCP applies to inspectors, test personnel, and other personnel who are issued, use, or control the issuance of quality inspection/identification stamps.

3.0 APPLICABLE FORMS AND MATERIAL

3.1 Receipt For Quality Inspection Identification Stamps, Form 2.2.1-2.
3.2 Control Log For Quality Inspection Identification Stamps, Form 2.2.1-3.
3.3 Inspection Stamp, Form 2.2.1-1.

4.0 PROCEDURE

4.1 Quality inspection identification stamps will be made of one of two types of material:

4.1.1 Steel - For items requiring an incised stamp mark and for use on multiple copy forms.

4.1.2 Rubber - For items that would be damaged by the use of a steel stamp. To be used with permanent ink.

4.2 Each stamp will be identified by the number on the face of the stamp. The stamp will be issued to a specific person and will be identified to that person by the number that appears on the face of the stamp.

QUALITY CONTROL PUBLICATION	QCP NO. 2.2.1
	PAGE NO. 2 OF 4
	ISSUE DATE:
TITLE: QUALITY STAMPS	APPROVED BY:
	REVISION NO: 0
	REVISION DATE:

4.3 The types of stamps to be used are illustrated in Form 2.2.1-1, Quality Inspection Identification Stamps. The use for these stamps are as follows:

4.3.1 Source Inspection Acceptance Stamp

This stamp indicates materials have been inspected and accepted at a subcontractors, suppliers facility.

4.3.2 In-Process Acceptance Stamp

This stamp is used to indicate that partially processed materials, subassemblies have been inspected at their current stage of completeness and have been found conforming to the drawing or specification.

4.3.3 Final Inspection Acceptance Stamp

This stamp is used to identify the acceptance of completed product that has been inspected prior to shipment or storage.

4.3.4 Test Acceptance Stamp

This stamp is used to indicate that parts, subassemblies, assemblies that have been tested were found to be conforming in every aspect to the drawing, specification and requirement.

4.3.5 Discrepant Material Stamp

This stamp is used to identify material that is not in conformance with the drawing, specification and/or requirement.

4.3.6 Material Review Board Acceptance Stamp

This stamp is used to identify materials that have been found in conformance to the drawing, specification and/or requirement by the material review board.

4.3.7 Material Review Board Rejection Stamp

This stamp is used to mark/identify materials that have been found nonconforming to the drawing, specification and/or requirements.

QUALITY CONTROL PUBLICATION	QCP NO. 2.2.1
	PAGE NO. 3 OF 4
	ISSUE DATE:
TITLE: QUALITY STAMPS	APPROVED BY:
	REVISION NO: 0
	REVISION DATE:

4.3.8 Equipment Calibration Stamp
This stamp is used to identify measuring and test equipment that have been calibrated and meet the standards as prescribed.

4.3.9 Quality Engineering Approval Stamp
This stamp indicates approval by Quality Engineering.

4.4 The Quality Assurance Department is responsible for issuing and controlling all quality stamps.

4.5 One or more stamps with the same identification number may be issued to personnel authorized to use them. When the stamps are issued the following information will be recorded on Form 2.2.1-2, as follows:

1. Date the stamp is issued.
2. The stamp identification number that is assigned.
3. The name, job title, department, and employee number that the stamp is issued to.
4. An impression of the stamp on the form when issued.
5. Description of the stamp (use).
6. Signature of the employee receiving the stamp.
7. Signature of the authorized issuer of the stamp.

4.6 The quality assurance department will keep control logs of all quality stamps in the company. The Control Log Form 2.2.1-3, will be filled out as follows:

1. The stamp number (the number on the face of the stamp).
2. Quantity of stamps made with the same number.
3. Stamp type.

QUALITY CONTROL PUBLICATION TITLE: QUALITY STAMPS	QCP NO. 2.2.1
	PAGE NO. 4 OF 4
	ISSUE DATE:
	APPROVED BY:
	REVISION NO: 0
	REVISION DATE:

4. Who the stamp has been issued to.
5. The date the stamp was issued.
6. Date the stamp was returned.
7. Date the stamp was reported lost.

SOURCE INSPECTION ACCEPTANCE STAMP

IN-PROCESS INSPECTION ACCEPTANCE STAMP

FINAL ACCEPTANCE STAMP

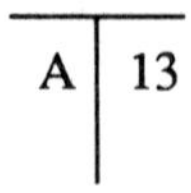

TEST ACCEPTANCE STAMP

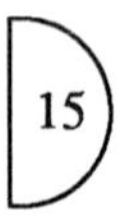

DISCREPANT MATERIAL STAMP

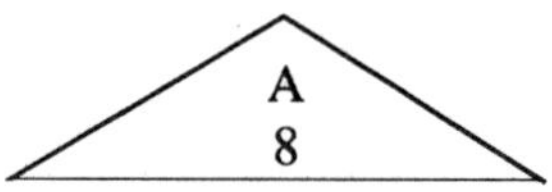

MATERIAL REVIEW BOARD ACCEPTANCE STAMP

MATERIAL REVIEW BOARD REJECTION STAMP

EQUIPMENT CALIBRATION STAMP

QUALITY ENGINEERING STAMP

FORM 2.2.1-1 QUALITY INSPECTION IDENTIFICATION STAMPS

RECEIPT
FOR
QUALITY INSPECTION IDENTIFICATION STAMPS

DATE: ______ (1) ______ STAMP(S) NO. ______ (2) ______

ISSUED TO: ______ (3) ______

JOB TITLE: ____________

DEPARTMENT: ____________

IMPRESSION AND DESCRIPTION OF EACH STAMP ISSUED

(4) STAMP	(5) DESCRIPTION
____________	____________
____________	____________
____________	____________
____________	____________

STAMPS ARE TO BE USED ONLY AS SPECIFIED BY QC PUBLICATION

ACKNOWLEDGED:

(7) ____________	(6) ____________
ISSUER - Q.C.	STAMP RECEIVED BY

*ONLY ONE STAMP NUMBER IS TO BE SHOWN. A SEPARATE RECEIPT WILL BE FILLED OUT FOR EACH ADDITIONAL NUMBER.

FORM 2.2.1-2

CONTROL LOG
FOR
QUALITY INSPECTION STAMPS

STAMP NO: ① ____________

QUANTITY MADE: ②

APPLICATION	RUBBER		STEEL	
	NO	QTY	NO	QTY
SOURCE INSP. ACCEPTANCE STAMP	A34		SA34	
IN-PROCESS ACCEPTANCE STAMP	A11		SA11	
FINAL INSP. ACCEPTANCE STAMP	A31		SA31	
TEST ACCEPTANCE STAMP	A13		SA13	
DISCREPANT MATERIAL STAMP	15		SA15	
MATERIAL BD. ACCEPTANCE STAMP	A08		SA08	
MATERIAL REV. REJECTION STAMP	03		SA03	
EQUIPMENT CALIBRATION STAMP	CAL2		SCA2	
QUALITY ENGINEERING STAMP	QE5		SQE5	

ISSUE INFORMATION

STAMP TYPE	ISSUED TO	DATES		
		ISSUED	RETURNED	LOST
③	④	⑤	⑥	⑦

FORM 2.2.1-3

QUALITY AUDITS

MIL-HDBK-H50, paragraph 1.2(c), Criteria for Evaluation, states, "All supplies and services under the contract, whether manufactured or performed within the contractors plant or at any other source, shall be controlled at all points necessary to assure conformance to contractual requirements. The program shall provide for the prevention and ready detection of discrepancies and for timely and positive corrective action. The contractor shall make evidence of quality conformance readily available to the Government Representative. Instructions and records for quality must be controlled."

Most contractors use, Quality Audits, as one of the means for the early detection of quality problems and deficiencies. Audit plans are prepared, taking into consideration every aspect in the way the company does it business. If any defects are found during these audits, immediate corrective action is to be implemented to correct these discrepancies. This means the root cause for the defects have been found and effective corrective action must be taken to prevent the reoccurrence of the defects. The audit system does not have to take the form of an audit system used by the government. The audit system should be planned to meet the needs and requirements of the company. The following QCP 2.3.1, will help contractors format and write a procedure that will meet a contractors needs.

NASA's requirements for the use of Quality Program Audits follows NHB 5300.4(1B), Quality Program Provisions. Paragraph 1B205, states, "The contractor shall conduct audits of personnel, procedures, and operations which implement the quality program. Each audit shall be performed by a team of contractor personnel familiar with all written procedures and standards applicable to the operation or work areas being audited and shall include personnel not having specific line responsibilities in those areas. Each audit shall include examination of all operations and documentation, evaluation of actual operations as compared with established requirements, recommendations for remedial and preventive action, and follow-up to assess results of recommendations. Audits shall include examination of articles and materials to verify the effectiveness of the contractor's efforts...Random unscheduled audits shall be performed in order to effectively assess existing conditions and operations...The results of audits in each area shall be documented in a report to contractor higher management with appropriate recommendations for correction of deficiencies. Management action shall be taken to ensure effective correction of the reported deficiencies. Follow-up reviews shall be made to ensure that required corrections have been implemented." NHB 5300.4(1D-2), paragraph 1D200.6, states, "NASA audit teams will periodically audit the contractor's safety activities. The contractor shall support these audits as required." Paragraph 1D300.33, states, "The contractor shall conduct audits of the internal reliability activity and those activities of the suppliers. These reviews shall evaluate progress and effectiveness and shall determine the need for adjustments or changes in the reliability activities. Audits shall be conducted at appropriate intervals." Paragraph 1D501, states, "The contractor shall conduct audits of personnel, procedures, and operations which implement the quality program."

QUALITY CONTROL PUBLICATION TITLE: QUALITY AUDITS	QCP NO. 2.3.1
	PAGE NO. 1 OF 4
	ISSUE DATE:
	APPROVED BY:
	REVISION NO: 0
	REVISION DATE:

1.0 PURPOSE

This quality control publication establishes the method for periodically verifying the quality system established by the company. The audit system is one of the methods used by the Quality Assurance Department in determining the effectiveness of the company's policies and procedures that are used to implement product quality.

2.0 INTENT

The intent of this QCP is to describe the method that will be used by the quality assurance department in auditing the following functions within the company:

1. Purchasing department
2. Receiving department
3. Receiving inspection
4. Stores
5. Production, manufacturing, assembly
6. Plating, welding, soldering and all other special processes
7. Engineering controls
8. Calibration laboratory
9. All other inspection and test functions
10. Shipping
11. Automatic Testing Equipment (ATE).

QUALITY CONTROL PUBLICATION	QCP NO. 2.3.1
	PAGE NO. 2 OF 4
	ISSUE DATE:
TITLE: QUALITY AUDITS	APPROVED BY:
	REVISION NO: 0
	REVISION DATE:

And all other company functions that have an effect on product quality. The quality auditing of subcontractors, vendors, and all other suppliers of material and product is covered by QCP 2.3.2.

3.0 APPLICABLE FORMS AND PUBLICATIONS

3.1 Quality Assurance Audit Log, Report and Findings, Forms 2.3.1-1A, 2.3.1-1B, 2.3.1-1C, and 2.3.1-1D

3.2 Corrective Action Process, see QCP 3.5.1.

4.0 DEFINITION

4.1 Quality Audit

4.1.1 A quality audit is an examination by the quality assurance department of all functions within the company that would affect product quality, and to verify the effectiveness of company's quality program.

5.0 PROCEDURE

5.1 The quality assurance department is responsible for planning and conducting the Quality Audits.

5.2 A Yearly Quality Audit Log, Form 2.3.1-1A will be filled out as follows:

1. The year the quality audits are to be accomplished.
2. Audit plan number and department number.
3. Dates of proposed audits.
4. Process, requirement, product, etc. to be audited.
5. Specification or requirement to be used in audit.

QUALITY CONTROL PUBLICATION	QCP NO. 2.3.1
	PAGE NO. 3 OF 4
	ISSUE DATE:
TITLE: QUALITY AUDITS	APPROVED BY:
	REVISION NO: 0
	REVISION DATE:

6. Is the audit to be performed in-house?
7. Is the audit to be performed at a vendor's or subcontractor's facility? (check one)
8. Audit report number. (prior to starting audit)
9. Date audit was completed.
10. Audit schedule approved by (QA manager.)

5.3 The director of quality assurance will review the log, and after possible corrections, will sign Log (10), indicating approval, and date of approval.

5.4 The audit will be accomplished as shown in Form 2.3.1.-1B:

1. Date of audit.
2. Audit report number.
3. Department audited.
4. Log number.
5. Department number.
6. Requirement audited.
7. Specifications used for audit.
8. Audit acceptable. (check if appropriate).
9. Discrepancy(ies) found. (check if appropriate).
10. In-house audit. (check if appropriate).
11. Vendor, subcontractor audit. (check if appropriate).
12. Vendor number (as assigned by the Purchasing Department).
13. Personnel contacted.
14. Personnel performing audit.

QUALITY CONTROL PUBLICATION	QCP NO. 2.3.1
	PAGE NO. 4 OF 4
	ISSUE DATE:
TITLE: QUALITY AUDITS	APPROVED BY:
	REVISION NO: 0
	REVISION DATE:

5.5 The quality Audit Report Findings form will be used to describe all nonconformances in detail and the corrective action to be taken before the report can be finalized. The report in Form 2.3.1-1C will be filled out as follows:

1. Audit report number.
2. Audit log number.
3. Date of report.
4. Specification or requirement in nonconformance.
5. Description of nonconformance.
6. Description of corrective action.
7. Audited by (quality assurance auditor).
8. Approved by (director/manager of quality assurance).
9. Date of approval.

5.6 The report is reviewed by the director or manager of the quality assurance department and is approved by signing and dating the report (8).

5.7 The auditor will follow-up on all corrective action until it is completed, and compliance to the corrective action has been verified, (see QCP 3.5.1 - Corrective Action Process).

5.8 Form 2.3.1-1D, Cover Sheet, will be filled out by the appropriate management personnel and attached to the front of the completed audit

YEARLY QUALITY AUDIT LOG

Year ① ____

AUDIT LOG ②		DATE OF AUDIT	PROCESS ETC. TO BE AUDITED	SPECIFICATION USED FOR AUDIT	CONDUCTED		AUDIT REPORT NUMBER
DEPT.	DEPT. NO.				IN HOUSE	VENDOR	
ACCOUNTING	05	③	④	⑤	⑥	⑦	⑧
ASSEMBLY	10						
CAD	15						
CAL LAB	20						
ENGINEERING	25						
MACH. SHOP	30						
MOLDING	35						
NDT	40						
PC BOARDS	45						
PLATING	50						
PRODUCTION	55						
PURCHASING	60						
RECEIVING	65						
REC'V. INSP.	70						
SHIPPING	75						
STOCK	80						
WELDING	85						
POTTING	90						

APPROVED BY: ⑩ ____

DATE: ⑨ ____

FORM 2.3.1-1A

PAGE 1 OF 2

QUALITY AUDIT REPORT

DATE OF AUDIT ① ____________

AUDIT REPORT NUMBER	DEPT. AUDITED	LOG NO.	DEPT. NO.	REQUIREMENT AUDITED	SPECIFICATION USED FOR AUDIT	RESULT OF AUDIT		TYPE OF AUDIT	
						GOOD	DISCREP.	IN-HOUSE	VENDOR
②	③	④	⑤	⑥	⑦	⑧	⑨	⑩	⑪

VENDOR NO: ⑫ ____________

PERSONNEL CONTACTED: ⑬ ____________

PERSONNEL PERFORMING AUDIT: ⑭ ____________

FORM 2.3.1-1B

QUALITY AUDIT REPORT

PAGE 2 OF 2

AUDIT REPORT NO. ____ ① AUDIT LOG NO. ____ ② DATE OF REPORT ____ ③

SPECIFICATION OR REQUIREMENT	DESCRIPTION OF DEFICIENCY	DESCRIPTION OF CORRECTIVE ACTION
④	⑤	⑥

⑦ AUDITED BY: ____ DATE: ____

⑧ APPROVED BY: ____ ⑨ DATE: ____

FORM 2.3.1-1C

COVER SHEET

QUALITY AUDITS

QUALITY PLAN ACCEPTANCE

QUALITY ASSURANCE DIRECTOR	DATE
PROGRAM MANAGER	DATE
PURCHASING DEPARTMENT	DATE
QUALITY ENGINEER	DATE

FORM 2.3.1-1D

QUALITY CONTROL PUBLICATION	QCP NO. 2.3.2
	PAGE NO. 1 OF 2
	ISSUE DATE:
TITLE: VENDOR QUALITY AUDITS	APPROVED BY:
	REVISION NO:
	REVISION DATE:

1.0 PURPOSE

This quality control publication establishes the method for periodically verifying the quality performance of subcontractors, suppliers, and vendors. This includes verifying that the terms and specifications as well as the quality requirements of the company's purchase orders are being complied with.

2.0 INTENT

This QCP applies specifically to subcontractors/suppliers who supply materials, goods, and services to the company.

3.0 DEFINITIONS

3.1 QCP 2.3.1, Paragraph 4.1.1

4.0 APPLICABLE FORMS AND PUBLICATIONS

4.1 Quality Assurance Audit Log, Report/Findings, (see QCP 2.3.1, paragraph 3.0). To prevent duplication, these forms will be used for vendor audit.

4.2 Supplier Corrective Action, QCP 3.5.2.

5.0 PROCEDURE

5.1 The quality assurance department in conjunction with the purchasing department, is responsible for planning and conducting quality audits at all subcontractors, supplier, and vendors facilities.

5.2 Quality engineering will select the subcontractors, suppliers and vendors, for auditing based on first buy, and on the basis of prior quality problems with that supplier.

QUALITY CONTROL PUBLICATION	QCP NO. 2.3.2
	PAGE NO. 2 OF 2
	ISSUE DATE:
TITLE: VENDOR QUALITY AUDITS	APPROVED BY:
	REVISION NO:
	REVISION DATE:

5.3 The director/manager of quality assurance will assign the personnel from the quality assurance department who will be responsible for conducting these audits. The purchasing department manager is responsible for (if necessary) the assignment of purchasing department personnel who will participate in these audits.

5.4 A cover sheet, Form 2.3.1-1D, will be filled out as required. This cover sheet contains all of the necessary approvals needed to implement the audits.

5.5 The auditor will make the necessary plans utilizing Forms 2.3.1-1A, 2.3.1-1B, 2.3.1-1C and 2.3.1-1D. The necessary information needed to fill out these forms are in QCP 2.3.1, paragraph 5.2, 5.3, 5.4, 5.5, 5.6 and 5.7.

5.6 The purchasing department buyer in conjunction with quality assurance will make all of the necessary arrangements with the company/facility to be audited to verify that the subcontractor, vendor or supplier has the necessary key personnel available to assist in conducting the audit.

5.7 Following the audit, the reports are to be coordinated with the purchasing department. The purchasing department is responsible for the transmission of the results of the survey to the subcontractor, vendor, or supplier.

5.8 The quality assurance auditor is responsible for the initiation and follow-up of *supplier corrective action requests* that are due to any nonconformances/discrepancies found during the audit, and for the timely resolution of all corrective actions.

QUALITY WORKSHOPS

The importance of the following statements should not be underestimated. They require that definite actions be taken by the contractor that will assure the government obtains a product or service that is conforming in every respect to the contract requirements.

MIL-HDBK-H50, states, "Among the characteristics of an effective quality program are delegation of authority, responsibility, and accountability for decisions affecting quality in a clear and precise manner which assures the proper functioning of the quality program. Contractors also recognize that the quality programs must be responsive to changing needs. Accordingly, contractors ordinarily provide for the continuous acquisition of current data on the status of quality."

The above quotation from MIL-HDBK-H50 serves to show the concern that the government has in the ability of contractors to provide the current and latest quality data to all of their personnel. For a quality system to succeed, contractors personnel have to be kept informed as to the latest quality policies and procedures of the company and to the latest data available. New and innovative quality control theories, as publicized in various magazines, newsletters, and books on this subject are being implemented into practical use throughout the world. This trend will last for a long period of time. The implementation of quality control in the workplace encompasses all facets of a company's method of doing business. Without a knowledgeable workforce this control could not be implemented easily or without resistance. QCP 2.4.1 was written as a guide in the writing of a procedure that establishes the way in which the employees of the company are exposed to the quality objectives of the company, as it relates to government requirements and specifications.

Paragraph 1B202 of NHB 5300.4(1B), relates NASA's requirement for personnel training. It states, "The contractor shall have trained competent personnel for the implementation of the quality program. The contractor shall develop, maintain, and implement necessary training for engineering, fabrication, test, procurement, quality assurance, and other personnel who may have an effect upon or who are responsible for the determination of quality or to meet cited requirements of this publication. Training activities shall be documented and shall provide for:

a. Excellence of workmanship and personnel skills.

b. Careful and safe operations.

c. Maintenance and improvement, where necessary, of article and material quality."

Paragraph 1D500.7, states, "The contractor shall develop, maintain, and implement necessary quality training...The training for critical processes shall include, as applicable, adhesive and resin application, welding, brazing, soldering, electrical connector operations, contamination control operations, and nondestructive testing evaluations. The contractor shall utilize the list of critical processes (refer to paragraph 1D504-4C) to develop training requirements." This paragraph is found in NHB 5300.4(1D-2), Safety, Reliability, Maintainability and Quality Provisions for the Space Shuttle Program.

QUALITY CONTROL PUBLICATION TITLE: QUALITY WORKSHOPS	QCP NO. 2.4.1
	PAGE NO. 1 OF 3
	ISSUE DATE:
	APPROVED BY:
	REVISION NO: 0
	REVISION DATE:

1.0 PURPOSE

The purpose of this quality control publication is to establish a method for familiarizing new employees with the company's Quality Assurance policies and procedures, and updating this training for all personnel on an annual basis or as needed/required.

2.0 INTENT

This QCP applies to all personnel, whether, a new hire, or as a yearly update to the company's quality assurance policies and procedures and to new government requirements as applicable.

3.0 APPLICABLE FORMS AND PUBLICATIONS

3.1 Quality Manual.

3.2 Quality Workshop Entry/Update Notice, Form 2.4.1-1.

3.3 Quality Assurance Entry/Update Log, Form 2.4.1-2.

4.0 PROCEDURE

4.1 The quality assurance department will establish a quality workshop to familiarize new employees of the company with its quality assurance method of operation.

4.2 A refresher workshop will be given at intervals, as determined by the quality assurance department to be necessary, to update all personnel in new quality assurance policies that have been established in the interim.

4.3 The contents and the materials presented at these workshops is the responsibility of the quality assurance department. The material included in the workshops will be, the company's organization, the

QUALITY CONTROL PUBLICATION	QCP NO. 2.4.1
	PAGE NO. 2 OF 3
	ISSUE DATE:
TITLE: QUALITY WORKSHOPS	APPROVED BY:
	REVISION NO: 0
	REVISION DATE:

quality assurance organization and its function, the reason for and the use of quality inspection and identification stamps, the purpose of quality assurance audits, certification programs, the method of quality planning, the use and application of work/inspection/test instructions and documentation, the calibration system, material review and corrective action process, drawing control, engineering change proposals, and all other policies and procedures as applicable.

4.4 Quality assurance personnel will be notified when all workshops will be held through the use of the Quality Workshop Entry/Update Notice, Form 2.4.1-1. This form will be filled out as follows:

1. The name of the employee that is to receive this notice.
2. The employee's number.
3. The department where the employee works.
4. The date of this notice.
5. The date of the workshop.
6. The starting time of the workshop.
7. The completion time of the workshop.
8. Where the workshop will be held (location).
9. The signature of the employee acknowledging the receipt of this notice.
10. The reason (if applicable), for not being able to attend the workshop.
11. The name of the initiator of this notice.
12. The department of the initiator.
13. The phone number where the initiator can be reached.

QUALITY CONTROL PUBLICATION	QCP NO. 2.4.1
	PAGE NO. 3 OF 3
	ISSUE DATE:
TITLE: QUALITY WORKSHOPS	APPROVED BY:
	REVISION NO: 0
	REVISION DATE:

Upon the employee signing the acknowledgement portion of this notice, the notice will be returned to the initiator, with a copy of the notice retained by the employee and supervisor.

4.5 If an employe is unable to attend the workshop as scheduled, the supervisor must arrange a new date for attending the workshop, along with an explanation as to the reason for not being able to attend. This information must be sent to the initiator of the notice using the above form.

4.6 The quality assurance department will maintain a log of all quality assurance personnel who are scheduled to attend the quality workshops and the dates of attendance. The Quality Workshop Entry/Update Log Sheet, Form 2.4.1-2, will be filled out as follows:

1. The name of the employee scheduled to attend the workshop.
2. The employee's number.
3. The department where the employee works.
4. The department number.
5. The ate of the scheduled workshop.
6. The date the employee attended the workshop.
7. The date(s) of scheduled or re-scheduled workshops to be attended by the employee.

QUALITY WORKSHOP
ENTRY/UPDATE NOTICE

EMPLOYEE NAME: ①	NOTICE: YOU HAVE BEEN SCHEDULED TO ATTEND A QUALITY WORKSHOP ON THE DATE BELOW, STARTING TIME OF WORKSHOP, COMPLETION TIME AND LOCATION AS STATED BELOW.
EMPLOYEE NUMBER ②	
DEPARTMENT ③	
DATE OF NOTICE ④	

DATE OF WORKSHOP: ⑤ ______________

STARTING TIME: ⑥ ______________

COMPLETION TIME: ⑦ ______________

LOCATION OF WORKSHOP: ⑧ ______________

All employees are required to attend one of the workshops when employed. A follow-up workshop will be held annually, or more often, when new policies or procedures make it imperative to do so.

If you are unable to attend the specified workshop, please have your supervisor contact the initiator of this notice by filling in the reason below.

REASON FOR NON-ATTENDANCE:	ACKNOWLEDGEMENT:
⑩ ______________	⑨ ______________
______________	(Signature of Employee)
______________	______________
	(Date Signed)

NAME OF INITIATOR:	DEPT:	PHONE:
⑪	⑫	⑬

FORM 2.4.1-1

QUALITY WORKSHOP
ENTRY/UPDATE LOG

EMPLOYEE NAME	EMPLOYEE NUMBER	DEPARTMENT	DEPT. NO.	DATE OF WORKSHOP	DATE COMPLETED	⑦ DATE OF NEXT WORKSHOP			
①	②	③	④	⑤	⑥				

FORM 2.4.1-2

EMPLOYEE TRAINING AND CERTIFICATION

MIL-Q-9858A and its associated MIL-HDBK-H50 clearly states the need for contractors to determine the extent of the skills required by their employees in order to meet the needs of a contract, and for providing the necessary training to, and, certification of, their employees in order to meet the requirements of the contract.

Paragraph 3.2 of MIL-HDBK-H50, states, "The contractor, during the earliest practical phase of contract performance, shall conduct a complete review of the requirements of the contract to identify and make timely provision for the special controls, processes, test equipment, fixtures, tooling and skills required for assuring product quality." All contractors doing business with the government should have training programs established to meet the special requirements of the contract. These requirements include, soldering standards, welding (fusion and resistance), non-destructive testing (x-ray, magnetic particle inspection, liquid penetrant, etc.), metrology (calibration), and other special processes. Most of the requirements for certification of employees in contracts, also require recertification of these employees as a continuation of the quality process to keep pace with changing technology (e.g. changing requirements).

NHB 5300.4(1B), NASA's Quality Program Provisions, paragraph 1B202-2, states, "Contractor personnel controlling selected processes and personnel performing selected operations shall be certified. Certification by the contractor may be reviewed or repeated by the procuring NASA installation or it's designated government quality representative to verify the adequacy of such certifications. Certification of personnel shall be based upon objective evidence which includes training and testing. Certified personnel shall be given a card, badge or similar evidence of certification." Paragraph 1B202-3, states, "Contractor personnel shall be recertified based on contractor or government observation of unsatisfactory quality of articles or services; changes in techniques, parameters or required skills; or interruption of work period as established for the process or operation involved. Recertification shall require retesting of the individual to the testing procedure to demonstrate continuing proficiency. Persons failing the retest shall not be permitted to perform these processes or operations until provided with additional training and required proficiency has been demonstrated...Records shall be maintained of the training, testing, and certification status of personnel." NHB 5300.4(1D-2), paragraph 1D500.7.b, states, "Contractor personnel controlling critical processes and personnel performing critical operations shall be certified. Certification shall include satisfactory completion of a NASA approved written examination and/ or a performance demonstration which may be repeated by NASA, or it's designated representative, to verify the adequacy of such certification. Personnel certified by the contractor shall be given a card, badge, or similar evidence of certification to be carried on their person while performing their duties. Paragraph 1D500.7c, Recertification, states, "Contractor personnel controlling critical processes and personnel performing critical operations shall be certified. Certification shall include satisfactory completion of a NASA approved written examination and/or a performance demonstration which may be repeated by NASA, or it's designated representative, to verify the adequacy of such certification. Personnel certified by the contractor shall be given a card, badge, or similar evidence of certification to be carried on their person while performing their duties. Paragraph 1D500.7c, Recertification, states, "Contractor personnel shall be recertified based on contractor or government observation of unsatisfactory quality or articles or services; changes in techniques, parameters, or required skills; or interruption of work period as established for the process or operation involved."

The contractor should check the requirements and specifications of the contract in order to determine the length that a particular certification is good for, in order to plan for recertification of personnel prior to the actual need for recertification. The forgoing statement will usually be found in the process specification as called out in the contract.

QUALITY CONTROL PUBLICATION	QCP NO. 2.4.2
	PAGE NO. 1 OF 4
	ISSUE DATE:
TITLE: EMPLOYEE TRAINING AND CERTIFICATION	APPROVED BY:
	REVISION NO: 0
	REVISION DATE:

1.0 PURPOSE

This quality control publication establishes a procedure for the training and certification of those company employees that are engaged in job skills where contractual requirements call for military specifications that require special and extensive controls.

2.0 INTENT

It is the intent of this QCP to specify the ways in which employees are to be trained and certified.

3.0 APPLICABLE FORMS AND PROCEDURES

3.1 Employee Training And Certification Notice, Form 2.4.2-1.

3.2 Employee Certification Record, Form 2.4.2-2.

3.3 Employee Certification Card, Form 2.4.2-3.

4.0 PROCEDURE

4.1 The quality assurance and production engineering departments are responsible for the planning and writing of the applicable courses and for the training of employees.

4.2 The quality assurance department is responsible for monitoring and auditing all job functions that require training and certification.

4.3 Employee Training/Certification Notice, Form 2.4.2-1 will be used to notify employees of the training sessions they are scheduled to attend. This form will be filled out as follows:

QUALITY CONTROL PUBLICATION	QCP NO. 2.4.2
	PAGE NO. 2 OF 4
	ISSUE DATE:
TITLE: EMPLOYEE TRAINING AND CERTIFICATION	APPROVED BY:
	REVISION NO: 0
	REVISION DATE:

1. The employee's name.
2. Assigned employee number.
3. Department where employee works.
4. Date of notice.
5. Training or retraining (check one).
6. To be certified or to maintain certification (check one).
7. Area to be trained and/or certified in. (Example: welding).
8. Date of training.
9. Starting time of training.
10. Location of training.
11. Reason for non-availability.
12. Name of initiator of notice.
13. Department of initiator.
14. Phone number of initiator.

4.4 If an employee is unable to attend the training session, that person's supervisor is to fill in (11) above, and return the notice to the initiator, retaining a copy for the supervisor's files.

4.5 The quality assurance department is responsible for maintaining employee training and certification records. The Employee Certification Record, Form 2.4.2-2 is to be filled out as follows:

1. The employee's name.
2. His or her employee number.
3. Department where employee works.

QUALITY CONTROL PUBLICATION TITLE: EMPLOYEE TRAINING AND CERTIFICATION	QCP NO. 2.4.2 PAGE NO. 3 OF 4 ISSUE DATE: APPROVED BY: REVISION NO: 0 REVISION DATE:

Fill out training/certification area and dates as follows:

4. Process or area of certification.
5. Date of certification.

Fill out certification expiration blocks as follows:

6. Process or area of certification.
7. Date of expiration.
8. Comments pertaining to training/certification.

4.6 Employees who have been certified will receive a Certification Card, as pictured in Form 2.4.2-3. This card will be filled out as follows:

1. Expiration date of certification.
2. Job area certified in.
3. Certification number.
4. Date of issue of card.
5. Name of the employee certified.
6. His or her employee number.
7. Department where employee works.
8. What company requirement or government specifications is covered by this card.
9. Signature of the person approved to sign (approve) the certification card.

<table>
<tr><td rowspan="6">QUALITY CONTROL PUBLICATION

TITLE: EMPLOYEE TRAINING AND CERTIFICATION</td><td>QCP NO. 2.4.2</td></tr>
<tr><td>PAGE NO. 4 OF 4</td></tr>
<tr><td>ISSUE DATE:</td></tr>
<tr><td>APPROVED BY:</td></tr>
<tr><td>REVISION NO: 0</td></tr>
<tr><td>REVISION DATE:</td></tr>
</table>

4.7 A re-certification of any employee will be required if:

1. The nature and degree of the specification requiring certification has changed.
2. The employee is being certified in a different geographical area.
3. Due to non-conformances/discrepancies found.

EMPLOYEE TRAINING/CERTIFICATION NOTICE

TO: EMPLOYEE NAME ①	EMPLOYEE NUMBER: ②
DEPARTMENT ③	DATE: ④

⑤ You are scheduled for a training ☐ retraining ☐ course

⑥ To be certified ☐ Maintain your certification ☐

⑦ In the following job function: ____________________

____

DATE OF TRAINING: ⑧ ____________________

STARTING TIME: ⑨ ____________________

LOCATION OF TRAINING: ⑩ ____________________

____

All new employees must be trained and certified who are engaged in job skills where contractual requirements or company policy mandate these requirements. Retraining and recertification will be required as necessary. If for some reason you will be unavailable for this training, please have your supervisor return this form to the initiator, explaining below the reasons for your not being able to attend this session.

REASON FOR NON-AVAILABILITY:

⑪ ______________________________________

____

____

____

____
SUPERVISOR'S SIGNATURE

____
DATE

NAME OF INITIATOR ⑫	DEPARTMENT OF INITIATOR ⑬	DATE ⑭

FORM 2.4.2-1

EMPLOYEE TRAINING/CERTIFICATION RECORD

EMPLOYEE NAME: ①	EMPLOYEE NUMBER: ②	DEPARTMENT: ③

TRAINING/CERTIFICATION AND DATES

AREA CERTIFIED	DATE	AREA CERTIFIED	DATE
④	⑤	④	⑤

CERTIFICATION EXPIRATION DATES

CERTIFICATE NUMBER	EXPIRATION DATE	CERTIFICATE NUMBER	EXPIRATION
⑥	⑦	⑥	⑦

COMMENTS: ⑧ ____________________

FORM 2.4.2-2

XYZ COMPANY
EMPLOYEE CERTIFICATION CARD

EXPIRATION DATE: ①______________

AREA OR PROCESS CERTIFIED: ②______________

CERTIFICATION NUMBER: ③______ ISSUE DATE: ④______

EMPLOYEE NAME: ⑤______________

EMPLOYEE NUMBER: ⑥______ DEPARTMENT: ⑦______

HAS BEEN CERTIFIED PER: ⑧______________

⑩ ______________
MANAGER OF PRODUCTION ENGINEERING

⑨ ______________
DIRECTOR OF QUALITY ASSURANCE

FORM 2.4.2-3

CHAPTER SIX

Organizational Structure

THE ORGANIZATIONAL STRUCTURE

Paragraph 3.1, organization, MIL-1-9858A and MIL-HDBK-H50, states "Although practically all contractors now have quality control and/or inspection departments which are focal points for quality matters, these departments cannot satisfy all of the quality program requirements of MIL-Q-9858A. Many other departments of a contractor's organization contribute to the quality efforts. Their actions, together with those of the quality and/or inspection departments, constitute the quality programs to which MIL-Q-9858A applies."

The following quality control publications, QCP's 3.1.1, 3.1.2, and 3.1.3, describe a company's organizational structure. While quality is not the realm of any one department, and MIL-Q-9858A and MIL-HDBK-H50 do not preclude assignment of the responsibility for the coordination and management of the implementation of a quality program to any one organizational component, the following QCPs set the procedures by which all management functions are to be a part of the total quality system of a contractor.

NASA's NHB 5300.4(1B), Reliability and Quality Assurance Publication - Quality Program Provisions for Aeronautical and Space System Contractor, paragraph 1B201, states, "The contractor shall make functional assignments to implement each element of his quality program. Personnel performing quality program functions shall have sufficient, well-defined responsibility and the organizational freedom to assess problems and to recommend and/or effect solutions. The effectiveness of quality program functions and the ability of assigned personnel to objectively assess, document, and report findings shall be maintained during all phases of the contract work and shall not be reduced by other considerations, such as the influence of engineering changes, rework, or rescheduling. The contractor shall designate one individual responsible for directing or managing the quality program. He shall have direct, unimpeded access to high management and shall report regularly to higher management on the status and adequacy of the program." NHB 5300.4(1D-2), Safety, Reliability, Maintainability and Quality Provisions for the Space Shuttle Program, paragraph 1D500-2, states, "The contractor shall ensure that the effectiveness of quality functions and the ability of assigned personnel to objectively assess, document, and report findings is not hampered by other considerations (such as, the overt influence of engineering changes, rework, or rescheduling), during all phases of the contract work...The contractor shall maintain an effective and timely quality assurance activity planned and developed in conjunction with all other contractors' functions necessary to satisfy the contract requirements." Paragraph 1D300, states, "The contractor shall maintain a reliability activity planned and developed in conjunction with other contractor elements. Reliability functions shall be an integral part of the design and development process and shall include the evaluation of hardware reliability through analysis, review, and assessment" (this includes the software and firmware controls that are required for such hardware that includes software and firmware). NHB 5300.4(1B), paragraph 1B206-2 states the requirement for a complete organizational plan for contractors. "Charts and narrative statements describing each element of the contractor's organization (eg., Procurement, Engineering, Reliability, Fabrication, Test, Safety, and Quality Assurance) which implement the quality program and detailed statements of duties, functions, and responsibilities relating to each quality program task. The Plan shall show the relationship of the individual managing the quality program with each element performing quality program tasks, including his authority to control and monitor cited tasks...Narrative descriptions which describe the contractor's execution and management of each task."

QUALITY CONTROL PUBLICATION TITLE: COMPANY ORGANIZATIONAL STRUCTURE	QCP NO. 3.1.1
	PAGE NO. 1 OF 4
	ISSUE DATE:
	APPROVED BY:
	REVISION NO: 0
	REVISION DATE:

1.0 PURPOSE

This quality control publication establishes the overall organizational structure of the company. It will also establish the need for all of management to take an active part in the total quality system.

2.0 INTENT

It is the intent of this QCP to describe the responsibilities of all departments within the company.

3.0 COMPANY ORGANIZATIONAL STRUCTURE

3.1 The company is made up of various organizational sections. Each of these sections interact with each other to provide a complete organization that is quality oriented. Form 3.1.1-1 is a chart of the company's organizational structure.

3.1.1 Marketing/Sales Department, provides for:

a. Market research.

b. Sales.

c. Contract Management.
   1. Contract managers.
   2. Project coordinators.

3.1.2 Accounting Department, provides for:

a. Fiscal policies.

b. Accounting.

c. Data Processing.

d. Preparation of invoices and billing.

QUALITY CONTROL PUBLICATION	QCP NO. 3.1.1
	PAGE NO. 2 OF 4
	ISSUE DATE:
TITLE: COMPANY ORGANIZATIONAL STRUCTURE	APPROVED BY:
	REVISION NO:0
	REVISION DATE:

e. Collects the cost center data. The cost center data when accumulated, is transmitted to the quality assurance department for its quarterly cost of quality reports.

3.1.3 The Personnel Department is responsible for:

a. Employment and records.

b. Employee benefits.

c. Hourly wage and salaried payroll and payroll records.

d. Labor relations.

e. Safety and security.

f. Training - Records pertaining to employee training.

3.1.4 The Engineering Department:

a. Research and development.

b. Product design.

c. Tool and equipment design.

d. Drawing and drawing controls.

e. Engineering standards and control.

f. Production engineering.

g. Facilities engineering.

h. Methods engineering.

i. Training and certification.

j. Configuration management (hardware & software).

k. Materials control and materials laboratory.

QUALITY CONTROL PUBLICATION **TITLE:** COMPANY ORGANIZATIONAL STRUCTURE	QCP NO. 3.1.1
	PAGE NO. 3 OF 4
	ISSUE DATE:
	APPROVED BY:
	REVISION NO: 0
	REVISION DATE:

3.1.5 Purchasing Department:

a. Purchasing of materials and goods.

b. Vendor, supplier, subcontractor contacts and records.

c. Vendor, supplier, subcontractor control. This includes material/goods certifications and proof of material analysis.

d. Transmission of quality requirements with the applicable purchase orders.

3.1.6 Receiving Department:

a. The receiving of all materials and goods. If material is received that is suspect of transit damage, the purchasing and quality departments will be notified immediately.

3.1.7 Shipping Department:

a. Final count of all material/product to be shipped.

b. Packaging of all material/product to the specific packaging requirements.

c. Preservation of material/product as per the applicable specification and/or contract requirement(s).

d. Shipping Documents.

e. Contact with and control of all shippers.

f. Mailroom responsibilities (if so assigned).

3.1.8 Manufacturing/Production Department;

a. Tool fabrication.

b. Tool control (tool crib/stockroom).

QUALITY CONTROL PUBLICATION	QCP NO. 3.1.1
	PAGE NO. 4 OF 4
	ISSUE DATE:
TITLE: COMPANY ORGANIZATIONAL STRUCTURE	APPROVED BY:
	REVISION NO: 0
	REVISION DATE:

c. Production planning and control.

d. Parts, subassembly, assembly fabrication and records.

e. Overhaul.

f. Repair.

3.1.9 Quality Assurance Department:

a. Quality management.

b. Quality engineering.

c. Reliability engineering.

d. Quality planning and procedures, including inspection and test instructions and documentation.

e. Calibration laboratory controls.

f. Training and certification of all quality functions.

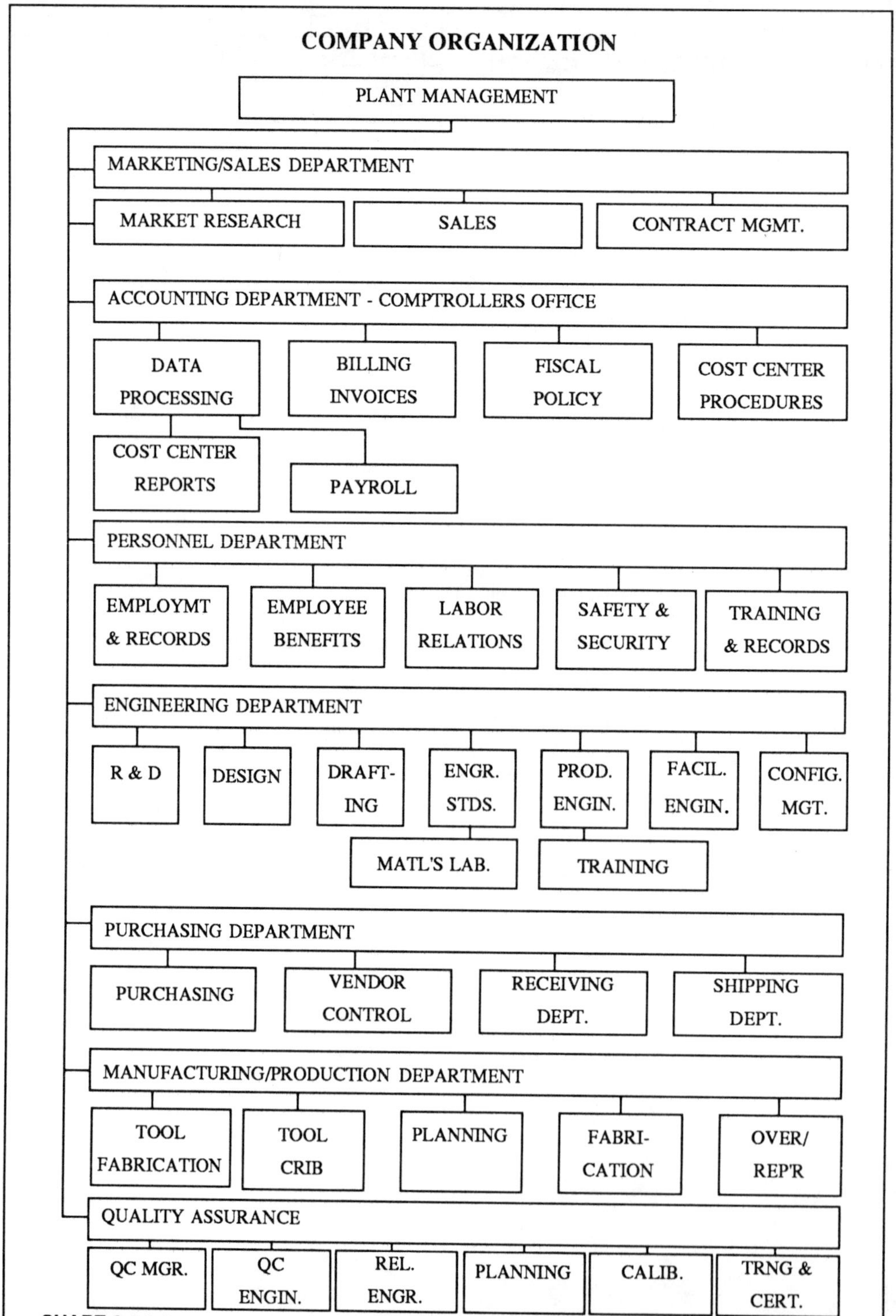
COMPANY ORGANIZATION
PLANT MANAGEMENT
MARKETING/SALES DEPARTMENT
MARKET RESEARCH
SALES
CONTRACT MGMT.
ACCOUNTING DEPARTMENT - COMPTROLLERS OFFICE
DATA PROCESSING
BILLING INVOICES
FISCAL POLICY
COST CENTER PROCEDURES
COST CENTER REPORTS
PAYROLL
PERSONNEL DEPARTMENT
EMPLOYMT & RECORDS
EMPLOYEE BENEFITS
LABOR RELATIONS
SAFETY & SECURITY
TRAINING & RECORDS
ENGINEERING DEPARTMENT
R & D
DESIGN
DRAFT-ING
ENGR. STDS.
PROD. ENGIN.
FACIL. ENGIN.
CONFIG. MGT.
MATL'S LAB.
TRAINING
PURCHASING DEPARTMENT
PURCHASING
VENDOR CONTROL
RECEIVING DEPT.
SHIPPING DEPT.
MANUFACTURING/PRODUCTION DEPARTMENT
TOOL FABRICATION
TOOL CRIB
PLANNING
FABRI-CATION
OVER/ REP'R
QUALITY ASSURANCE
QC MGR.
QC ENGIN.
REL. ENGR.
PLANNING
CALIB.
TRNG & CERT.

CHART 3.1.1-1

QUALITY CONTROL PUBLICATION	QCP NO. 3.1.2
	PAGE NO. 1 OF 3
	ISSUE DATE:
TITLE: QUALITY ASSURANCE ORGANIZATIONAL STRUCTURE	APPROVED BY:
	REVISION NO: 0
	REVISION DATE:

1.0 PURPOSE

This Quality Control Publication defines the quality assurance departments functions and responsibilities within the company's organization.

2.0 INTENT

It is the intent of this QCP to define the functions of each section within the quality organization. This quality control publication will establish the relationship between the quality assurance department and other departments within the company's infrastructure.

3.0 APPLICABLE FORMS AND PUBLICATIONS

3.1 Quality Assurance Organizational Chart, Form 3.1.2-1.

4.0 POLICIES AND PROCEDURES

4.1 The organizational chart in Form 3.1.1-1 shows the relationship between the quality assurance department and other departments of the company. The quality assurance director reports directly to the plant manager (or other top official of the company that the other departmental heads report to). The quality assurance director has an equal impact in the way the company functions.

4.2 All sections within the quality assurance department report directly to the quality assurance director. The various sections of the quality assurance department are depicted in Form 3.1.2-1.

4.3 The quality assurance director is responsible for establishing and maintaining the quality plan and all quality directives as they relate to the various sections of the quality assurance department, and their relationship with other functional departments within the company.

QUALITY CONTROL PUBLICATION	QCP NO. 3.1.2
	PAGE NO. 2 OF 3
	ISSUE DATE:
TITLE: QUALITY ASSURANCE ORGANIZATIONAL STRUCTURE	APPROVED BY:
	REVISION NO: 0
	REVISION DATE:

4.4 Quality Administration is responsible for:

4.4.1 Quality Data Analysis.

4.4.1.1 Cost of quality data collection, analysis and reporting.

4.4.1.2 Quality assurance reporting, see QCP 3.4.2.

4.4.2 Inspection Stamp Control, see QCP 2.2.1.
4.4.3 Quality Audits, QCP's 2.3.1, 5.1.1, 6.1.1.
4.4.4 Assignment of projects to quality assurance personnel.
4.4.5 Training and Certification, QCP 2.4.2.

4.5 Quality Engineering is responsible for:

4.5.1 Manufacturing Process Evaluation.

4.5.1.1 Evaluation of nonconformances in process, see QCP 6.5.3.

4.5.1.2 Evaluation of vendors, QCP 5.1.3.

4.5.2 Product Design Evaluation, QCP 3.2.2.
4.5.3 Material Review, see QCP 3.5.1.
4.5.4 Inspection/Testing, see QCP's 3.3.2, 3.4.1, 4.3.1, 5.2.1, 6.1.2, 6.1.4, 6.2.1, 6.3.3, 6.7.1, 7.1.1.
4.5.5 Measuring and test equipment.

4.5.5.1 Metrology, QCP 4.2.1 thru 4.2.7.

4.6 Reliability Engineering is responsible for:

4.6.1 See QCP 3.2.3 for discussion of responsibilities.
4.6.2 Material review and analysis, Corrective action, QCP's 2.3.2, 3.2.1, 3.4.3, 3.5.1, 4.1.1, 5.2.2, 6.1.3, 6.1.4, 6.5.3.

<table>
<tr><td rowspan="6">QUALITY CONTROL PUBLICATION
TITLE: QUALITY ASSURANCE ORGANIZATIONAL STRUCTURE</td><td>QCP NO. 3.1.2</td></tr>
<tr><td>PAGE NO. 3 OF 3</td></tr>
<tr><td>ISSUE DATE:</td></tr>
<tr><td>APPROVED BY:</td></tr>
<tr><td>REVISION NO: 0</td></tr>
<tr><td>REVISION DATE:</td></tr>
</table>

4.7 The quality planning section is responsible for:

4.7.1 The initiation of quality publications and their up-date and revision. Inspection routines and procedures. Testing instructions and record of inspections and tests. Statistical quality control. The review of contracts and purchase orders for the quality requirements, and the transmittal of those requirements to other departments, vendors, suppliers, etc.

QUALITY DEPARTMENT ORGANIZATIONAL CHART

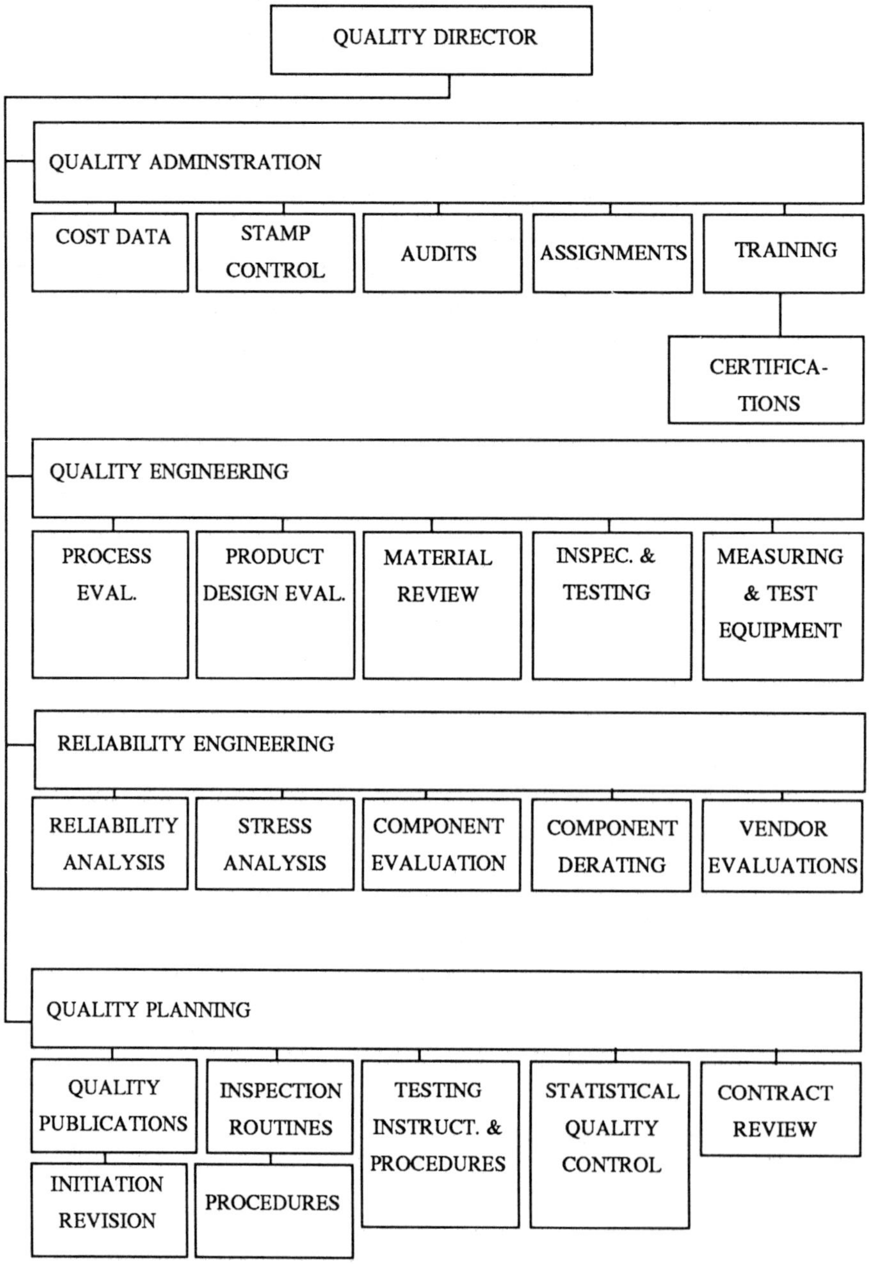

CHART 3.1.2-1

<table>
<tr><td rowspan="3">QUALITY CONTROL PUBLICATION</td><td>QCP NO. 3.1.3</td></tr>
<tr><td>PAGE NO. 1 OF 3</td></tr>
<tr><td>ISSUE DATE:</td></tr>
<tr><td rowspan="3">TITLE: QUALITY ASSURANCE OF THE CONTRACT CYCLE</td><td>APPROVED BY:</td></tr>
<tr><td>REVISION NO: 0</td></tr>
<tr><td>REVISION DATE:</td></tr>
</table>

1.0 PURPOSE

This quality control publication describes the quality assurance department's involvement with contracts and purchase orders. This involvement starts with a request for bid or a solicitation from a procuring activity, thru the delivery of the product or service and to the end of the functional life of the product or service.

2.0 INTENT

It is the intention of this QCP to acquaint all personnel of the company, with the quality assurance department's role in the contract/purchase order cycle of operations.

3.0 APPLICABLE FORMS, PUBLICATIONS AND CHARTS

3.1 Quality Assurance Contract/Purchase Order Life Cycle Chart, Form 3.1.3-1.

4.0 PROCEDURE

4.1 The Quality Assurance Department is responsible for analyzing (in conjunction with other departments within the company), and verifying the limits of variation of each characteristic of a product or service that is to be delivered. This includes the monitoring of these established limits, the reporting of discrepancies and the obtaining of corrective action to eliminate such discrepancies and nonconformances.

4.2 To determine the limits of variation and what actions are required to protect product quality, the following steps are taken:

4.2.1 Planning Stage

4.2.1.1 To determine the planning effort needed.

4.2.1.2 Analyzing the products/services contract requirements.

QUALITY CONTROL PUBLICATION	QCP NO. 3.1.3
	PAGE NO. 2 OF 3
	ISSUE DATE:
TITLE: QUALITY ASSURANCE OF THE CONTRACT CYCLE	APPROVED BY:
	REVISION NO: 0
	REVISION DATE:

4.2.1.3 Determining the training, tooling, equipment, supplies, methodology, etc. needed to fulfill the requirements and specifications of the contract/ purchase order.

4.2.2 Design Stage

4.2.2.1 Evaluate the design for conformance to quality requirements and specifications.

4.2.3 Manufacturing Process Development

4.2.3.1 Evaluate proposed process control for conformance to quality requirements and specifications.

4.2.4 Production Planning

4.2.4.1 Evaluate the production plan for conformance to quality requirements and specifications.

4.2.5 Fabrication Procedures For Tooling and Equipment

4.2.5.1 Evaluate the design of tools, equipment, either fabricated in-house or purchased.

4.2.5.2 Establish a calibration control system for tools, gauges, other equipment.

4.2.6 Raw materials, parts purchasing and control

4.2.6.1 Evaluate the control of purchases to verify conformance to specifications.

QUALITY CONTROL PUBLICATION	QCP NO. 3.1.3
	PAGE NO. 3 OF 3
	ISSUE DATE:
TITLE: QUALITY ASSURANCE OF THE CONTRACT CYCLE	APPROVED BY:
	REVISION NO: 0
	REVISION DATE:

4.2.7 Receiving

4.2.7.1 Evaluate the controls established to verify either at vendor's facility or in-house that the supplies received or to be received conform to the applicable specifications, and to obtain corrective action for all discrepancies and nonconformances.

4.2.8 Production

4.2.8.1 In-process inspection and testing and documentation.

4.2.8.2 Analyze discrepant corrective action to prevent re-occurrence.

4.2.8.3 Verify that repair, rework procedures are adequate and have been approved.

4.2.9 Shipping

4.2.9.1 Verify shipping and packaging procedures and instructions are approved, to the contract requirements, and being followed properly.

4.2.10 Post Shipping Controls

4.2.10.1 Evaluate returns and/or customer complaints.

4.2.10.2 Take the necessary corrective action to prevent re-occurrence.

LIFE CYCLE CHART

PRODUCT LIFE CYCLE	QUALITY ASSURANCE INVOLVEMENT
1 PLANNING STAGE	DETERMINE THE PLANNING EFFORT ANALYZE CONTRACT REQUIREMENTS
2 DESIGN STAGE	EVALUATE THE DESIGN FOR QUALITY REQURIEMENTS
3 MANUFACTURING PROCESS DEVELOPMENT	EVALUATE PROCESS CONTROLS
4 PRODUCTION PLANNING	EVALUATE PRODUCTION PLAN
5 FABRICATION PROCEDURES	EVALUATE ALL FABRICATION
6 PURCHASING CONTROLS	EVALUATE THE CONTROLS ESTABLISHED FOR PURCHASING RAW MATERIALS, ETC.
7 RECEIVING	EVALUATE THE CONTROLS FOR RECEIVING GOODS AND MATERIALS
8 PRODUCTION	EVALUATE PRODUCTION AND PROCESS CONTROLS
9 SHIPPING	EVALUATE SHIPPING CONTROLS AND PROCEDURES
10 POST SHIPPING CONTROLS	EVALUATE CUSTOMER RETURNS AND COMPLAINTS

CHART 3.1.3-1

QUALITY CONTROL PUBLICATION	QCP NO. 3.1.4
	PAGE NO. 1 OF 1
	ISSUE DATE:
TITLE: INSPECTION AND TESTING LOCATIONS	APPROVED BY:
	REVISION NO: 0
	REVISION DATE:

1.0 PURPOSE

The purpose of this Quality Control Publication is to show where the various inspection and test areas are located in the plant.

2.0 INTENT

It is the intent of this QCP to guide company personnel and customers, in locating the various inspection and test areas in the plant.

3.0 APPLICABLE PUBLICATIONS AND CHARTS

3.1 Inspection and Testing Location Chart, Form 3.1.4-1.

4.0 PROCEDURE/LOCATIONS

4.1 The inspection area for electronic assembly, hand soldering and wave soldering is located as depicted in Form 3.1.4-1.

4.2 The plating inspection area is located in the plating department.

4.3 Final quality control (QC) inspection is located next to the shipping department.

4.4 Receiving inspection and test is located next to the receiving department.

4.5 Fabrication inspection is located in the fabrication department.

4.6 Molding inspection is located in the molding department.

4.7 The machine shop and sheet metal inspection area is located in the machine shop.

4.8 In-process and final testing is centrally located near various assembly areas.

4.9 The environmental test area is located next to the materials laboratory.

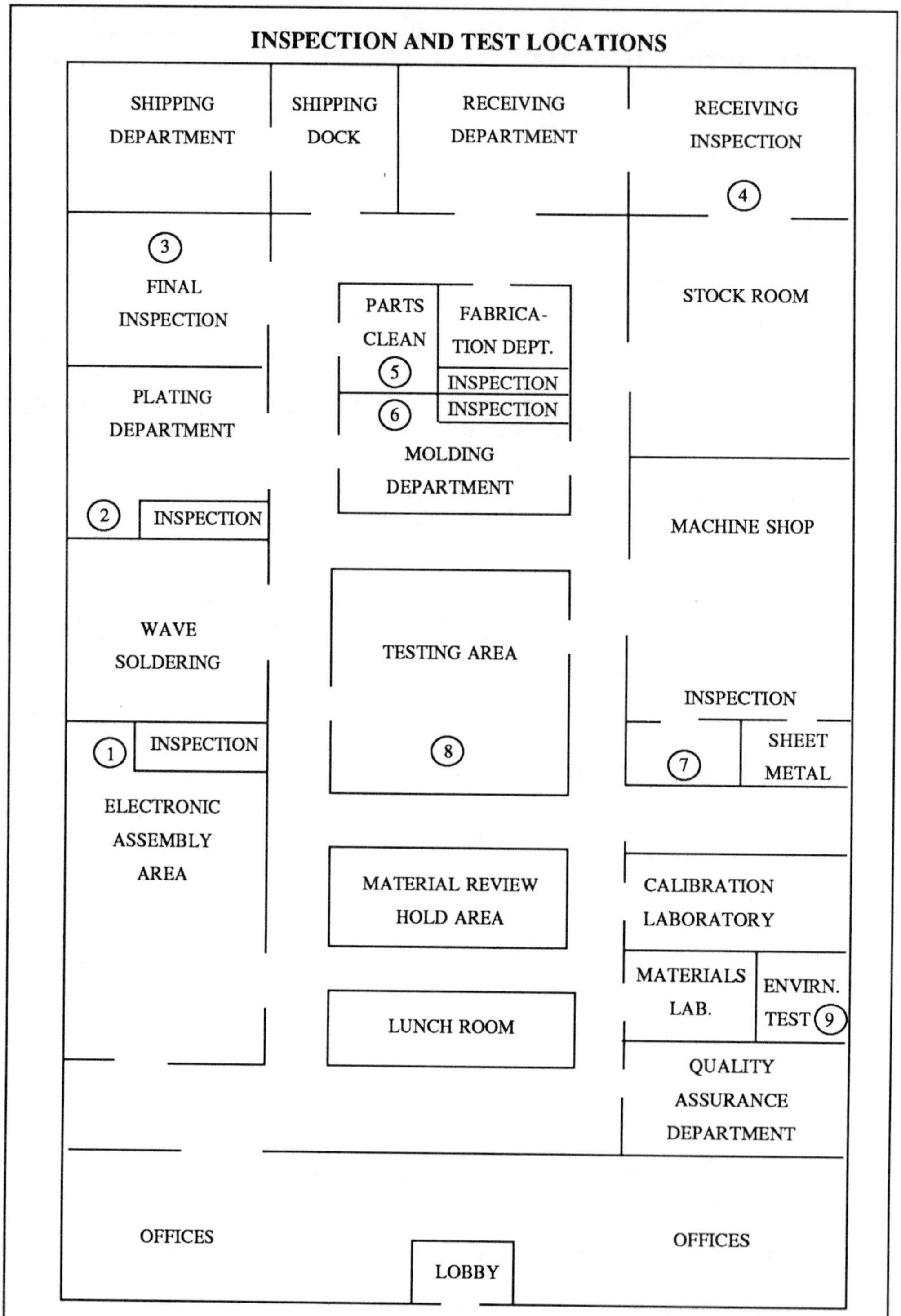
INSPECTION AND TEST LOCATIONS
SHIPPING DEPARTMENT
SHIPPING DOCK
RECEIVING DEPARTMENT
RECEIVING INSPECTION
4
3
FINAL INSPECTION
PARTS CLEAN
FABRICA-TION DEPT.
5
INSPECTION
6
INSPECTION
STOCK ROOM
PLATING DEPARTMENT
MOLDING DEPARTMENT
2
INSPECTION
MACHINE SHOP
WAVE SOLDERING
TESTING AREA
INSPECTION
1
INSPECTION
8
7
SHEET METAL
ELECTRONIC ASSEMBLY AREA
MATERIAL REVIEW HOLD AREA
CALIBRATION LABORATORY
MATERIALS LAB.
ENVIRN. TEST
9
LUNCH ROOM
QUALITY ASSURANCE DEPARTMENT
OFFICES
LOBBY
OFFICES

CHART 3.1.4-1

CHAPTER SEVEN

Organizational Planning

ORGANIZATIONAL PLANNING

MIL-Q-9858A, Paragraph 3.2, Initial Quality Planning, states, "The contractor during the earliest practical phase of contract performance, shall conduct a complete review of the requirement of the contract to identify and make timely provision for the special controls, processes, test equipment, fixtures, tooling and skills required for assuring product quality...Initial quality planning should take place as early as possible, preferably prior to the start of contract performance. The contractor's quality program is not complete unless it is planned and developed in conjunction with all other functions such as research and development, production, engineering, and subcontracting...As each new special requirement is identified. the means for testing and proving successful compliance with the unique requirements must be considered."

NHB 5300.4(1B), states, "The contractor shall prepare, maintain, and implement a Quality Program Plan, which describes how the contractor will ensure compliance with cited quality requirements." Paragraph 1B206-1, states, "The Quality Program Plan shall be submitted as required by the *Request For Proposal* or *Contract*. The plan format shall be readily identified with each cited requirement." NHB 5300.4(1D-2), Space Shuttle Program, cites various plans that are required by contract when this publication is cited in the contract as an applicable requirement and/or specification.

Paragraph 1D200-1, Safety Plan, states, "The contractor shall prepare a *Safety Plan* which complies with the requirements identified in this document. The contractor shall place special emphasis on describing how he/she will assure the identification, elimination and/or control of potential hazards which lead to injury, loss of personnel and/or damage or loss of flight or ground hardware throughout the complete cycle of the program. This *Safety Plan* will integrate and describe the relationship of all safety activities. Existing documents may be referenced and submitted as part of the *Safety Plan*. The Industrial Safety/ Occupational Health and Safety Plan shall be incorporated or attached to the *Safety Plan*."

Paragraph 1D300-2, states, "The contractor shall prepare and maintain a documented Reliability Plan which describes how the reliability requirements will be implemented and controlled. The plan shall be prepared in accordance with the applicable information requirements list/information requirement description (IRL/IRD)."

Paragraph 1D400, states, "The contractor shall prepare Maintainability Plan which describes how the program will be accomplished, including necessary participation of subcontractors and suppliers. The plan shall be prepared and submitted in accordance with the applicable IRL/IRD."

Paragraph 1D500-1, states, "The contractor shall maintain an effective and timely quality assurance activity planned and developed in conjunction with all other contractor's functions necessary to satisfy the contract requirements...The contractor shall prepare, maintain (documented plan), and implement a Quality Plan which describes how he/she will ensure compliance with the requirements set forth herein. The plan shall be submitted as specific in the IRL/IRD. The plan content shall be readily identifiable with each cited requirement and shall cover all quality activities for the contract."

The planning activities in NASA contracts requires documented planning efforts and have to be submitted to the NASA procurement office for approval. This is in contrast to the requirement of MIL-Q-0958A contracts. In NASA contracts this requirement is a line item in the contract and requires NASA's approval.

QUALITY CONTROL PUBLICATION	QCP NO. 3.2.1
	PAGE NO. 1 OF 3
	ISSUE DATE:
TITLE: CONTRACT QUALITY REQUIREMENTS ANALYSIS	APPROVED BY:
	REVISION NO: 0
	REVISION DATE:

1.0 PURPOSE

The purpose of this quality control publication is to establish a procedure for conducting a complete review of the requirements and specifications of a contract prior to the commencing of the production cycle.

2.0 INTENT

The intent of the this QCP is to provide a method for the quality analysis of the contract requirements, and for the transmittal of these requirements to the purchasing, engineering, production, manufacturing, etc. department, so that effective controls can be established to protect the overall quality of the product or service being purchased by the Government.

3.0 APPLICABLE FORMS AND PUBLICATIONS

3.1 Quality Contract Requirements Analysis, Form 3.2.1-1.

3.2 Quality Contract Req. Analysis Continuation Sheet, Form 3.2.1-1A.

3.3 Existing Quality Capabilities Inventory Form, Form 3.2.1-2.

3.4 Quality Design Review Participation, see QCP 4.1.2.

4.0 PROCEDURE

4.1 The marketing/sales department will provide the quality assurance department with copies of all contracts/purchase orders upon receipt. This includes all requests for bids and solicitations received.

4.2 The quality assurance department's planning section will review the contracts when received, for all requirements that will have an impact on the quality of the finished product. This includes the quality clauses, (FAR Clauses included in the contract/purchase order), that give the quality requirements FAR clause number, (such as 52.246-1, 52.246-2, (MIL-I-45208A or MIL-Q-9858A) preservation and packaging requirements, qualified products listing (QPL) for purchases, etc., and the transmittal of these requirements to the applicable departments.

QUALITY CONTROL PUBLICATION	QCP NO. 3.2.1
	PAGE NO. 2 OF 3
	ISSUE DATE:
TITLE: CONTRACT QUALITY REQUIREMENTS ANALYSIS	APPROVED BY:
	REVISION NO:0
	REVISION DATE:

Included in this analysis is the impact areas that need to be addressed due to the requirements and specifications of the contracts, such as, the need for new tooling, fixtures, test equipment, advanced metrology requirements, training workload (the possible need for new personnel), existing capabilities or product that can either be used or modified for the contract, etc.

4.3 While performing the required analysis of a request for bid, solicitation, or contract award, the Quality Contract Requirements Analysis, Form 3.2.1-1 is to be filled out as follows:

1. Customer name.
2. Contract or purchase order number.
3. Part number or National Stock Number.
4. Description of product or service required.
5. Estimated starting date of production.
6. Date final product or service is due to be delivered (as per contract/solicitation requirements.
7. Quantity ordered or to be ordered.
8. Scheduled intermediate delivery dates (as per contract).
9. Existing product available to use as is. Modification required prior to use. No existing product or service may be used (check one).
10. In this block list similar product and/or modifications needed to use existing product. References to existing drawings to be used.
11. Are quality requirements in the contract clear? Are there discrepancies in the requirements? Is a request for a deviation needed to clear up quality requirements? (Check one.)
12. Statements applicable to blocks 9, 10, 11.
13. Advanced metrology requirements determined in contract (explain).
14. Special equipment/fixtures/gauges etc. required (explain).
15. Special or new test equipment required (explain).
16. Special skills/training required (explain).

QUALITY CONTROL PUBLICATION	QCP NO. 3.2.1
	PAGE NO. 3 OF 3
	ISSUE DATE:
TITLE: CONTRACT QUALITY REQUIREMENTS ANALYSIS	APPROVED BY:
	REVISION NO: 0
	REVISION DATE:

17. Workload requires new personnel to be hired (explain).
18. Special requirement(s) for preservation and packaging that are required in the contract (explain).
19. Contract analysis initiated by:
    Name ________. Date __________.
20. Analysis reviewed by Name ____________ .
    Date ________ . (QA Management).

For other observations and continuation of blocks use the continuation sheet, Form 3.2.1-1A.

4.4 After the quality contract requirements analysis form has been distributed and coordinated with all applicable departments, and all changes have been acted on, the Existing Product/Service Capability Form is to be filled out by the quality assurance as follows: Form 3.2.1-2.

1. The name of the customer/procurement office.
2. The contract or purchase order number.
3. The part number or Nation Stock Number.
4. Product or service description.
5. Block number applicable to blocks of Form 3.2.1-1.
6. Specific contract requirement.
7. Specific existing requirement or requirement worked to in the past.
8. Location of parts or material being used that could be used for new contract.
9. List modifications needed to use existing parts or material.
10. Estimated cost of modifying existing parts or material.
11. Names of personnel assigned to this project.
12. Due date of this analysis.

QUALITY CONTRACT REQUIREMENTS ANALYSIS

CUSTOMER NAME (1)	CONTRACT/PURCHASE ORDER (2)	PART OR NSN NO. (3)	
DESCRIPTION OF PRODUCT OR SERVICE REQUIRED: (4)			
START DATE OF PROD. (5)	SHIPPING DATE (6)	QUANTITY ORD. (7)	REQUIRED DELIVERY (8)
SAME AS PROD. OR SERV. SOLD? (9) SAME ☐ SIMILAR ☐ DIFF. ☐			
LIST THE SIMILARITIES OR MODIFICATIONS NEEDED TO MAKE NEW PRODUCT: (10)			
ARE QUALITY REQ.: (11) IN CONT. ☐ MISSING OR CONFLICTING REQ. ☐ DEVIATION REQUESTED ☐			
STATEMENTS APPLICABLE TO BLOCKS 9, 10, 11: (12)			
ADVANCED METROLOGY REQUIREMENTS: (13)			
SPECIAL EQUIP/FIXTURES/GAUGES REQUIRED (explain): (14)			
SPECIAL OR NEW TEST EQUIPMENT REQUIRED (explain): (15)			
SPECIAL SKILLS/TRAINING REQUIRED (explain): (16)			
NEED MORE PERSONNEL (explain): (17)			
SPECIAL PRESERVATION AND PACKAGING PROCEDURES REQUIRED BY CONTRACT: (18)			
ANALYSIS INITIATED BY: (19) DATE:			
REVIEWED BY: (20) DATE:			

FORM 3.2.1-1

QUALITY CONTRACT REQUIREMENTS ANALYSIS CONTINUATION SHEET
BLOCK NUMBER: ☐
BLOCK NUMBER: ☐
BLOCK NUMBER: ☐
SEE PREVIOUS CONTINUATION SHEET NUMBERS: **FORM 3.2.1-1A**

EXISTING PRODUCT/SERVICE CAPABILITY FORM

<table>
<tr><td colspan="2">CUSTOMER (1)</td><td colspan="2">CONTRACT.P.O. NUMBER (2)</td><td>PART NO. OR NSN NO. (3)</td><td colspan="3">PRODUCT/SERVICE DESCRIPTION (4)</td></tr>
<tr><td>BLOCK NO.</td><td>CONTRACT REQ.</td><td>EXISTING REQUIREMENT</td><td>LOC. OF EXISTING PARTS/MATERIAL</td><td>MODIFICATION REQUIRED</td><td>EST. COST</td><td>PERSONNEL ASST. TO PROJECT</td><td>DUE DATE</td></tr>
<tr><td>(5)</td><td>(6)</td><td>(7)</td><td>(8)</td><td>(9)</td><td>(10)</td><td>(11)</td><td>(12)</td></tr>
<tr><td colspan="8">FORM 3.2.1-2</td></tr>
</table>

QUALITY CONTROL PUBLICATION TITLE: INSPECTION AND TEST PLANNING	QCP NO. 3.2.2 PAGE NO. 1 OF 4 ISSUE DATE: APPROVED BY: REVISION NO: 0 REVISION DATE:

1.0 PURPOSE

This quality control publication establishes the method for the development of a detailed inspection and test plan by the quality engineering section of the quality assurance department to verify that all products and services offered to the government for acceptance meet the requirements and specifications of the contract.

2.0 INTENT

The intent of this QCP is to detail a systematic method for the gathering of all pertinent data from the purchasing, design engineering, production/ manufacturing engineering, quality assurance department, in order to develop comprehensive inspection and test procedures and instructions that are to be used throughout the life cycle of all products and services contracted for by the government.

3.0 APPLICABLE FORMS AND PUBLICATIONS

3.1 Quality Contract Requirements Analysis, Form 3.2.1-1.

3.2 Existing Quality Capabilities Inventory, Form 3.2.1-2.

3.3 Manufacturing/production Outline (provided by the production/ manufacturing planning engineering department).

3.4 Test Plan (provided by production/manufacturing section of the engineering department).

3.5 Quality Plan/Reliability Analysis, Form 3.2.2-1A.

3.6 Quality Plan/Reliability Analysis - Continuation Sheet, Form 3.2.2-1B.

4.0 PROCEDURE

4.1 The quality assurance department will analyze the contract quality requirements, the engineering drawings, the manufacturing and

QUALITY CONTROL PUBLICATION	QCP NO. 3.2.2
	PAGE NO. 2 OF 4
	ISSUE DATE:
TITLE: INSPECTION AND TEST PLANNING	APPROVED BY:
	REVISION NO:0 0
	REVISION DATE:

production procedures and instructions, the requirements for purchased parts, test equipment and test fixture requirements, calibration and maintenance equipment requirements.

4.2 After analyzing all of the necessary requirements and making out Forms 3.2.1-1 and 3.2.1-2, a quality inspection and testing plan will be made out in conjunction with the reliability engineering section, utilizing the forms depicted in Forms 3.2.2-1A and 3.2.2-1B. These forms will be filled out as follows:

1 The number assigned to the quality inspection/planning/ reliability analysis.

3. The name of the customer and/or government procurement office.

4. Name of the program/project that has been given to describe the program/project.

5. The contract or purchase order number.

6. Part, assembly or completed project description (Name).

7. Part, assembly part number.

8. Is the part/assembly a *qualified product listing* item.

9. Is a first article inspection/test required by contract and/or purchase order?

10. Has the required reliability study of all parts, material, etc. to become part of the final item been concluded?

11. Is there a previous history of producing this item?

12. Nation Stock Number of item (if applicable).

13. Give a brief description of previous history here.

QUALITY CONTROL PUBLICATION	QCP NO. 3.2.2
	PAGE NO. 3 OF 4
	ISSUE DATE:
TITLE: INSPECTION AND TEST PLANNING	APPROVED BY:
	REVISION NO: 0
	REVISION DATE:

14. This block relates to the reliability engineering functions input into this form, to indicate whether or not the various reliability methods of proving parts/material are conforming to existing specifications.

15. This block indicates whether or not there is a history of failures/ nonconformances if this item has been manufactured previously.

16. Is there a record of effective corrective action if prior failures/ nonconformances existed.

17. The name of the proposed vendor, supplier of parts material, sub-assemblies, etc.

18. The manufacturing operation number assigned to a particular manufacturing/production operation.

19. Inspection and/or test station number where the particular inspection and/or test is to take place for the operation described in block 18.

20. The particular characteristic to be verified at the inspection/test location described in block 19.

21. The specification number that describes that characteristic described in block 20.

22. The paragraph where the particular characteristic in the specification is located.

23. A description of the inspection and/or test equipment that is to be used to verify the characteristic as described in block 20.

24. Has the inspection/test equipment as described in block 23 been calibrated or is calibration due?

QUALITY CONTROL PUBLICATION	QCP NO. 3.2.2
	PAGE NO. 4 OF 4
	ISSUE DATE:
TITLE: INSPECTION AND TEST PLANNING	APPROVED BY:
	REVISION NO:0
	REVISION DATE:

25. The estimated time that it will take to accomplish the inspections and/or tests in block 19. Or the actual time if this inspection/test has been accomplished previously.

26. Under Notes -
    1. A continuation of block 14 may be inserted here if other reliability proof methods are being or are planned to be accomplished.
    2. Any other notes applicable to this form.

27. Name of quality planning coordinator for this project.

28. Name of reliability engineer responsible for the reliability part of the project.

29. The signature and date of the director of quality assurance department indicating approval of this planning form.

4.3 Form 3.2.2-1B - Continuation Sheet is to be filled out according to the block numbers and instructions as described above for Form 3.2.2-1A.

QUALITY PLAN/RELIABILITY/ANALYSIS FORM

PLAN/ANALYSIS NO. ______ (1)

CUSTOMER NAME: (3)	PROG. NAME (4)	CONTRACT NO. (5)	PART/ASSEMBLY NAME (6)	PART NUMBER (7)
QPL ITEM (8) YES ☐ NO ☐	FIRST ART. REQ. DATE (9) YES ☐ NO ☐	RELIABILITY STUDY COMPLETE (10)	PREVIOUS HISTORY (11) YES ☐ NO ☐	NATIONAL STOCK NO. (12)

DESCRIPTION OF PREVIOUS HISTORY (13)	RECORD OF FAILURES (15) YES ☐ NO ☐	CORRECTIVE ACTION TAKEN (16) YES ☐ NO ☐	VENDOR/SUPPLIER NAME (17)

METHOD OF PROVING RELIABILITY STRESS TEST ☐ (14) VIBRATION ☐ ENVIRON. ☐ BURN-IN ☐ CHEMICAL ☐

MFR. OPER. NO.	INSP./TEST STA. NO.	CHARACTERISTIC TO BE VERIFIED	CONTRACT SPEC. NO.	CONTRACT PARA. NO.	INSP./TEST EQUIP TO BE USED	INSP./TEST EQUIP. CALIBRATION DATES	EST. INSP/ TEST TIME
(18)	(19)	(20)	(21)	(22)	(23)	(24)	(25)

NOTES (26)

QUALITY PLAN COORDINATOR (NAME) (27)	RELIABILITY ENGINEER DATE (28)	APPROVED BY: (NAME - TITLE - DATE) (29)

FORM 3.2.2-1A

QUALITY PLAN/RELIABILITY/ANALYSIS
CONTINUATION SHEET

PAGE NO. ______ OF ______

MFG. OPER. NO.	INSP/TST STATION NO.	CHARACTERISTICS TO BE VERIFIED	CONTRACT SPEC. NO.	CONTRACT PARA. NO.	INSP./TEST EQUIP. TO BE USED	INSP./TEST EQUIP. CALIB. DATES	ESTIM. INSP./TST TIME
(18)	(19)	(20)	(21)	(22)	(23)	(24)	(25)

NOTES:

FORM 3.2.2-1B

RELIABILITY PLANNING

Reliability planning is an important part of the planning cycle. MIL-HDBK-H50, Paragraph 3.2, states, "Old familiar products and processes may be adapted to new, unknown applications. Ordinary applications may take on new aspects because of use in new environments. For instance, the use of paper as a material might present new problems to the textile industry." And, "As each new special requirement is identified, the means for testing and proving successful compliance with the unique requirement *must* be considered."

The *must* in the above quotation shows the emphasis on the requirement for the testing and proving that parts and material used are in compliance with the specifications.

MIL-HDBK-H51 that is used as a guide to the requirements of MIL-I45208A, Military Inspection System Requirements, contains various paragraphs that make reference to the need for reliability of the items that are to be offered to the government for its acceptance and subsequent use. Paragraph 3.8, Qualified Products, states, "The inclusion of a product on the Qualified Produces List only signifies that at one time the manufacturer made a product which met specification requirements. It does not relieve the contractor of his responsibility for furnishing supplies that meet all specification requirements or for performing specified inspections and tests for such material."

NASA reliability requirements are specific and discussed in detail in NASA publication NHB 5300.4(D-2). It states, "The contractor shall maintain a reliability activity planned and developed in conjunction with other contractor elements. Reliability functions shall be an integral part of the design and development process and shall include the evaluation of hardware reliability through analysis, review, and assessment. Timely status reporting will be utilized to facilitate control of the reliability effort." Paragraph 1D301, states, "The contractor shall accomplish the following reliability engineering tasks on all flight equipment and as specified on flight GFE (Government Furnished Equipment). The reliability engineering tasks to support Chapter 2 safety requirement of assuring fail safe design and operation of GFE, are limited to GFE used at or common to the launch-landing and retrieval sites, and are identified in paragraphs 1D301-3, Failure Mode and Effects Analysis (FMEA) and Critical Items List (CIL), 1D301-4, Reliability-Maintainability Interface, 1D301-6, Problem Reporting and Corrective Action, and 1D301-7, Reporting and Resolving NASA Parts and Materials Problems (ALERTS)."

The following Quality Control Publication can be used as a guide to fulfill the requirements as stated above, and help to format and write a procedure that will meet the needs of the organization.

QUALITY CONTROL PUBLICATION	QCP NO. 3.2.3
	PAGE NO. 1 OF 5
	ISSUE DATE:
TITLE: RELIABILITY ENGINEERING'S PLANNING CYCLE	APPROVED BY:
	REVISION NO: 0
	REVISION DATE:

1.0 PURPOSE

The purpose of this Quality Control Publication is to establish and maintain a reliability engineering section that operates under the control of the quality assurance department.

2.0 INTENT

The intent of this QCP is to define reliability engineering's functions, in providing accurate and documented information as to the ability of components, material, etc., to function throughout the functional life of the items offered to the government for its acceptance and use.

3.0 APPLICABLE FORMS AND PUBLICATIONS

3.1 Quality Control Publication 3.2.2.

3.2 Quality Planning/Reliability Analysis, Forms 3.2.2-1A and 1B.

3.3 Organizational Chart, Form 3.1.1-1.

3.4 Reliability-Materials Laboratory-Inspection/Test/Analysis, Form 3.2.3-1A.

3.5 Reliability-Materials Laboratory-Inspection/Test/Analysis, Form 3.2.3-1B.

3.6 Reliability-Inspection/Test/Analysis-Log, Form 3.2.3-2.

4.0 PROCEDURE

4.1 Reliability Analysis Study - Contract Planning Stage.

4.1.1 The reliability engineering section will prepare those parts of Form 3.2.2-1A, that pertain to the reliability analysis/study function. The blocks that reliability engineering is to fill out are as follows:

QUALITY CONTROL PUBLICATION	QCP NO. 3.2.3
	PAGE NO. 2 OF 5
	ISSUE DATE:
TITLE: RELIABILITY ENGINEERING'S PLANNING CYCLE	APPROVED BY:
	REVISION NO: 0
	REVISION DATE:

1. Block 10 fill out as stated in QCP 3.2.2.
2. Block 14 fill out as stated in QCP 3.2.2.
3. Block 20 Fill out in conjunction with the planning section of quality.
4. Blocks 23 & 24 plan with the engineering department materials laboratory (See Form 3.1.1-1).
5. Block 26 include notes taken during the performance above and/or additional actions taken.
6. Block 28 signature of reliability engineer and date analysis/study performed.

4.1.2 The Forms 3.2.3-1A, -1B, -2 are used as part of the planning cycle and for reliability engineering analysis of failures and/or nonconformances. The filling out of these forms is discussed in paragraph 4.2 below.

4.2 Reliability Analysis/Study - Engineering Analysis of Questionable and/or Nonconforming Material.

4.2.1 Forms 3.2.3-1A and 3.2.3-1B are used by the reliability engineering section to analyze, inspect and test all parts, materials and products in making a determination as to the functional life of these items, and for analyzing problem areas or areas or nonconformances to the applicable requirements and specifications. These forms are to be filled out as follows:

4.2.2 Form 3.2.3-1A

1. The identification number assigned to this report.
2. The contract or purchase order number.

QUALITY CONTROL PUBLICATION	QCP NO. 3.2.3
	PAGE NO. 3 OF 5
	ISSUE DATE:
TITLE: RELIABILITY ENGINEERING'S PLANNING CYCLE	APPROVED BY:
	REVISION NO: 0
	REVISION DATE:

3. The department requesting the action.
4. The date this report is required.
5. The name of the person making the request to reliability engineering.
6. The date this report is filled out.
7. The part number or national stock number of the material, part, item under investigation.
8. The material, part, item description.
9. The reason for this request. Place a check mark in the applicable box.
10. The drawing or specification number is placed in this box.
11. The type of test requested (stress, chemical, physical, vibration, environmental, etc.)
12. The specification number of the particular requirement for the test(s) in block 11.
13. The paragraph number of the specification in Block 12 (if applicable).
14. Results of the inspection/test/analysis for the particular time under investigation.
15. The disposition recommendation of the item under investigation.
16. The name of the person making the recommendation and date of the recommendation.
17. All comments or observations as applicable to this report is written into this box.
    A continuation sheet is to be used if needed.

QUALITY CONTROL PUBLICATION	QCP NO. 3.2.3
	PAGE NO. 4 OF 5
	ISSUE DATE:
TITLE: RELIABILITY ENGINEERING'S PLANNING CYCLE	APPROVED BY:
	REVISION NO: 0
	REVISION DATE:

18. The signature of the reliability engineer assigned to this project and date, when report is completed, indicating acceptance of the report.
19. The signature of the director of quality and the date of acceptance of this report.

4.2.3 Form 3.2.3-1B

1. The number as assigned on Form 3.2.3-1A.
2. The applicable part or national stock number.
3. The parameters and/or characteristics as depicted by the applicable specification or requirement in Form 3.2.3-1A.
4. The actual parameters observed during the inspection/test/analysis.
5. The differences between what is required by the specification and what has been observed during the inspection/test/analysis.
6. Comments, observations, or other types of testing utilized that is applicable to this investigation. Continuation of remarks from Form 3.2.3-1A.

4.3 A log sheet will be maintained to indicate the status of all projects that are being or have been accomplished. This log sheet, Form 3.2.3-2, will be filled out as follows.

1. The contract or purchase order number.
2. The customer's name.
3. The applicable drawing or specification number.
4. The reason for this inspection/test/analysis is to be in the applicable box.

QUALITY CONTROL PUBLICATION	QCP NO. 3.2.3
	PAGE NO. 5 OF 5
	ISSUE DATE:
TITLE: RELIABILITY ENGINEERING'S PLANNING CYCLE	APPROVED BY:
	REVISION NO: 0
	REVISION DATE:

5. The part or national stock number.
6. The inspection/test/analysis report number as assigned in Form 3.2.3-1A.
7. The specification number as assigned in (1) of Form 3.2.3-1A.
8. The date the report is due.
9. The completion date of the report.
10. The place and/or location where the inspections/tests/analysis are to be accomplished.
11. The date the report was issued to the departments and/or personnel that are responsible for the applicable actions due to this report.
12. Comments that pertain to this report.
13. Name of the reliability engineer assigned to this project and the date of review.
14. Name of the reliability engineer assigned to this project and the date of submission of this report.
15. The signature of the director of the quality assurance department and the date of acceptance of this report.

INSP/TEST/ANALYSIS REPORT NUMBER (1) ____________

RELIABILITY - MATERIALS LABORATORY
INSPECTION/TEST/ANALYSIS FORM

CONTRACT NO. (2)	REQ. DEPT. (3)	DATE REPORT REQ. (4)	NAME OF PERSON MAKING REQ. (5)	DATE REPORT FILLED OUT (6)

PART NO. (7)	ITEM DESC. (8)	REASON FOR REQUEST: (9) PLANNING ☐ QUAL. ☐ FAILURES ☐	APPLICABLE DRAWING NO. (10)

TYPE OF TEST REQ.	APPLICABLE SPECIFICATION	SPEC. PARAGRAPH	RESULTS OF INSP/TEST/ANALYSIS
(25)	(12)	(13)	(14)
REL. SIG. DATE (18) QUAL. DIR. SIG. DATE (19)	COMMENTS: (17)		(15) RECOMMENDED DISPOSITION ACCEPT ☐ REJECT ☐ NAME OF PERSON RECOMMENDING DISPOSITION (16) DATE ______

FORM 3.2.3-1A

INSP/TEST/ANALYSIS REPORT NO. ① ____________________

RELIABILITY - MATERIALS LABORATORY
INSPECTION/TEST/ANALYSIS
CONTINUATION SHEET

PART NUMBER	REQUIRED PARAMETERS/CHAR	ACT. PARAM. OBSERV. AND/OR CHARACTERISTICS	DIFFERENCES BETWEEN REQUIRED AND ACTUAL CHARACTERISTICS
②	③	④	⑤

COMMENTS/OBSERVATIONS/OTHER:

⑥

FORM 3.2.3-1B

RELIABILITY - INSPECTION /TEST/ANALYSIS LOG

CONTRACT/PO NO. (1)	CUSTOMER NAME (2)	DRAWING NO. (3)	REASON FOR INSP/TEST/ANALYSIS PLANNING ☐ QUALIFICATION ☐ FAILURE ☐ (4)			
PART NO.	INSP/TEST ANAL. REPORT NO.	SPECIFICATION USED IN ANALYSIS	DATE REQ.	DATE COMP.	WHERE INSP/TEST ANALYSIS IN ACCOMP.	DATE REPORT ISSUED
(5)	(6)	(7)	(8)	(9)	(10)	(11)

COMMENTS:

(12)

NAME OF QC ENGINEER DATE (13)	NAME OF RELIABILITY ENGINEER DATE (14)	SIGNATURE OF QC DIRECTOR DATE (15)

FORM 3.2.3-2

DESIGN REVIEW PARTICIPATION

Reliability engineering participation in the product design review stage of the planning cycle is not only important, but, is required in many contracts. MIL-STD-786B, Reliability Program for Systems and Equipment Development and Production, page 101-1, Purpose, states "The purpose of task 101 is to develop a reliability program plan which identifies, and ties together, all program management tasks required to accomplish program requirements." Paragraph 101.2, Task: The following statements have been selectively picked out to emphasize this quality control publication's policy statement and instructions.

1. A description of how the reliability program will be conducted to meet the requirements of the SOW (Statement of Work).
2. A detailed description of how each specified reliability accounting and engineering design task will be performed or complied with.
3. The designation of reliability milestones (includes design and test).
4. The method by which the reliability requirements are disseminated to designers and associated personnel.
5. Statement of what source of reliability design guidelines or reliability design review checklist will be utilized.
6. Description of how reliability contributes to the total design, and the level of authority and constraints on this engineering discipline.
7. Page 102-1, paragraph 102.2 - Attend and participate in subcontractors' design review.

QUALITY CONTROL PUBLICATION	QCP NO. 3.2.4
	PAGE NO. 1 OF 5
	ISSUE DATE:
TITLE: DESIGN REVIEW PARTICIPATION	APPROVED BY:
	REVISION NO: 0
	REVISION DATE:

1.0 PURPOSE

The purpose of the quality control publication is to define and establish the role of the reliability engineering section in participating in design reviews in accordance with the contractual milestones and that the system, subsystem, equipment, or component quantitative reliability requirements will be achieved.

2.0 INTENT

It is the intent of this QCP to define the reliability responsibilities in product (item) design reviews.

3.0 PROCEDURE

3.1 Formal reviews and assessments of contract reliability requirements are conducted at major program points, identified as system program reviews (design reviews are part of the overall program reviews), as specified by the contract. As the program develops, reliability progress shall also be assessed by the use of additional reliability program/design reviews as necessary to identify the major milestones that have been accomplished or are due to be accomplished.

3.2 The reviews will identify and discuss all pertinent aspects of system program, as applicable, and as defined below:

A. Preliminary Design Review (PDR).

1. *Updated reliability status including:*

a. Reliability modeling.
A reliability mathematical model is based on system/subsystem/equipment functions. As the design evolves, a reliability block diagram is developed and maintained for the system/subsystem with associated allocations and predictions for all items in each

QUALITY CONTROL PUBLICATION	QCP NO. 3.2.4
	PAGE NO. 2 OF 5
	ISSUE DATE:
TITLE: DESIGN REVIEW PARTICIPATION	APPROVED BY:
	REVISION NO: 0
	REVISION DATE:

reliability block. The reliability block diagram is keyed and traceable to the functional block diagram, schematics, and drawings, and provide the basis for accurate mathematical representation of reliability. The reliability mathematical model is updated with information resulting from reliability and other relevant tests as well as changes in item configuration, mission parameters and operational constraints. Inputs and outputs of the reliability mathematical model is to be compatible with the input and output requirements of the system and subsystem level analysis models.

b. Reliability apportionment.
The purpose of this task is to assure that once quantitative system requirements have been determined, they are allocated or apportioned to lower levels. Both basic reliability and mission reliability requirements are allocated to the level specified, and is used to establish the baseline requirements for designers. Requirements consistent with the allocations are imposed on the subcontractors and suppliers.

c. Reliability predictions.
The purpose of this task is to estimate the basic reliability and mission reliability of the system/subsystem/equipment, and to make a determination of whether these reliability requirements can be achieved with the proposed design. Failure rates other than those established at contract award may be used only upon approval of the procuring activity. The permissible failure rate adjustment factors for standby operation and storage shall be as specifically agreed to by the procuring activity. When the individual part operating

QUALITY CONTROL PUBLICATION	QCP NO. 3.2.4
	PAGE NO. 3 OF 5
	ISSUE DATE:
TITLE: DESIGN REVIEW PARTICIPATION	APPROVED BY:
	REVISION NO: 0
	REVISION DATE:

conditions are defined, the prediction procedure in section 2 of MIL-HDBK-217, or procurement activity approved alternative, is to be used. If the part type and quantity is the only information available, the prediction procedure of section 3 of MIL-HDBK-217, or procurement activity approved alternative, shall be used.

d. Failure modes, effects, and criticality analysis.
The purpose of this task is to identify potential design weaknesses through systematic, documented consideration of the following: all likely ways in which a component or equipment can fail; causes for each mode; and the effects of each failure (which may be different for each mission phase.)

e. Reliability content of specification.

f. Design guideline criteria.

g. Other tasks as identified.

2. *Other Problems Affecting Reliability.*

   a. Sneak Circuit Analysis (SCA).

   b. Electronic parts/circuits tolerance analysis.

3. *Parts Program Progress.*

   The purpose of this task is to control the selection and use of standard and nonstandard parts. A parts control program is established accordance with MIL-STD-965 procedures, as designated in the contract. Reliability design guidelines shall be developed and documented to include derating criteria, junction temperatures, and parts application

QUALITY CONTROL PUBLICATION	QCP NO. 3.2.4
	PAGE NO. 4 OF 5
	ISSUE DATE:
TITLE: DESIGN REVIEW PARTICIPATION	APPROVED BY:
	REVISION NO: 0
	REVISION DATE:

criteria. Safety margins for nonelectronic parts will also be included when appropriate. The guidelines shall be consistent with guidance provided by the Procuring Activity.

4. *Reliability Critical Items Program.*
   The purpose of this task is to identify and control those items which require "special attention" because of complexity, application of advanced state-of-the-art techniques, and the impact of potential failure on safety, readiness, mission success, and demand for maintenance/logistics support.

5. *Effects of Functional Testing, Storage, Handling, Packaging, Transportation, and Maintenance.*
   The purpose of this task is to determine the effects of storage, handling, packaging, transportation, maintenance, and repeated exposure to functional testing on hardware reliability. Procedures are established, maintained, and implemented to determine by test and analysis, or estimation, the effects of storage, handling, packaging, transportation, maintenance, and repeated exposure to functional testing on the design and reliability of the hardware. The results of this effort shall include items such as:

   a. Identification of equipments and their major or critical characteristics which deteriorate with storage age or environmental conditions (including shock and vibration).

   b. Identification of procedures for periodic field inspection or tests (including recall for test) or stockpile reliability evaluation. The procedures shall include

QUALITY CONTROL PUBLICATION	QCP NO. 3.2.4
	PAGE NO. 5 OF 5
	ISSUE DATE:
TITLE: DESIGN REVIEW PARTICIPATION	APPROVED BY:
	REVISION NO: 0
	REVISION DATE:

suggested quantity of items for test and acceptable levels of performance for the parameters under test.

c. Identification of special procedures for maintenance or restoration.

The results of this effort shall be used to support long term failure rate predictions, design trade-offs, etc.

CHAPTER EIGHT

Completed Item Inspection and Tests

FINAL INSPECTION AND TESTING

Paragraph 6.3 of MIL-Q-9858A and MIL-HDBK-H50, states, "The quality program shall assure that there is a system for final inspection of completed products. Final inspection shall provide for reporting to designers any unusual difficulties, deficiencies or questionable conditions. When modifications, repairs or replacements are required after final inspection, there shall be reinspection of any characteristics affects.

Paragraph 3.2.1 of MIL-I-45208A and MIL-HDBK-H51, states, "Inspection shall be prescribed by clear, complete and current instructions. The instructions shall assure inspection of materials and completed articles as required by the item specification and the contract. In addition, criteria for approval and rejection of product shall be included."

AQAP-1, states, "The contractor shall perform inspection and testing on the finished product or service necessary to complete the evidence of conformance with contract requirements. Procedures for final inspection and testing shall ensure that inspections and tests that should have been conducted at earlier stages, have, in fact, been performed and that the data is acceptable and available from applicable records."

AQAP-4, paragraph 211, states, "The contractor shall perform all inspection on the finished product or service necessary to complete the evidence of full conformance with contract requirements. Procedures for final inspection shall ensure that inspections that should have been conducted at earlier stages have, in fact, been performed and that the data is acceptable."

NHB 5300.4(1B), states, "Separate end-time inspection and test specifications and procedures shall be prepared and utilized for each end-item. These inspections and tests shall be conducted in a manner and under conditions which simulate end-use and environments to the highest degree practical without damage to the end-item, and which provide a valid measure of the overall quality of the end-time. The degree, duration, and number of tests performed on each end-time shall be sufficient to provide assurance that the end-item is capable of meeting contract requirements, and that the required quality and workmanship is present."

NHB 5300.4(1C) paragraph 1C304, states, "Procured and fabricated articles and materials shall be inspected and tested to ensure conformance to contract requirements, including applicable drawings, specifications and changes thereto. These inspections shall occur during receiving, processing, fabrication, assembly, and shipping phases. Written inspection and test procedures shall be prepared, supplementing contract requirements, to clarify details of the inspection and measuring equipment required, the detailed operations to be performed, the criteria for determining quality conformance or rejection of articles and materials and the results to be documented."

QUALITY CONTROL PUBLICATION	QCP NO. 6.3.1
	PAGE NO. 1 OF 3
	ISSUE DATE:
TITLE: FINAL INSPECTION AND TESTING	APPROVED BY:
	REVISION NO: 0
	REVISION DATE:

1.0 PURPOSE

This quality control publication establishes the method and responsibilities for the final inspection of deliverable parts, material, subassemblies and assemblies for compliance to the requirements and specifications of the contract or purchase order.

2.0 INTENT

It is the intent of this QCP to show the relationship between the design, production, manufacturing, and quality engineering functions in the establishment of a cohesive inspection system.

3.0 APPLICABLE FORMS AND PROCEDURES

3.1 Inspection/Test Instructions, Form 3.3.1-2.

3.2 Laboratory Analysis/Test Report, Form 3.3.3-1.

3.3 Failure Report, Form 6.5.1-1.

3.4 Inspection Report, Form 3.3.3-2.

3.5 Accepted tag, QCP 6.7.1.

3.6 Rejection and Disposition Tag, QCP 6.7.1.

4.0 PROCEDURE

4.1 Work orders direct the flow of all items throughout the complete work cycle via the operation codes specified on the work order.

4.2 All completed material, parts and other items are forwarded to the applicable final inspection areas (via the work order) to verify that the items conform to the applicable specifications and contract requirements.

QUALITY CONTROL PUBLICATION	QCP NO. 6.3.1
	PAGE NO. 2 OF 3
	ISSUE DATE:
TITLE: FINAL INSPECTION AND TESTING	APPROVED BY:
	REVISION NO: 0
	REVISION DATE:

4.3 All final inspections are accomplished as required by the Inspection/Test Instructions, Form 3.3.1-2, which are specified on the work order in the form of operation codes.

4.4 Parts, material, subassemblies, assemblies and completed systems will not be accepted by Final Inspection unless all operations as called out on the operations sheet have been completed and each operation has been signed/stamped for by the applicable operator or inspector as provided for on the operation sheet and accompanying inspection reports and production/inspection instructions.

4.5 The final inspection is to include (as above) and examination of the accompanying paper work for completeness, correctness, and shall include verification that all operations were accomplished using the latest revision drawings and specifications. The final inspection shall include verification of the workmanship, physical and functional characteristics, and for the proper marking and protection of all items as called out in the drawings and specifications.

4.6 If special tests or laboratory analysis are to be performed prior to final inspection, a Laboratory Analysis/Test Request, Form 3.3.3-1 is to be filled out and submitted to the appropriate department for accomplishment (see QCP 3.3.3).

4.7 Material, parts, subassemblies, assemblies found to be acceptable for shipment at final inspection are to be marked or tagged as required by the inspection procedure for those items.

4.8 The Accepted Tag, Form 6.7.1-2 is to be attached to all completed and accepted items, and the acceptance or rejection of all units is to be so noted on the accompanying routing sheets and other documentation.

4.9 The Inspection Report, Form 3.3.3-2 (QCP 3.3.3), is to be filled out when parts, units, etc. are found to be discrepant. The instructions for the use of this form is found in QCP 3.3.3.

QUALITY CONTROL PUBLICATION	QCP NO. 6.3.1
	PAGE NO. 3 OF 3
	ISSUE DATE:
TITLE: FINAL INSPECTION AND TESTING	APPROVED BY:
	REVISION NO: 0
	REVISION DATE:

4.10 A preliminary review board will be held by manufacturing, production, quality engineering along with the responsible department supervision, to determine if the parts can be reworked to the applicable drawing and/or specification.

4.11 If it has been determined by the preliminary review board that the material, units, etc. can be reworked to the applicable drawing and/or specification, the material/units will then be routed to the appropriate department along with an approved rework procedure for the accomplishment of the rework.

4.12 After the rework has been accomplished, the material/unit must be inspected to the applicable inspection instruction before the material can be accepted.

4.13 Materials/Units that can not be reworked to drawing/specification as determined by the preliminary review board, are to be routed to the material review board holding area along with a Nonconforming Material and Disposition Report, in QCP 6.5.2, Form 6.5.2-1, with the appropriate sections filled out along with the paperwork that accompanies the material.

4.14 A copy of the NCMDR will be kept in the department affected by this action until disposition of the material/unit and corrective action has been taken.

4.15 No action can be taken with the above material/units until all approved dispositions, recommendations are completed.

FINAL ACCEPTANCE

MIL-Q-9858A and MIL-HDBK-H50, section 6.3 states the requirement for the Final Testing of end items. "The quality program shall assure that there is a system for final test of completed products. Such testing shall provide a measure of the overall quality of the completed product and shall be performed so that it simulates, to a sufficient degree, product end use and functioning...Sufficiently thorough testing must be done to assure that completed products will perform as intended during use...Deficiencies or deviations from established design requirements shall be reported. When any inspected item is reworked, repaired or modified, it must be reinspected or retested...Contractors usually find that final testing is a useful source of information for improving both manufacturing methods and products."

MIL-I-45208A and MIL-HDBK-H51, section 3.2.1, states the requirement for Inspection and Testing Documentation. "Inspection and testing shall be prescribed by clear, complete and current instructions...To meet the objective of the requirements in this paragraph, the contractor's inspection instructions may either be oriented along product lines or along functional lines (e.g., receiving, in-process, final inspection). Either method or a combination of both is acceptable, including the variations described, provided the instructions assure the performance of the inspections needed to prove compliance with the contractual and specification requirements."

AQAP-1, paragraph 213 (b), states, "The contractor shall perform inspection and testing on the finished product or service necessary to complete the evidence of conformance with contract requirements. Procedures for final inspection and testing shall ensure that inspections and tests that should have been conducted at earlier states, have, in fact, been performed and that the data is acceptable and available from applicable records. Any unusual difficulties found during inspection and testing shall be reported to the QAR (Government Quality Assurance Representative).

AQAP-4, paragraph 211, states, "The contractor shall perform all inspection on the finished product or service necessary to complete the evidence of full conformance with contract requirements. Procedures for final inspection shall ensure that inspections that should have been conducted at earlier stages have, in fact, been performed and that the data is acceptable."

QUALITY CONTROL PUBLICATION	QCP NO. 6.3.2
	PAGE NO. 1 OF 3
	ISSUE DATE:
TITLE: FINAL ACCEPTANCE, INSPECTION AND TEST	APPROVED BY:
	REVISION NO: 0
	REVISION DATE:

1.0 PURPOSE

This Quality Control Publication establishes the method and responsibilities for the final testing of deliverable material, parts, sub-assemblies, assemblies to prove their compliance to the applicable specifications and requirements of the contract or purchase order.

2.0 INTENT

It is the intent of this QCP to establish the method and instructions for the final testing of all items prior to either the stocking of these items or the delivery of these items.

3.0 APPLICABLE FORMS AND PROCEDURES

3.1 Inspection/Test Instructions, Form 3.3.1.

3.2 Laboratory Analysis/Test Report, Form 3.3.3-1.

3.3 Failure Report, Form 6.5.1-1.

3.4 Test Report, Form 3.3.3-2.

3.5 Accepted Tag - QCP 6.7.1.

3.6 Rejection and Disposition Tag - QCP 6.7.1.

3.7 Non-Conforming Material and Disposition Report, Form 6.5.2-1.

4.0 PROCEDURE

4.1 Work orders direct the flow of all items throughout the complete work cycle via the operation codes specified on the work order.

4.2 All completed material, parts and other items are forwarded to the applicable final test areas (via the work order) to verify that the items conform in all respects to the drawings, specifications and the requirements of the contract or purchase order.

QUALITY CONTROL PUBLICATION	QCP NO. 6.3.2
	PAGE NO. 2 OF 3
	ISSUE DATE:
TITLE: FINAL ACCEPTANCE, INSPECTION AND TEST	APPROVED BY:
	REVISION NO: 0
	REVISION DATE:

4.3 All final testing is accomplished as required by the Inspection/Test Instructions, Form 3.3.1-2, which are specified on the work order in the form of operation codes.

4.4 No item is to be accepted for final testing unless all operations that precede the final tests are signed/stamped for on the work order by the applicable operator or inspector and there are no open items or problems that have to be addressed prior to final testing.

4.5 The quality assurance department is responsible for monitoring the test area to make sure no uncalibrated equipment is either being used or is present in the area where the tests are to be conducted. If such equipment is present, it should be removed to the calibration department or tagged with the Out-Of-Service Decal, Form 4.2.2-4 of QCP 4.2.2.

4.6 When conditions exist that may interfere with the testing in progress, a Test-In-Process, notice will be posted on all entrances to the test area, see QCP 3.3.3.

4.7 A test report is to be prepared for each item tested (as required by the specification, contract, purchase order).

4.8 At the completion of acceptance testing, product found to be acceptable is tagged with the Accepted Tag (if practical), refer to Form 6.7.1-2. If lot testing has been accomplished, the Accepted Tag, will accompany the lot.

4.9 If customer source inspection is a requirement for the final inspection/ test, the customer will be notified within 72 hours prior to the start of the testing, or as specified in the contract or purchase order.

4.10 A Failure Report, Form 6.5.1-1, is to be filled out when items, units tested are found to be non-conforming. The instructions for the use of this form are found in QCP 6.5.1.

QUALITY CONTROL PUBLICATION	QCP NO. 6.3.2
	PAGE NO. 3 OF 3
	ISSUE DATE:
TITLE: FINAL ACCEPTANCE, INSPECTION AND TEST	APPROVED BY:
	REVISION NO: 0
	REVISION DATE:

4.11 A Preliminary Review Board will be held by manufacturing, production, quality engineering along with the responsible department supervision, to determine if the part/item can be reworked to the applicable drawing/ specification and contract/purchase order requirement.

4.12 Paragraphs 4.11 thru 4.15 of QCP 6.3.1 apply to the balance of the procedures in this QCP. In trying to avoid un-necessary repetition, reference to procedural actions that are the same will be made, instead of stating the same procedures over again.

QUALITY CONTROL PUBLICATION	QCP NO. 6.3.3
	PAGE NO. 1 OF 3
	ISSUE DATE:
TITLE: FINAL ACEPTANCE PROCESSING AND DOCUMENTATION	APPROVED BY:
	REVISION NO: 0
	REVISION DATE:

1.0 PURPOSE

This Quality Control Publication establishes the method and procedures for the final acceptance processing of in-house documentation, deliverable documentation, publications, and finished product by the final quality control unit of the quality assurance department prior to forwarding the documentation and finished product to the shipping department.

2.0 INTENT

It is the intent of this QCP to instruct the final quality control unit in the way in which to verify the completeness of all documentation that describes the supplied material, that instructs the customer on how to use the equipment, that instructs the customer's technical personnel on how to install, maintain, and repair the equipment, that explains the theory of operation of the equipment/ unit, and provides schematics, drawings, reliability/maintainability studies, and other documentation that may be contractually required. These final quality control actions include. the final acceptance processing of in-house documentation and finished product and the acquiring of customer source inspection acceptance of deliverable items, units and documentation as required by the contract or purchase order.

3.0 APPLICABLE FORMS AND PROCEDURES

3.1 Deliverable Material and Documentation Checklist, Form 6.3.3-1.

3.2 Inspection/Test Instructions, QCP 3.3.1.

3.3 Inspection Report, QCP 3.3.3-2.

3.4 Accepted Tag - QCP 6.7.1.

3.5 Rejection Tag - QCP 6.7.1.

3.6 Non-Conforming Material and Disposition Report, Form 6.5.2-1.

QUALITY CONTROL PUBLICATION	QCP NO. 6.3.3
	PAGE NO. 2 OF 3
	ISSUE DATE:
TITLE: FINAL ACEPTANCE PROCESSING AND DOCUMENTATION	APPROVED BY:
	REVISION NO: 0
	REVISION DATE:

4.0 PROCEDURE

4.1 Quality engineering is responsible for verifying the accuracy of all technical documentation prior to the release of the documentation to the final quality control (QC).

4.2 Final QC is responsible for the verification of the presence and completeness of all inspection/test documentation, manuals and other contractually required publications prior to the release of all items to the shipping department for delivery.

4.3 The Final Quality Documentation Checklist, Form 6.3.3-1, is to be filled out as follows:

1. The name of the project.
2. The purchase order or contract number.
3. The work order number, as posted on the work order for the items/ materials delivered with the documentation.
4. Name of the customer.
5. Part/completed item name.
6. Part/completed item number.
7. Serial numbers (if applicable).
8. Date of processing this report.
9. Item number of the documentation to be delivered.
10. The actual documentation names to be verified.
11. Is the item required per the purchase order or contract? The items to be checked are filled in on this form during the initial planning stages of the purchase order or contract.

QUALITY CONTROL PUBLICATION	QCP NO. 6.3.3
	PAGE NO. 3 OF 3
	ISSUE DATE:
TITLE: FINAL ACCEPTANCE PROCESSING AND DOCUMENTATION	APPROVED BY:
	REVISION NO: 0
	REVISION DATE:

12. Final QC stamp indicating completeness and acceptance of each item on the checklist.
13. Remarks applicable to the checklist findings.
14. The final QC inspector's name.
15. The date this report was filled out by the inspector.
16. The name of the person that prepared this form during the planning stages.
17. The date this form was prepared.
18. Approving authority name.
19. Date of the approval.

4.4 In the planning stages of the contract the above form was prepared in the following way.

1. The purchase order/contract was examined in order to determine for each deliverable item, the documentation that was to accompany the finished product when delivered to the customer(s).

4.5 An Inspection Report, Form 3.3.3-2, QCP 3.3.3, is to be filled out after all final inspections/tests have been completed. This report is filled out by the final QC unit to verify the following:

4.5.1 Documentation is complete and meets the requirements of purchase order/contract. (As determined by the quality assurance department).

4.5.2 Inspection stamps have been used where required, throughout the complete production/inspection cycle.

4.5.3 Workmanship requirements have been fulfilled, i.e. cleanliness, finished surfaces meet the specification/drawing, no obvious damage has occurred during handling of the item/product.

4.5.4 All markings, identification plates/labels, instructions, conform to the requirements of the contract.

DOCUMENTATION REVIEW CHECKLIST

PROJECT NAME (1)	CONTRACT/PO NO. (2)	WORK ORDER NO. (3)	CUSTOMER (4)

PART NAME (5)	PART NUMBER (6)	SERIAL NO. (7)	DATE (8)

ITEM NO. (9)	DOC. NO. (10)	DOCUMENT NAME (11)	(12) CHECKMARK(S)		
			REQ'D.	INSP.	DATE
1	XXX-200	SERVICE MANUAL			
2	XXX-210	PARTS MANUAL			
3	XXX-220	ASSEMBLY MANUAL			
4	XXX-230	OPERATING MANUAL			
5	XXX-240	OPER. TEST REPORT			
6	XXX-250	ENVIR. TEST REPORT(S)			
7	XXX-260	RELIABILITY/MAINTAINABILITY			
8	XXX-270	CERT. OF CONFORMANCE			
9	XXX-280	INSPECTION REPORT(S)			
10	XXX-290	PURCHASING DOCUMENTATION			
11	XXX-300	NON-DESTRUCT. TEST REPORT(S)			
12	XXX-310	MATERIAL ANALYSIS REPORT(S)			
13	XXX-320	DISCREPANCY REPORT(S)			
14	XXX-330	CORRECTIVE ACTION REPORT(S)			
15	XXX-340	WAIVER(S)/DEVIATION(S)			
16	XXX-350	ENGINEERING CHG PROPOSAL(S)			
17	XXX-	OTHER(S)			
18	XXX-	OTHER(S)			

NOTES: (13)

QC INSPECTOR'S NAME (14)	DATE	INSPECTOR'S SIGNATURE (15)	DATE
FORM PREPARED BY (16)	DATE	APPROVED BY (17)	DATE

FORM 6.3.3-1

CHAPTER NINE

Corrective Action

CORRECTIVE ACTION

MIL-Q-9858A and MIL-HDBK-H50, section 3.5, Corrective Action, MIL-HDBK-H50, states, "Prompt, effective corrective action is essential to a quality program. Segregating defective material from acceptable material is not enough: the cause of the defects must be found and corrected. Occasionally the cause of infrequent or non-repetitive defects cannot be determined and the only action possible is to reject the defective items...It is imperative that the contractor make effective use of all data regarding defects, whether the data comes from using activities or is generated by his own operation. Data from users may concern defects caused by the prime contractor or by his suppliers. In either case, the contractor is responsible for assuring that corrective action is taken. Engineering, production control, purchasing, or any other function found to have caused the defect is charged with the responsibility for devising and implementing corrective measures. The interests of both the contractor and the government demand close attention to the effectiveness of corrective actions. Likewise, both the contractor and the government must monitor *fixes* carefully to be certain of their continued effectiveness."

Paragraph 3.2.3 of MIL-HDBK-H51, states, "The contractor is required to correct promptly any assignable inadequacies in his inspection system which have resulted or could result in non-conforming products or services being offered to the government for acceptance...To meet the objective of the requirements in this paragraph, the contractor's inspection system must provide for both the detection of potential, as well as actual, causes of defects and the elimination, as soon as practical, of those causes that are detected."

Paragraph 206 of AQAP-1, states, "The contractor shall establish and maintain procedures designed to detect and correct deficiencies and conditions that adversely affect quality, and, where appropriate their causes, in operations pertaining to design, purchasing, manufacturing, inspecting or other elements of contract performance."

Paragraph 213, of AQAP-4, states, "The contractor shall take prompt action to correct conditions that have caused or could cause either nonconformance of material or services, or deviations from agreed procedures and practices, or from the requirements of this document."

Quality control publication 3.5.1 is a sample procedure that will be useful in addressing corrective action in your quality manual, this is true of all the sample procedures in this book.

NHB 5300.4(1B), paragraph 1B802, states, "The contractor shall:

a. Conduct timely and effective remedial action to ensure the correction of the article or material.

b. Conduct timely and effective preventive action to prevent recurrence of the nonconformance including correction of technical documents, correction of other identical articles or materials at all locations and the prevention of detrimental side effects.

c. Assign responsibility for followup of remedial and preventive actions to ensure accomplishment.

d. Notify responsible contractor of supplier organizational elements of nonconformances and the need for remedial and preventive actions."

QUALITY CONTROL PUBLICATION	QCP NO. 3.5.1
	PAGE NO. 1 OF 4
	ISSUE DATE:
TITLE: CORRECTIVE ACTION	APPROVED BY:
	REVISION NO: 0
	REVISION DATE:

1.0 PURPOSE

This Quality Control Publication establishes the procedures for the implementation of *timely* and *effective corrective action* that will prevent recurrence of defects, discrepancies and nonconformances in material/product that is to be presented to the government and other customers for acceptance of such material and/or product.

2.0 INTENT

It is the intent of this QCP to provide the *method* for the implementation of the corrective action procedures.

3.0 APPLICABLE FORMS AND PUBLICATIONS

3.1 Failure Report, Form 6.5.1-1.

3.2 Nonconforming Material and Disposition Report, Form 6.5.2-1.

3.3 Corrective Action Request, Form 3.5.1-1.

3.4 Corrective Action Status Log, Form 3.5.1-2.

4.0 PROCEDURE

4.1 When a discrepancy, failure or nonconformance is found during any phase of the production life cycle (which includes purchasing, receiving, receiving inspection and shipping departments), a Failure Report, as depicted in QCP 6.5.1, will be filled out and forwarded to the Material Review Board, along with the discrepant material/product (if feasible due to the nature and/or size of the discrepant material/product) along with the associated documentation for a review and disposition of the nonconformances and discrepancies. If the material or product is of such a nature that the moving of the item would take extreme measures, it will be segregated and stored in that area until final disposition and corrective action has been obtained as described in this QCP and QCP's 6.5.1 through 6.5.5.

QUALITY CONTROL PUBLICATION TITLE: CORRECTIVE ACTION	QCP NO. 3.5.1
	PAGE NO. 2 OF 4
	ISSUE DATE:
	APPROVED BY:
	REVISION NO: 0
	REVISION DATE:

4.2 Corrective Action is initiated following the procedures and steps taken in QCP's 6.5.1 through 6.5.4, QCP 6.5.2. Form 6.5.2-1 is the first step taken in the Corrective Action Process. This is followed by the procedures in this QCP, and documented on Form 3.5.1-1 as required in 4.3 of this QCP.

4.3 The Corrective Action Request, Form 3.5.1-1, is to be filled out as follows:

1. The corrective action request number.
2. The department function where the discrepancy/nonconformance occurred.
3. The date of this request.
4. The material review board is the requestor of the report.
5. When the reply to this request is due. (Timely corrective action is required to keep product moving).
6. Program or project affected.
7. Material, part, assembly, item name/description.
8. Part number.
9. Failure report number.
10. Nonconforming material and disposition report, Form 6.5.2-1.
11. Description of deficiency/nonconformance. (Blocks 1 through 11 are to be filled in by the material review board).
12. The cause of the discrepancy/nonconformance as determined by the department responsible.
13. That department's recommended corrective action to be taken to prevent the recurrence of the discrepancy/nonconformance.

QUALITY CONTROL PUBLICATION	QCP NO. 3.5.1
	PAGE NO. 3 OF 4
	ISSUE DATE:
TITLE: CORRECTIVE ACTION	APPROVED BY:
	REVISION NO: 0
	REVISION DATE:

14. Department supervisor's signature.
15. Supervisor's title.
16. Date of signature.
17. MRB approval, disapproval (check one.)
18. Date of approval/disapproval.
19. Quality assurance department representative's signature.

4.4 All recommendations, approvals and disapprovals are to be recorded on the Nonconforming Material and Disposition Report, Form 6.5.2-1 and follow-up action taken to resolve the discrepancy or discrepancies/ nonconformance.

4.5 All corrective action requests are to be logged into the corrective action status log, Form 3.5.1-2 for record keeping and to keep track of the status of all open items that involve product quality. No open items or product will be submitted to the Government or other customers until all actions have been finalized and all appropriate approvals have been obtained. A review of the status logs will be accomplished by quality engineering prior to requesting acceptance of any material or finished product from the government or other customers.

4.6 The Corrective Action Status Log will be filled in as follows:

1. Corrective action report number.
2. Failure report number.
3. Nonconforming material and disposition report number.
4. Department/organization responsible for the corrective action.
5. Date of request for corrective action.

QUALITY CONTROL PUBLICATION	QCP NO. 3.5.1
	PAGE NO. 4 OF 4
	ISSUE DATE:
TITLE: CORRECTIVE ACTION	APPROVED BY:
	REVISION NO: 0
	REVISION DATE:

6. Date corrective action is due. (Timely action is mandatory. No material/product will be moved until correction and corrective action has been accomplished).
7. Date of correction and corrective action.
8. Material review board approval/disapproval - check one.)
9. Pertinent remarks.
10. Follow-up recommendations and actions.
11. Date all corrections and corrective actions have been completed.

CORRECTIVE ACTION REQUEST			
DATE: ③		CAR NO. ①	
TO: ②		FROM: ④	
NAME OF PROGRAM ⑥	PART NAME/DESCRIPTION ⑦	PART NO. ⑧	REPLY DUE DATE ⑤
FAILURE REPORT NO. ⑨		NCMDR NO.: ⑩	
DESCRIPTION OF DEFICIENCY/NONCONFORMANCE: ⑪			
CAUSE OF DEFICIENCY/NONCONFORMANCE: ⑫			
ACTION TO BE TAKEN TO PREVENT RECURRENCE OF DEFICIENCY/ NONCONFORMANCE: ⑬			
APPLICABLE REMARKS:			
SIGNATURE: ⑭	TITLE: ⑮		DATE: ⑯
MRB APPROVAL ☐ DISAPPROVAL ☐ ⑱ DATE		Q.C. REP. SIG. ⑲	
FORM 3.5.1-1			

CORRECTIVE ACTION LOG

CAR NO.	FAILURE REPORT NUMBER	NCMDR NO.	DEPARTMENT RESPONSIBLE FOR REPORT	DATE REQ.	DATE DUE	DATE OF ACTION	APPROVED ☐ DISAPPROVED ☐	REMARKS	FOLLOW UP	COMP DATE
①	②	③	④	⑤	⑥	⑦	⑧	⑨	⑩	⑪

FORM 3.5.1-2

QUALITY CONTROL PUBLICATION	QCP NO. 3.5.2
	PAGE NO. 1 OF 3
	ISSUE DATE:
TITLE: SUPPLIER/VENDOR CORRECTIVE ACTION	APPROVED BY:
	REVISION NO: 0
	REVISION DATE:

1.0 PURPOSE

This quality control publication establishes the procedure for the obtaining of vendor/supplier corrective action to prevent the recurrence of defects and to notify vendors suppliers when defects are found.

2.0 INTENT

It is the intent of this QCP to provide for a method of notifying vendors/ suppliers when there are defects in delivered material, parts, subassemblies, etc.

3.0 APPLICABLE FORMS AND PUBLICATIONS

3.1 Failure Report, Form 6.5.1-1.

3.2 Nonconforming Material and Disposition Report, Form 6.5.2-1.

3.3 Vendor Corrective Action Request, Form 3.5.2-1.

4.0 PROCEDURE

4.1 When a defect, nonconformance, etc. is found that is traceable to a vendor/supplier whether it is found in receiving inspection, stock or at any other point, the material is subject to the same procedures as depicted in QCP 3.5.1 with one additional step. A Vendor Corrective Action Request, Form 3.5.2-1, will be made out notifying the vendor/supplier that discrepant material was received and dispositioned as stated on the form. The Vendor Corrective Action Request will be filled out as follows:

1. The Vendor Corrective Action Request report number (assigned by the purchasing department).
2. The date of the request.
3. The name and address of the supplier.

QUALITY CONTROL PUBLICATION	QCP NO. 3.5.1
	PAGE NO. 2 OF 3
	ISSUE DATE:
TITLE: SUPPLIER/VENDOR CORRECTIVE ACTION	APPROVED BY:
	REVISION NO: 0
	REVISION DATE:

4. The name and address of the initiator of the request.
5. The part/assembly number of the discrepant material.
6. The part/assembly name/description.
7. The quality of part/material received.
8. The quantity of part/material rejected.
9. The name of the project the part/material is to be used on.
10. The purchase order number that the part/material was supplied under.
11. A description of the discrepancy, including the discrepant characteristics.
12. A check mark indicating the authorized disposition of the discrepant part/material.
13. The signature of the person authorized to disposition the part/material (purchasing department).
14. The signature of the person authorized to disposition the part/material (quality engineering).

4.2 After logging the request, Form 3.5.1-2, the request is sent to the purchasing department for transmittal to the vendor/supplier for action.

4.3 The purchasing department will notify the vendor/supplier as to the timeliness and the answer required. If an amount of time elapses and causes a slowdown in production and in delivery requirements, a monetary adjustment in the purchase order will be obtained, and the vendor/supplier could be dropped from the recommended vendor/supplier list.

QUALITY CONTROL PUBLICATION	QCP NO. 3.5.1
	PAGE NO. 3 OF 3
	ISSUE DATE:
TITLE: SUPPLIER/VENDOR CORRECTIVE ACTION	APPROVED BY:
	REVISION NO: 0
	REVISION DATE:

4.4 Blocks 15, 16, 17, 18, 19 are filled in by the vendor/supplier indicating the cause of the discrepancy and the corrective action being taken to eliminate the root cause of the discrepancies.

4.5 Upon receipt of the completed Vendor Corrective Action request, the purchasing department will make a copy of it for filing and forward the original to quality engineering.

4.6 Quality engineering will review all actions taken by the vendor/supplier and determine if the returned material/goods and actions taken are thorough and correct. If there is any doubt or proof that the vendor/supplier has not taken the appropriate actions, quality engineering may request additional data/information or could request a joint audit at the vendor's/supplier's place of business (see QCP 5.1.1).

VENDOR CORRECTIVE ACTION REQUEST

VCAR NO. ① ________	DATE ② ________
TO: ③	FROM: ④

PART/ASSY.NO.	PART NAME/DESCRIPTION	QTY. RECV'D	QTY. REJ.
⑤	⑥	⑦	⑧

PROJECT:	PURCHASE ORDER NUMBER
⑨	⑩

CHARACTERISTICS DISCREPANT/NON-CONFORMING TO SPEC/DRAWING/ PRINT/CONTRACT:

⑪

DISPOSITION ⑫

- ☐ RETURNED TO VENDOR FOR CREDIT
- ☐ RETURNED TO VENDOR FOR REWORK
- ☐ USED AS IS
- ☐ REWORKED AT VENDOR'S EXPENSE
- ☐ OTHER (SPECIFY)
- ☐ CREDIT DUE TO (EXPLAIN)

⑬ ________ PURCHASING DEPART. APPROVAL

⑭ ________ QUAL. ASSUR. DEPT. APPROVAL

VENDOR TO FILL OUT BLOCKS 15, 16, 17

CAUSE OF DISCREPANCY/NONCONFORMANCE

⑮

VENDOR CORRECTIVE ACTION: (USE SEPARATE SHEET IF NECESSARY)

⑯

AUTHORIZED VENDOR SIGNATURE ⑰ ________ TITLE ⑱ ________ DATE ⑲ ________

FORM 3.5.2-1

CHAPTER TEN

Costs Related To Quality

COSTS RELATED TO QUALITY

The following QCP establishes the relationship between the various sections of MIL-Q-9858A and the planning of a Cost of Quality system that is contractually required. The latest interpretation of the Cost of Quality requirements is presented here in order to understand what the full impact of not being able to control all facets of the way in which a company does its business will impact on the profit margin. The lack of adequate planning affects overall system approach and adversely affects profit margin. The lack of adequate production controls creates nonconformances and discrepancies in the product and does adversely affect profit margin. A Cost of quality system is developed in order to track difficiencies and costs and, is a major concern to the government due to the effects of these costs on price.

The following paragraphs from MIL-Q-9858A and MIL-STD-1520 are presented here to show how the government evaluates a contractor's Cost of Quality system. The evaluation takes two steps: 1. The amount of nonconforming material/product the government is receiving. The cause and prevention of these nonconformances. 2. The impact of cost to the government and the reclaiming of these costs.

MIL-Q-9858A, paragraph 1.3, states "The quality program shall facilitate determination of the effects of the quality deficiencies and quality costs on prices." MIL-Q-9858A, paragraph 3.4, states "The contractor shall maintain and use any records or data essential to the economical an effective operation of his quality program. Inspection records shall, as a minimum, indicate the nature of observations and the number and type of deficiencies found. The quality program shall provide for the analysis and use of records as a basis for management action."

MIL-Q-9858A, paragraph 3.5, states "The quality program shall detect promptly and correct assignable conditions adverse to quality. Design, manufacturing, testing, or other operation which could result in or have resulted in defective supplies which could create excessive losses or costs must be identified and changed. Corrective action shall include as a minimum:

1. Analysis of data and examination of product scrapped or reworked to determine extent and causes.
2. Analysis of trends to prevent nonconforming product.
3. Introduction of required improvements and monitoring of the effectiveness of corrective action taken."

MIL-Q-9858A, paragraph 3.6, states "The contractor shall maintain and use quality cost data as a management element of the quality program. These data shall serve the purpose of identifying the cost of both the prevention and correction of nonconforming supplies (e.g., labor and material involved in material spoilage caused by defective work, correction of defective work and for the quality control caused to be exercised) by the contractor at subcontractor's or vendor's facilities."

MIL-Q-9858A, paragraph 6.1, states "Supplier's materials and products shall be subjected to inspection upon receipt to the extent necessary to assure conformance to technical requirements."

MIL-Q-9858A, paragraph 6.3, states "The quality program shall assure that there is a system for final inspection and test of completed products."

MIL-Q-9858A, paragraph 6.5, states "The contractor shall make known to the government upon request the data associated with the costs and losses in connection with scrap and with rework necessary to reprocess nonconforming material to make ti conform completely."

MIL-STD-1520, paragraph 4.11.6, "the contractor shall assure the collection of the costs associated with nonconforming material. The contractor shall use a system employing actual costs, relative cost constants, estimates by qualified personnel or any combination thereof. The objective of generating this cost data is to provide current and trend data to be used for contractor and Government management review and appropriate action. Cost collection shall consist of:

1. Total scrap costs.
2. Total rework costs.
3. Total repair costs.

MIL-STD-1520, paragraph 5, states "The requirements of this standard shall be implemented by the contractor through the preparation, publication and maintenance of detailed written procedures. These procedures shall be acceptable to the Government Representative and be available for his review."

MIL-Q-9858A, paragraph 3.1, requires that the broad umbrella of management shall regularly review the status and adequacy of the quality program. The discussion of cost of quality must therefore extend to high management levels.

Finally, looking at the total cost of quality system, even though the contractors quality assurance department may have designed the cost of quality system monitor the system, and input data into the system, the most common actual users of the data are non-quality people. This fact points to the importance of clear, complete procedures prescribing the use of the system. In monitoring the system, all areas of a facility will have to be monitored due to the requirements of MIL-Q-9858A and the requirements of MIL-STD-1520. This monitoring is tied into most of the other Alpha Designators of 8200.1 in this book.

QUALITY CONTROL PUBLICATION	QCP NO. 3.6.1
	PAGE NO. 1 OF 4
	ISSUE DATE:
TITLE: COSTS RELATED TO QUALITY	APPROVED BY:
	REVISION NO: 0
	REVISION DATE:

1.0 PURPOSE

This quality control publication establishes the methods and procedures for the collection and utilization of cost data, which is utilized to facilitate management determinations as to the effects of system, material and product deficiencies on the total cost of producing a product versus the total sales profits of the company and the most effective method for taking positive corrective action to prevent recurring defects.

2.0 INTENT

The intent of this QCP is to provide a foundation for a systematic approach to the Cost of Quality system.

3.0 APPLICABLE FORMS AND PUBLICATIONS

3.1 QCP 3.4.1 - Records

3.2 QCP 3.5.1 - Corrective Action

3.3 QCP 3.6.2 - Quality Assurance Reports

3.4 QCP 6.1.1 - Material and Materials Control

3.5 QCP 6.2.1 - Process Control

3.6 QCP 6.3.1 - Final Inspection

3.7 QCP 6.5.1 thru 6.5.5 - Nonconforming Material

4.0 DEFINITION

4.1 All costs incurred as a result of nonconformances (cost of failure) and all costs incurred as a result of corrective actions taken specifically to prevent future occurrences (cost of prevention).

QUALITY CONTROL PUBLICATION	QCP NO. 3.6.1
	PAGE NO. 2 OF 4
	ISSUE DATE:
TITLE: COSTS RELATED TO QUALITY	APPROVED BY:
	REVISION NO: 0
	REVISION DATE:

5.0 PROCEDURE

5.1 The quality assurance department and the cost accounting function of the accounting department (under the comptrollers office) are responsible for the methods and procedures whereby defects, discrepancies, nonconforming material/product and all other cost factors are recorded wherever they appear during the total life of receiving and producing a product, making changes to existing material/product and the associated documentation and in the determining the disposition of defective material/product.

5.2 Various cost centers related to the type and location of the defects have been established and are organized into eight categories. These categories are as depicted below:

1. Material costs due to scrap and the replacement of such material and the cost of dispositioning the material.
2. Cost of all repairs along with the dispositioning costs and planning costs (repair procedures)
3. The cost of rework along with the disposition and planning costs (rework procedures).
4. Cost of generating, Engineering Change Orders, and Proposals, Waivers and Deviations.
5. Cost of investigations due to deficiencies. This includes man-hours expended, material costs, inside/outside labor costs.
6. Reinspection and retesting costs.
7. Customer price adjustment costs due to defective/discrepant product.
8. Warranty and its associated costs.

QUALITY CONTROL PUBLICATION TITLE: COSTS RELATED TO QUALITY	QCP NO. 3.6.1
	PAGE NO. 3 OF 4
	ISSUE DATE:
	APPROVED BY:
	REVISION NO: 0
	REVISION DATE:

5.3 All salaried personnel are to record their time charges as depicted in the above cost centers. An explanation of the various cost centers follows below.

5.3.1 Material Costs - The costs of replacing material due to damage, production of nonconforming material, process failures, machining failures, vendor supplied material/parts.

5.3.2 Repair Costs - The costs of repairing material due to nonconformances. Definition of repair: Even when fixed, the material does not meet the specification/drawing in all aspects.

5.3.3 Rework Costs - The costs of reworking material to the specification/drawing in all aspects.

5.3.4 ECO, ECP, Waiver/Deviation Costs - The costs of generating, Engineering Change orders, Engineering Change Proposals, Waivers and Deviations due to the misunderstanding or oversight of technical requirements by the engineering department, lack of complete planning, faulty work or process instructions and controls.

5.3.5 Investigation Costs - The costs of investigating in-house and customer complaints due to material/product nonconformances/ discrepancies and the corrective action taken to correct the deficiencies.

5.3.6 Reinspection and Retesting Costs - The costs incurred in the reinspection/ retesting of product after rework and/or repairs have been completed.

5.3.7 Customer Price Adjustment Costs - The costs incurred when a negotiated price settlement has been made due to faulty/ discrepant material being sent to customers.

5.3.8 Warranty Costs - The costs incurred due to the repair/rework of product that was under warranty.

5.4 Failure codes (as provided by manufacturing and quality engineering), Work Order Numbers, Part Numbers, will also be recorded for each operation accomplished.

QUALITY CONTROL PUBLICATION	QCP NO. 3.6.1
	PAGE NO. 4 OF 4
	ISSUE DATE:
TITLE: COSTS RELATED TO QUALITY	APPROVED BY:
	REVISION NO: 0
	REVISION DATE:

5.5 Material Review Board Dispositioning and corrective action time will also be recorded as above.

5.6 The accounting department's Failure Data Accumulation Procedure is used by the accounting department in order to provide a weekly and quarterly report to the Quality Assurance Department for the compilation of a Cost Related To Quality report that is used to brief the top management of the company as to the status of all quality costs incurred during that quarter, and the corrective action that has been accomplished to eliminate those costs. It is up to top management to make the final decisions as the the policies and practices that will be put into effect by the company to control these costs.

5.7 The quality assurance department is responsible for the establishment of a procedure that will summarize accurately and completely all present costs/historical records that show a yearly comparison through the use of cost center breakdowns, bar charts, the use of other tools that will reflect an accurate and complete analysis of the Costs Related to Quality.

5.8 As stated in Chapter 4, Amendments and Revisions, in this book, the government will be provided, quarterly, with the cost related to quality reports and summaries as requested by the government.

CHAPTER ELEVEN

Drawings, Documentation and Change

DRAWINGS, DOCUMENTATION AND CHANGE

MIL-Q-9858A, paragraph 4.1, states "A procedure shall be maintained that concerns itself with the adequacy, the completeness and the correctness of drawings and with the control of changes in design." This requirement is relevant to the control of drawings and the documentation of those drawings:

1. Adequacy of drawings - Have all drawings been reviewed for adequacy? Do the drawings meet the requirements of the contract. If MIL-D-100 and/or MIL-D-1000 is required by contract, do the drawings meet these requirements?

2. Completeness/Correctness of drawings - Have design reviews been accomplished to verify the design and dimensional requirements meet the requirements of the contract? Is there adequate control of revisions and changes to prevent obsolete drawings from being used?

Paragraph 4.1, further states, "The quality program shall assure that there is complete compliance with contract requirements for proposing, approving, and effecting engineering changes...The quality program's responsibility for drawings and changes extend to the drawings and changes provided by the subcontractors and vendors for the contract." Are engineering changes, requests for waivers and deviations adequately controlled? If MIL-STD-480 and/or MIL-STD-481 is a contract requirement, are adequate procedures available and reviewed that provides for a documented method for obtaining government approval? Are internal engineering changes approved, documented and reviewed regularly? Are there procedures and controls for the documentation and revision of inspections, tests, special processes, nondestructive testing, environmental testing etc.?

Methods and procedures for the control of all documentation have to be established and reviewed on a regular basis to prevent the use of outdated drawings, inspection procedures, testing procedures, etc. from being utilized and therefore producing discrepant, nonconforming material/product.

MIL-I-45208A and MIL-HDBK-H51, paragraph 3.2.4, states "The contractor's inspection system shall provide for procedures which will assure that the latest applicable drawings, specifications and instructions required by the contract, as well as authorized changes thereto, are used for fabrication, inspection and testing." Here again is the requirement for a method and procedure for the control of all drawings, inspection and testing instructions, that will preclude the introduction of discrepant and nonconforming material/product.

AQAP 1, paragraph 208, Documentation Control and Change Control, states "The contractor shall establish and maintain control of all documentation essential to the accomplishment of work. The contractor's responsibility shall include where appropriate the documentation from his subcontractors...All changes to contractor documentation shall be in writing and processed in a manner which will ensure prompt action at the specified implementation point. The contractor shall maintain a record of changes as they are made."

AQAP-4, paragraph 203, Documentation - (b) Technical Data and Changes, states, "The contractor shall ensure that the latest applicable drawings and specifications required by the contract, as well as authorized changes thereto, are used for inspection."

NHB 5300.4 (1B), paragraph 1B402-2c(1), Procurement Controls-Changes, states, "The supplier shall be required to notify the contractor of any proposed changes in design, fabrication methods, or processes approved by the contractor, including changes which may affect the quality or intended end-use of the item, and obtain written approval of the change from the contractor before making the change."

Paragraph 1B302 states "The contractor shall ensure control of all documents, and changes thereto, affecting the quality program. Documents shall be distributed to the proper points at the proper times, and obsolete documents removed from operating areas. The change control system shall be documented. The control system shall provide for initiation of document change requests. Changes which involve interface relationships or which affect articles not under design control of the contractor shall be coordinated with the affected parties. The contractor shall effectively integrate these requirements with other document control requirements of the contract."

NHB 5300.4(1C), paragraph 1C202-1, states, "A change control system shall be maintained, providing for document distribution to the proper points at the proper time sand removal of obsolete documents from operating areas. The control system shall provide for initiation of document change requests. Changes which involve interface relationships or which affect articles and materials controlled by others shall be coordinated with the affected parties. These requirements shall be effectively integrated with other document control requirements of the contract."

QUALITY CONTROL PUBLICATION	QCP NO. 4.1.1
	PAGE NO. 1 OF 5
	ISSUE DATE:
TITLE: DRAWINGS, DOCUMENTATION AND CHANGE	APPROVED BY:
	REVISION NO: 0
	REVISION DATE:

1.0 PURPOSE

This quality control publication sets forth the methods and procedures for the establishment of a system that controls the adequacy, completeness, currentness and the control of changes to all drawings, documentation and verifies that any changes in design or baseline configurations are documented and the necessary approvals in regards to changes have been obtained.

2.0 INTENT

This QCP applies to all released documentation, including engineering drawings, specifications, process instructions, production engineering instructions, design-related work instructions, engineering change orders/ proposals and requests for deviations or waivers.

3.0 APPLICABLE FORMS, PROCEDURES AND PUBLICATIONS

3.1 MIL-STD-480A

3.1.1 Department of Defense Form 1692 and Department of Defense Form 1692-1 through 1692-5.

3.1.2 Department of Defense Form 1694 and 1695.

3.2 MIL-STD-481A

3.2.1 Department of Defense Forms 1693 and 1694.

3.3 Design Review Participation, QCP 3.2.4.

3.4 Quality Planning, QCP 3.2.2.

3.5 Inspection/Test Instructions, QCP 3.3.1

QUALITY CONTROL PUBLICATION	QCP NO. 4.1.1
	PAGE NO. 2 OF 5
	ISSUE DATE:
TITLE: DRAWINGS, DOCUMENTATION AND CHANGE	APPROVED BY:
	REVISION NO: 0
	REVISION DATE:

4.0 DEFINITIONS

4.1 Engineering Change
An alteration in the configuration of a configuration item or items, delivered, to be delivered, or under development, after formal establishment of its configuration identification.

4.2 Engineering Change Proposal (ECP)
A term which includes both a proposed engineering change and the documentation by which the change is described and suggested.

4.3 Configuration Item (CI)
An aggregation of hardware/software, or any of its discrete portions, which satisfies an end use function and is designated by the Government for configuration management. CIs may vary widely in complexity, size and type, from an aircraft, electronic or ship system to a test meter or round of ammunition. During development and initial production, CIs are only those specification items that are referenced directly in a contract (or an equivalent in-house agreement). During the operation and maintenance period, any repairable item designated for separate procurement is a configuration item.

4.4 Configuration Control
The systematic evaluation, coordination, approval or disapproval, and implementation of all approved changes in the configuration of a CI after formal establishment of its configuration identification.

4.5 Form, Fit and Function
That configuration comprising the physical and functional characteristics of the item as an entity but not including any characteristics of the elements making up the item.

5.0 PROCEDURE

5.1 The reliability engineering function of the quality assurance department has the responsibility for all engineering documentation

QUALITY CONTROL PUBLICATION	QCP NO. 4.1.1
	PAGE NO. 3 OF 5
	ISSUE DATE:
TITLE: DRAWINGS, DOCUMENTATION AND CHANGE	APPROVED BY:
	REVISION NO: 0
	REVISION DATE:

review and control. Quality/reliability engineering will participate in Design Reviews (QCP 3.2.4), and will be the quality assurance representative on the Change Control Board.

5.2 Engineering drawings, inspection/test instructions, work orders, process control instructions, and all other instructions are to be reviewed by quality engineering for adequacy, completeness and currentness (current revision level), and will take the appropriate corrective actions when discrepancies are found.

5.3 Quality audits are to be conducted periodically to verify that only drawings, documentation, etc. that are to the latest revision are being used. All obsolete drawings, etc. are to be removed from all areas where found and corrective action to prevent recurrence is to be taken.

5.4 Quality engineering is responsible for reviewing and analyzing records and reports. One purpose for these actions is to determine if a recommendation for a quality-related design improvement in the product is required due to a value engineering study and/or there are multiple defects and/or nonconformances in the product. All recommendations are forwarded to the design engineering department for the necessary actions.

5.5 As a participant on the change control board, quality engineering is to review Engineering Change Requests (ECR's), Engineering Change Orders (ECO's), Engineering Change Proposals (ECP's), Request(s) for Deviation(s)/Waiver(s), to determine if they are correct, complete, in compliance with standards, specifications, contractual requirements, and need.

5.6 The quality engineering function is to implement inspections/tests at those points in the production/manufacturing cycle, due to change approvals, as recommended by the engineering department or where quality engineering determines it will be the most effective. This is for approved engineering changes only.

QUALITY CONTROL PUBLICATION	QCP NO. 4.1.1
	PAGE NO. 4 OF 5
	ISSUE DATE:
TITLE: DRAWINGS, DOCUMENTATION AND CHANGE	APPROVED BY:
	REVISION NO: 0
	REVISION DATE:

5.7 Quality engineering is responsible for developing new inspection and test methods for acceptance of material/product. This occurs when engineering changes have been approved.

5.8 Production engineering is responsible for developing new testing methods (in-process), when the applicable engineering changes have been approved.

5.9 The quality planning function is responsible for altering quality plans, inspection and test instructions if such alterations are required by the approved engineering change (see QCP's 3.2.2 and 3.3.1).

5.10 Quality engineering will monitor the incorporation of production and assembly changes at the designated production/manufacturing points, and for taking corrective action where discrepancies are found. The nature of the monitoring will take the form of Quality Audits, and will be part of the quality audit function.

5.11 Receiving inspection, in-process inspection, materials laboratory, environmental laboratory, and all final inspection and testing points will verify the incorporation of the engineering changes by observing and documenting the results of their respective inspections and tests.

5.12 If an Engineering Change Proposal, or Request for Deviation, or Waiver is submitted to the government, the change request or waiver/deviation is to be routed through the local DCAS Government representative. If the contractor feels that the change, waiver or deviation requires immediate action, action can be initiated by teletype, telephone or by personal contact. This is to be followed by a written statement within (3) days, followed up by a written ECP no later than 30 days after the 1st communication.

5.13 A complete description of how Engineering Change Proposals (DD Forms 1692 and 1692-1 thru 1692-5) are filled out is found in MIL-STD-480A, Appendix A, pages 38 thru 52. Instructions for preparing DD

QUALITY CONTROL PUBLICATION	QCP NO. 4.1.1
	PAGE NO. 5 OF 5
	ISSUE DATE:
TITLE: DRAWINGS, DOCUMENTATION AND CHANGE	APPROVED BY:
	REVISION NO: 0
	REVISION DATE:

Form 1695, Notice of Revision, is found on pages 58 through 60. Instructions for the preparation of DD Form 1694, Request for Deviation/Waiver, are found on pages 54 through 57.

5.14 MIL-STD-480A is to be used for proposing engineering changes to configuration items which were developed, designed, or modified only for the department of defense activities, and will be used to control the form, fit, and function of items developed by the company and used in configuration items.

5.15 MIL-STD-481A is used when it has been determined by the purchasing government activity that a short form ECP is adequate, when changes are necessary for standard items which were not developed as parts of a larger system, and company developed (private) items.

DD FORM		LIFE CYCLE PHASES			
NO. AND PAGE	Usage	Program Initiation (Conceptual)	Demonstration and Validation	Full Scale Engineering Development	Production/ Deployment and Operational
1692 Pg. 1	Cover Sheet	REQUIRED only when functional characteristics are to be controlled	REQUIRED Cover sheet summarizes the ECP	REQUIRED Cover sheet summarizes the ECP	REQUIRED Cover sheet summarizes the ECP
1692-1 Pg. 2	Effects on Functional Allocated Configuration Identification	NOT REQUIRED	REQUIRED USED to: Describe proposed changes in functional configuration identification	REQUIRED USED to: Describe proposed changes in functional or allocated configuration identification as defined by system & appropriate item specifications	REQUIRED if: (a) System specification change is associated with design change (b) Two part specification method used & part I specification needs to be changed. (c) Development & product fabrication supecifications used & development specification need to be changed
1692-2 Pg. 3	Effects on Product Configuration Identification Operations & Logistics	NOT REQUIRED	NOT REQUIRED	REQUIRED when: Prototypes are undergoing operational or service testing USED to: Describe changes to hardware	REQUIRED USED to: Describe effects of change in product configuration identification & changes in parts and/ or assemblies
1692-3 Pg. 4	Estimated Net Total Cost Impact (one item)	NOT REQUIRED	NOT REQUIRED	NOT REQUIRED	REQUIRED USED to: Tabulate cost impact

DD FORM		LIFE CYCLE PHASES (Continued)			
NO. AND PAGE	Usage	Program Initiation (Conceptual)	Demonstration and Validation	Full Scale Engineering Development	Production/ Deployment and Operational
1692-4 Pg. 5	Estimated Cost/ Savings Summary Related	NOT REQUIRED	NOT REQUIRED	NOT REQUIRED	REQUIRED if: (a) There are related ECPs applying to two or more items (b) New trainers or items of support equipment are required USED to: Summarize cost impact of all related ECPs
1692-5 Pg. 6	Milestone Chart	NOT REQUIRED	NOT REQUIRED	NOT REQUIRED	REQUIRED if: There is a schedule change in more than deliverty date for item USED to: Show-inter-relationships in schedules

LIFE CYCLE APPLICATIONS OF DD FORM 1692

ENGINEERING CHANGE PROPOSAL, PAGE 1 *(SEE MIL-STD-480 FOR INSTRUCTIONS)*	DATE PREPARED	PROCURING ACTIVITY NO.		
1. ORIGINATOR NAME AND ADDRESS		2. CLASS OF ECP	3. JUST CODE	4. PRIORITY

5. ECP DESIGNATION							6. BASELINE AFFECTED
a. MODEL/ TYPE	b. MFR. CODE	c. SYS. DESIG.	d. ECP NO.	e. TYPE	f. REV.	g. CORR.	☐ FUNC- TIONAL ☐ ALLO- CATED ☐ PRODUCT
							7. OTHER SYS./CONFIG. ITEMS AFF. ☐ YES ☐ NO

8. SPECIFICATIONS AFFECTED - TEST PLAN				9. DRAWINGS AFFECTED			
	MFR CODE	SPEC./DOC. NO	SCN	MFR CODE	NUMBER	REV.	NOR. NO
a. SYSTEM							
b. ITEM							
c. TEST PLAN							

10. TITLE OF CHANGE	11. CONTRACT NO. & LINE ITEM
12. CONFIGURATION ITEM NOMENCLATURE	13. IN PRODUCTION ☐ YES ☐ NO
14. NAME OF PART OR LOWEST ASSEMBLY AFFECTED	15. PART NO. OR TYPE DESIGNATION

16. DESCRIPTION OF CHANGE

17. NEED FOR CHANGE

18. PRODUCTION EFFECTIVITY BY SERIAL NUMBER	19. EFFECT ON PRODUCTION DELIVERY SCHEDULE

20. RETROFIT	
a. RECOMMENDED ITEM EFFECTIVITY	c. SHIP/VEHICLE CLASS AFFECTED
b. ESTIMATED KIT DELIVERY SCHEDULE	d. LOCATIONS OR SHIP/VEHICLE NUMBERS AFFECTED

21. ESTIMATED COSTS/SAVINGS UNDER CONTRACT	22. ESTIMATED NET TOTAL COSTS
23. SUBMITTING ACTIVITY AUTHORIZING SIGNATURE	TITLE

24. APPROVAL/DISAPPROVAL			
a. CLASS I ☐ APPROVAL RECOMMENDED	b. CLASS II ☐ APPROVED ☐ DISAPPROVED	☐ CONCUR IN CLASSIFICATION OF CHANGE	☐ DO NOT CONCUR IN CLASSIFICATION OF CHANGE
c. GOVERNMENT ACTIVITY		SIGNATURE	

DD FORM 1 DEC 68 1692

ENGINEERING CHANGE PROPOSAL, PAGE 2 *(SEE MIL-STD-480 FOR INSTRUCTIONS)*	PROCURING ACTIVITY NO.
ORIGINATOR NAME AND ADDRESS	ECP NUMBER
EFFECTS ON FUNCTIONAL/ALLOCATED CONFIGURATION IDENTIFICATION	
25. OTHER SYSTEMS AFFECTED	26. OTHER CONTRACTORS/ACTIVITIES AFFECTED
27. CONFIGURATION ITEMS AFFECTED	
28. EFFECTS ON PERFORMANCE ALLOCATIONS AND INTERFACES IN SYSTEM SPECIFICATIONS	
29. EFFECTS ON EMPLOYMENT, INTEGRATED LOGISTIC SUPPORT, TRAINING, OPERATIONAL EFFECTIVENESS, ETC.	
30. EFFECTS ON CONFIGURATION ITEM SPECIFICATIONS	
31. DEVELOPMENTAL REQUIREMENTS AND STATUS	
32. TRADE OFFS AND ALTERNATIVE SOLUTIONS	
33. DATE BY WHICH CONTRACTUAL AUTHORITY IS NEEDED	

DD FORM 1 DEC 68 **1692-1**

ENGINEERING CHANGE PROPOSAL, PAGE 3 *(SEE MIL-STD-480 FOR INSTRUCTIONS)*	PROCURING ACTIVITY NO.
ORIGINATOR NAME AND ADDRESS	ECP NUMBER

EFFECTS ON PRODUCT CONFIGURATION IDENTIFICATION, OPERATION AND LOGISTICS

(X)	FACTOR	ENCL.	PAR.	(X)	FACTOR	ENCL.	PAR.
	34. EFFECT ON PRODUCT CONFIGURATION IDENTIFICATION OR CONTRACT						
	PERFORMANCE						
	WEIGHT-BALANCE-STABILITY *(Aircraft)*				34. EFFECT ON OPERATIONAL EMPLOYMENT		
	WEIGHT-MOMENT *(Other equipment)*				SAFETY		
	DRAWINGS				SURVIVABILITY		
	NOMENCLATURE				MAINTAINABILITY		
					SERVICE LIFE		
					OPERATING PROCEDURES		
	35. EFFECT ON INTEGRATED LOGISTIC SUPPORT (ILS) ELEMENTS				ELECTROMAGNETIC INTERFERENCE		
	ILS PLANS				ACTIVATION SCHEDULE		
	MAINTENANCE CONCEPT AND PLANS				OPERATING INSTALLATIONS		
	MAINTENANCE PROCEDURES						
	INTERIM SUPPORT PROGRAM				37. OTHER CONSIDERATIONS		
	SPARES AND REPAIR PARTS				INTERFACE		
	TECH. MANUALS/PROGRAMMING TAPES				OTHER AFFECTED EQUIPMENT/GFE		
	FACILITIES				PHYSICAL CONSTRAINT		
	SUPPORT EQUIPMENT				OPERATIONAL COMPUTER PROGRAMS		
	OPERATOR TRAINING				REWORK OF OTHER EQUIPMENT		
	OPERATOR TRAINING EQUIPMENT				SYSTEM TEST PROCEDURES		
	MAINTENANCE TRAINING						
	MAINTENANCE TRAINING EQUIPMENT						
	PERSONNEL						
	CONTRACT ENGINEERING TECH. SVCS.						
	VERIFICATION AND DEMONSTRATION PLANS						

38. ALTERNATIVE SOLUTIONS

39. DEVELOPMENTAL STATUS

40. RECOMMENDATIONS FOR RETROFIT

41. MAN-HOURS PER UNIT TO INSTALL RETROFIT KITS
a. ORGANIZATION | b. INTERMEDIATE | c. DEPOT | d. OTHER

42. MAN-HOURS TO CONDUCT SYSTEM TESTS AFTER RETROFIT

43. THIS CHANGE MUST BE ACCOMPLISHED
☐ BEFORE ☐ WITH ☐ AFTER THE FOLLOWING CHANGES

44. IS CONT. FIELD SERVICE ENGR. REQUIRED?
☐ YES ☐ NO

45. OUT OF SERVICE TIME

46. EFFECT OF THE ECP AND PREVIOUSLY APPROVED ECP'S ON ITEM

47. DATE CONTRACTUAL AUTHORITY NEEDED FOR:
PRODUCTION ______________________
ILS ______________________

DD FORM 1 DEC 68 1692-2

ENGINEERING CHANGE PROPOSAL, PAGE 4 *(SEE MIL-STD-480 FOR INSTRUCTIONS)*	PROCURING ACTIVITY NO.
ORIGINATOR NAME AND ADDRESS	ECP NUMBER

48. ESTIMATED NET TOTAL COST IMPACT (USE MINUS SIGN FOR SAVINGS)

FACTOR	COSTS/SAVINGS UNDER CONTRACT					OTHER COSTS/SAVINGS TO GOVERNMENT (6)
	NON-RECURRING (1)	RECURRING			TOTAL (5)	
		UNIT (2)	QUANTITY (3)	TOTAL (RECURRING) (4)		
a. PRODUCTION COSTS/SAVINGS						
CONFIGURATION ITEM						
FACTORY TEST EQUIPMENT						
SPECIAL FACTORY TOOLING						
SCRAP						
ENGINEERING, ENGR. DATA REV.						
REVISION OF TEST PROCEDURES						
QUALIFICATION OF NEW ITEMS						
SUBTOTAL OF PROD. COSTS/SAVINGS						
b. RETROFIT COSTS						
ENGINEERING, ENGRG. DATA REV.						
PROTOTYPE TESTING						
KIT PROOF TESTING						
RETROFIT KITS						
PREP. OF MWO/TCTO/SC/ALT INSTR.						
SPECIAL TOOLING FOR RETROFIT						
CONTRACTOR FIELD SERVICE ENGRG.						
GOV'T PERSONNEL INSTALLATION						
TESTING ATER RETROFIT						
MODIFICATION OF GFE						
QUALIFICATION OF MODIFIED GFE						
SUBTOTAL OF RETROFIT COSTS						
c. INTEGRATED LOGISTIC SUPPORT COSTS/SAVINGS						
SPARES/REPAIRS PARTS REWORK						
NEW SPARES AND REPAIR PARTS						
RETROFIT KITS FOR SPARES						
OPERATOR TRNG. COURSES						
MAINTENANCE TRNG. COURSES						
REV. OF TECH. MAN./PROG. TAPES						
NEW TECH. MAN./PROG. TAPES						
PREP. OF MWO/TCTO/SC/ALT INSTR.						
INTERIM SUPPORT						
MAINTENANCE MANPOWER						
SUBTOTAL OF ILS COSTS/SAVINGS						
d. OTHER COSTS/ SAVINGS						
e. SUBTOTAL COSTS/SAVINGS						
SUBTOTAL UNDER CONTRACT						
f. COORDINATION OF CHANGES BY OTHER CONTRACTORS						
g. COORDINATION CHANGES BY GOVERNMENT						
ESTIMATED NET TOTAL COSTS/SAVINGS						

DD FORM 1 DEC 68 1692-3

ENGINEERING CHANGE PROPOSAL, PAGE 5 *(SEE MIL-STD-480 FOR INSTRUCTIONS)*	PROCURING ACTIVITY NO.
ORIGINATOR NAME AND ADDRESS	ECP NUMBER

49. ESTIMATED COSTS/SAVINGS SUMMARY. RELATED ECP'S (USE MINUS SIGN FOR SAVINGS)	MANUFACTURER'S CODE (1)	ECP NUMBER (2)	COSTS/SAVINGS UNDER CONTRACTS (3)	OTHER COSTS/ SAVINGS TO GOVERNMENT (4)
a. PRODUCTION COSTS/SAVINGS *(Subtotal of Costs/Savings Elements from block 48a applicable to aircraft, ship, tank, vehicle, missile or its subsystem)*				
SUB-TOTAL RETROFIT COSTS				
b. RETROFIT COSTS *(Applicable to aircraft, ship, tank, vehicle, missile or its subsystem)*				
SUB-TOTAL RETROFIT COSTS				
c. INTEGRATED LOGISTIC SUPPORT COSTS/SAVINGS				
REVISED REQUIREMENTS				
1. ITEM RETROFIT *(If not covered under "b") (Applicable to aircraft, ship, tank, vehicle, missile or its subsystem)*				
2. ILS SUBTOTAL *(Applicable to aircraft, ship, tank, vehicle, missile or its subsystem)*				
3. OPERATOR TRAINER *(Net total cost/saving from each ECP covering maintenance trainer)*				
4. MAINTENANCE TRAINER *(Net total cost/ saving from each ECP covering operator trainer)*				
5. OTHER TRAINING EQUIPMENT				
6. SUPPORT EQUIPMENT *(Net total cost/ saving from each ECP on support equipment)*				
7. ILS PLANS				
8. MAINTENANCE CONCEPT, PLANS, SYSTEM DOCUMENTS				
9. INTERIM SUPPORT PLAN				

NEW REQUIREMENTS	NON-RECURRING COSTS	RECURRING COSTS			
		UNIT	QTY.	TOTAL	
10. PROVISIONING DOCUMENTATION					
11. OPER. TRNR/TNG DEVICES/EQUIP					
12. MANUALS/PROGRAMMING TAPES. SPARES, REPAIR PARTS *(For 11)*					
13. MAINTENANCE TRNR/TRNG DEVICES/EQUIPMENT					
14. MANUALS/PROGRAMMING TAPES. SPARES, RPR PARTS *(For 13)*					
15. SUPPORT EQUIPMENT					
16. MANUALS/PRGMG TAPES *(For 15)*					
17. PROV. DOCUMENTATION *(For 15)*					
18. REPAIR PARTS *(For 15)*					

	MANUFACTURER'S CODE	ECP NUMBER		
SUB-TOTAL ILS COSTS/SAVINGS *(Sum of c.1 through c.18)*				
d. OTHER COSTS/SAVINGS *(Total from block 48d of related ECP's)*				
TOTAL OTHER COSTS/SAVINGS				
SUB-TOTALS OF COLUMNS				
SUB-TOTAL UNDER CONTRACT				
e. ESTIMATED NET TOTAL COSTS/SAVINGS *(a + b + c + d)*				

DD FORM 1 DEC 68 **1692-4**

ENGINEERING CHANGE PROPOSAL, PAGE 6 (MILESTONE CHART)

DATE PREPARED

PROCURING ACTIVITY NO.

ORIGINATOR NAME AND ADDRESS

MFR. CODE

ECP NUMBER

CONFIGURATION ITEM NOMENCLATURE

TITLE OF CHANGE

DATE AUTHORIZATION TO PROCEED RECEIVED ;BY CONTRACTOR

SYMBOL EXPLANATION

S START DELIVERY C COMPLETE DELIVERY ▽ PROGRESS POINT

	NO. OF MONTHS	1	2	3	4	5	6	7	8	9	10	11	12	13	14	15	16	17	18	19	20	21	22	23	24	25	26	27	28	29	30	31	32	33	34	35	36
CONFIGURATION ITEM	PRODUCTION																																				
	TECH. MANUALS/ PROG. TAPES																																				
	RETROFIT																																				
	MWO, TCTO, SC, ALT																																				
	SPARES/REPAIR, PARTS																																				
SUPPORT EQUIPMENT	PRODUCTION																																				
	TECH. MANUALS/ PROG. TAPES																																				
	RETROFIT																																				
	MWO, TCTO, SC, ALT.																																				
	REPAIR PARTS																																				
TRAINER	OPERATOR																																				
	MAINTENANCE																																				
	NO. OF MONTHS	1	2	3	4	5	6	7	8	9	10	11	12	13	14	15	16	17	18	19	20	21	22	23	24	25	26	27	28	29	30	31	32	33	34	35	36

DD FORM 1 DEC 68 1692-5

ENGINEERING CHANGE PROPOSAL (SHORT FORM) *(See MIL-STD-481 for instructions)*	DATE *(YYMMDD)*	*Form Approved* *OMB No. 0704-0188*
	PROCURING ACTIVITY NUMBER	

Public reporting burden for this collection of information is estimated to average 2 hours per response, including the time for reviewing instructions, searching existing data sources, gathering and maintaining the data needed, and completing and reviewing the collection of information. Send comments regarding this burden estimate or any other aspect of this collection of information, including suggestions for reducing this burden, to Washington Headquarters Services, Directorate for Information Operations and Reports, 1215 Jefferson Davis Highway, Suite 1204, Arlington, VA 22202-4302, and to the Office of Information and Regulatory Affairs, Office of Management and Budget, Washington, DC 20503.

1. ORIGINATOR NAME AND ADDRESS	2. CONTRACT NUMBER AND LINE ITEM	
	3. PROCURING CONTRACTING OFFICER	
	CODE	TEL

4. TITLE OF CHANGE

5. ECP NUMBER	REV	AMEND	6. CAGE CODE	7. CLASS OF ECP	8. JUST. CODE	9. PRIORITY

10. SPECIFICATIONS AFFECTED			11. DRAWINGS AFFECTED		
CAGE CODE	SPECIFICATION / DOCUMENT NO.	REV	CAGE CODE	NUMBER	REV.

12. CONFIGURATION ITEM NOMENCLATURE / TYPE DESIGNATION / WEAPON SYSTEM CODE	13. IN PRODUCTION
	☐ YES ☐ NO

14. LOWEST ASSEMBLY AFFECTED		
NOMENCLATURE	PART NO.	NSN

15. DESCRIPTION OF CHANGE

16. NEED FOR CHANGE

17. EFFECT ON ASSOCIATED EQUIPMENT

18. PRODUCTION EFFECTIVITY BY SERIAL NUMBER	19. EFFECT ON PRODUCTION DELIVERY SCHEDULE

20. RECOMMENDED RETROFIT EFFECTIVITY	21. ESTIMATED KIT DELIVERY SCHEDULE	22. ESTIMATED COSTS / SAVINGS

23. SUBMITTING ACTIVITY AUTHORIZED SIGNATURE	23.a. TITLE

24. APPROVAL / DISAPPROVAL	a. RECOMMEND ☐ APPROVAL	☐ DISAPPROVAL	
b. APPROVAL ☐ APPROVED ☐ DISAPPROVED	c. GOVERNMENT ACTIVITY	SIGNATURE	DATE *(YYMMDD)*
d. APPROVAL ☐ APPROVED ☐ DISAPPROVED	e. GOVERNMENT ACTIVITY	SIGNATURE	DATE *(YYMMDD)*

DD Form 1693, JUL 88 *Previous editions are obsolete.* 241 222

FIGURE 1. ECP Short Form (DD Form 1693).

NOTICE OF REVISION (NOR)
(SEE MIL-STD-480 FOR INSTRUCTIONS)

This revision described below has been authorized for the document listed.

1. ORIGINATOR NAME AND ADDRESS	DATE	MFR. CODE	NOR NO.

2. TITLE OF DOCUMENT	3. MFR. CODE	4. DOCUMENT NUMBER	
	5. REVISION LETTER (CURRENT)	(NEW)	6. ECP. NO.

7. CONFIGURATION ITEM (OR SYSTEM) TO WHICH ECP APPLIES

8. DESCRIPTION OF REVISION

9. THIS SECTION FOR GOVERNMENT USE ONLY

A. CHECK ONE

☐ EXISTING DOCUMENT SUPPLEMENTED BY THIS NOR MAY BE USED IN MANUFACTURE.

☐ REVISED DOCUMENT MUST BE RECEIVED BEFORE MANFUACTURER MAY INCORPORATE THIS CHANGE.

☐ CUSTODIAN OF MASTER DOCUMENT SHALL MAKE ABOVE REVISION AND FURNISH REVISED DOCUMENT TO:

B. ACTIVITY AUTHORIZED TO APPROVE CHANGE FOR GOVERNMENT	SIGNATURE AND TITLE	DATE
10. ACTIVITY ACCOMPLISHING REVISION	REVISION COMPLETED (SIGNATURE)	DATE

DD FORM 1 DEC 68 1695

QUALITY CONTROL PUBLICATION	QCP NO. 4.1.2
	PAGE NO. 1 OF 3
	ISSUE DATE:
TITLE: REQUESTS FOR DEVIATION AND WAIVER	APPROVED BY:
	REVISION NO: 0
	REVISION DATE:

1.0 PURPOSE

This quality control publication establishes the methods and procedures for the requesting of deviations/waivers due to inaccuracies found in drawings/specifications or due to nonconforming conditions that have been found in completed items.

2.0 INTENT

This QCP applies to the government or other customers, quality assurance, design/production engineering, manufacturing, sales and contract management departments of the company.

3.0 APPLICABLE FORMS, PROCEDURES, DOCUMENTS

3.1 MIL-STD-481A

3.2 QCP 6.5.2 and QCP 6.5.3

4.0 DEFINITIONS

4.1 Deviation

4.1.1 A specific written authorization, granted prior to the manufacture of an item, to depart from a particular performance or design requirement of a specification, drawing or other document for a specific number of units or a specific period of time. A deviation differs from an engineering change in that an approved engineering change requires corresponding revision of the documentation defining the affected item, whereas a deviation does not contemplate revision of the applicable specification or drawing. See Requirements for Deviations, MIL-STD-480A, page 21.

QUALITY CONTROL PUBLICATION	QCP NO. 4.1.2
	PAGE NO. 2 OF 3
	ISSUE DATE:
TITLE: REQUESTS FOR DEVIATION AND WAIVER	APPROVED BY:
	REVISION NO: 0
	REVISION DATE:

4.2 Waiver

4.2.1 A written authorization to accept a configuration item or other designated items, which during production or after having been submitted for inspection, are found to depart from specified requirements, but nevertheless are considered suitable for, USE-AS-IS, after repair by an approved repair method. A waiver if accepted is usually for a specific lot of unit(s) or for a specified amount of time to allow for corrective action to be taken and is minor nature/deficiency. See "Requirements for Waivers, MIL-STD-481A, page 24.

5.0 PROCEDURE

5.1 If an inaccuracy/mistake is found in a contractually required specification, drawing, requirement or where the requirement/ specification would invalidate or cause a problem that would not allow either further inspection/testing or production/manufacturing of the item(s), a Request for Deviation DD Form 1694 will be prepared utilizing the instructions in MIL-STD-480A, page 55. If a short form can be used, the instructions for preparing this form is found in MIL-STD-481A, page 13, Appendix B.

5.2 If a discrepancy/nonconformance is found in a finished items, and a decision has been made to submit the items for government acceptance as a USE-AS-IS, a Request for Waiver, DD Form 1694, will be prepared utilizing the instructions in MIL-STD-480A, page 57, Appendix C. If a short form, Request for Waiver, can be used, the instructions in MIL-STD-481A, page 15, Appendix C, are to be followed in preparing this form.

QUALITY CONTROL PUBLICATION	QCP NO. 4.1.2
	PAGE NO. 3 OF 3
	ISSUE DATE:
TITLE: REQUESTS FOR DEVIATION AND WAIVER	APPROVED BY:
	REVISION NO: 0
	REVISION DATE:

5.3 The Request for Deviation/Waiver form will be forwarded to the local government representative for concurrence as to the classification of the deviation/waiver and for further processing. A copy of the request will be sent to the government purchasing office in order to expedite actions, if, it is determined during personal contact, TWX's, telephone calls to the procurement office have resulted in an understanding that the deviation/waiver will be accepted. Full acceptance of the deviation/waiver can not be accomplished until it has been approved by all of the government offices involved.

REQUEST FOR DEVIATION / WAIVER (*See MIL-STD-480 or 481 for instructions*)	DATE (*YYMMDD*)	*Form Approved* *OMB No. 0704-0188*
Public reporting burden for this collection of information is estimated to average 2 hours per response, including the time for reviewing instructions, searching existing data sources, gathering and maintaining the data needed, and completing and reviewing the collection of information. Send comments regarding this burden estimate or any other aspect of this collection of information, including suggestions for reducing this burden, to Washington Headquarters Services, Directorate for Information Operations and Reports, 1215 Jefferson Davis Highway, Suite 1204, Arlington, VA 22202-4302, and to the Office of Information and Regulatory Affairs, Office of Management and Budget, Washington, DC 20503		PROCURING ACTIVITY NUMBER

1. ORIGINATOR NAME AND ADDRESS

2. ☐ DEVIATION ☐ WAIVER

3. ☐ MINOR ☐ MAJOR ☐ CRITICAL

4. DESIGNATION FOR DEVIATION / WAIVER

a. MODEL/TYPE	b. CAGE CODE	c. SYS. DESIG.	d. DEV/WAIVER NO.

5. BASELINE AFFECTED ☐ FUNCTIONAL ☐ ALLOCATED ☐ PRODUCT

6. OTHER SYSTEM / CONFIGURATION ITEMS AFFECTED ☐ YES ☐ NO

7. SPECIFICATIONS AFFECTED - TEST PLAN

	CAGE CODE	SPECIFICATION / DOCUMENT NO.	REV.
a. SYSTEM			
b. ITEM			
c. TEST PLAN			

8. DRAWINGS AFFECTED

CAGE CODE	NUMBER	REV

9. TITLE OF DEVIATION / WAIVER

9.a. WEAPON SYSTEM CODE OR DESIGNATION

10. CONTRACT NO. AND LINE ITEM

11. PROCURING CONTRACTING OFFICER

CODE | TEL

12. CONFIGURATION ITEM NOMENCLATURE

13. CLASSIFICATION OF DEFECT

a. CD NO.	b. DEFECT NO.	c. DEFECT CLASSIFICATION ☐ MINOR ☐ MAJOR ☐ CRITICAL

14. NAME OF LOWEST PART / ASSEMBLY AFFECTED

15. PART NO. OR TYPE DESIGNATION

16. LOT NO.

17. QTY

18. RECURRING DEVIATION / WAIVER ☐ YES ☐ NO

19. EFFECT ON COST / PRICE

20. EFFECT ON DELIVERY SCHEDULE

21. EFFECT ON INTEGRATED LOGISTICS SUPPORT, INTERFACE OR SOFTWARE

22. DESCRIPTION OF DEVIATION / WAIVER

23. NEED FOR DEVIATION / WAIVER

24. SERIAL NUMBER(S) AFFECTED

25. SUBMITTING ACTIVITY AUTHORIZED SIGNATURE

25.a. TITLE

26. APPROVAL / DISAPPROVAL a. RECOMMEND ☐ APPROVAL ☐ DISAPPROVAL

b. APPROVAL	c. GOVERNMENT ACTIVITY	SIGNATURE	DATE (*YYMMDD*)
☐ APPROVED ☐ DISAPPROVED			
d. APPROVAL	e. GOVERNMENT ACTIVITY	SIGNATURE	DATE (*YYMMDD*)
☐ APPROVED ☐ DISAPPROVED			

DD Form 1694, JUL 88 *Previous editions are obsolete.* 297 222

FIGURE 2. Request for Deviation/Waiver (DD Form 1694).

CHAPTER TWELVE

Government Property

GOVERNMENT PROPERTY

QCP 7.2.1, states the requirements of MIL-Q-9858A, MIL-I-45208A and AQAP 1, as they pertain to Alpha Designator - G, of the 8200.1, Government Property. This section is broken down into three (3) sub-paragraphs which include:

1.0 Paragraph 7.2.1 - Government Furnished Material

1.1 When material is furnished by the government, the contractor's procedures shall include at least the following:

1.1.1 Examination upon receipt, consistent with practicability to detect damage in transit.
1.1.2 Inspection for completeness and proper type.
1.1.3 Periodic inspection and precautions to assure adequate storage conditions and to guard against damage from handling and deterioration during storage.
1.1.4 Functional testing, either prior to or after installation, or both, as required by contract to determine satisfactory operation.
1.1.5 Identification and protection from improper use or disposition.

1.2 Government Furnished Material (GFM), is material owned by the government and furnished directly to contractors for their use in meeting the requirements of their contracts. A procedure written by the quality assurance department and/or the company's government property administrator addressing the methods that are to be used for the receipt, handling, storage and maintenance of such material has to be submitted to the local government property administrator to verify that the government furnished material is being dispositioned as prescribed in the company's procedures.

2.0 Paragraph 7.2.2 - Damaged Government-furnished Material

2.1 "The contractor shall report to the Government Representative any Government-furnished material found damaged, malfunctioning or otherwise unsuitable for use. In the event of damage or malfunctioning during or after installation the contractor shall determine and record probable cause and necessity for withholding from use."

2.1.1 "Contractors must report all unsuitable GFM to the authorized Government Representative. If unsuitability is found during or after installation, the contractor must determine the probable cause and determine if it is necessary to avoid use of the material. This information shall be reported to the Government Representative.

3.0 Paragraph 7.2.3 - Bailed Property

3.1 "The contractor shall, as required by the terms of the Bailment Agreement, establish procedures for the adequate storage, maintenance and inspection of bailed Government property. Records of all inspections and maintenance performed on bailed property shall be maintained. These procedures and records shall be subject to review by the Government Representative. Bailed Property refers primarily to equipment provided to the contractor for a special purpose and not for incorporation into deliverable products."

4.0 Paragraph 3.6 of MIL-I-45108A says essentially the same thing about the control of government furnished material as specified in MIL-Q-9858A, paragraph 7.2.1.

5.0 Paragraph 3.6.1 of MIL-I-45208A, Damaged Government-Furnished Material, has the same intent as paragraph 7.2.2 of MIL-Q-9858A.

6.0 AQAP-1, Paragraph 212 is slightly different, Purchaser Supplied Material, states, "The contractor shall establish and maintain procedures for the inspection, storage and maintenance of material provided by the purchaser for incorporation into supplies. Such material shall be inspected upon receipt as necessary to detect damage and to verify identity, completeness, and quantity. Any material lost, damaged or otherwise unsuitable for use shall be promptly reported to the QAR - (Government Quality Assurance Representative)."

NHB 5300.4(1B), paragraph 1B1300, states, "The contractor shall be responsible and account for all government property supplied by the government in accordance with the provisions of the contract, including property provided under such contract which may be in the possession or control of a supplier."

NHB 5300.4(1C), paragraph 1C204, states, "The contractor shall be responsible for all government property supplied by the government in accordance with the provisions of the contract."

QUALITY CONTROL PUBLICATION	QCP NO. 7.2.1
	PAGE NO. 1 OF 2
	ISSUE DATE:
TITLE: GOVERNMENT PROPERTY	APPROVED BY:
	REVISION NO: 0
	REVISION DATE:

1.0 PURPOSE

This quality control publication establishes the procedure for providing adequate inspection, storage, maintenance and use of government property, whether the property is on a return, repair, rework basis, consumption in a finished product, manufacturing, and inspection/testing use.

2.0 INTENT

This QCP applies to all government furnished materials and/or property unless excluded from these requirements by contractual agreement.

3.0 APPLICABLE FORMS AND PROCEDURES

3.1 QCP 3.3.1 - Inspection/Testing Instructions

3.2 QCP 6.5.1 - Failure Reporting

3.3 Form 6.1.3-1 - Receiving Inspection Report

4.0 PROCEDURE

4.1 Upon the receipt of government property, receiving inspection is to notify the quality assurance department that such property has been received. The quality assurance department will then notify the government property officers of the company, the government, and the local government quality assurance representative that such property has been received by the company.

4.2 The receiving department will then examine the government property as prescribed in QCP 6.1.3, and the results will be recorded on Form 6.1.3-1. Any transit damage, completeness/incompleteness of shipment and type, and proper identification of material is to be verified on the form. If any damage or discrepancies are noted, the quality assurance

QUALITY CONTROL PUBLICATION	QCP NO. 7.2.1
	PAGE NO. 2 OF 2
	ISSUE DATE:
TITLE: GOVERNMENT PROPERTY	APPROVED BY:
	REVISION NO: 0
	REVISION DATE:

department is to be notified, who will notify the company and government, government property officers, and the local government quality assurance representative.

4.3 If the inspection instructions or contract requirements require the material or items to be functionally tested to determine satisfactory operation prior to or after installation, incorporation or for use in inspection /tests, the quality assurance department is to supervise all such inspections and/or tests, and will have the inspection/tests results recorded on Form 6.1.3-1. If any discrepancies/nonconformances are found, Form 6.5.1-1 will be filled out and the discrepancies/ nonconformances will be noted on the form.

4.4 The quality assurance department is responsible for conducting periodic inspections to assure that the materials, units are being properly stored, adequately protected, subjected to periodic maintenance when required, and that precautions exist to protect all government material/property from improper use or disposition.

4.5 A secured storage area will be made available for the storage of all government property as required.

4.6 Quality assurance is responsible for reporting all incidences of damage, malfunction or other incidences of discrepant materials, devices, units that pertains to government property to the government property officers of the company, and the local government QA representative.

4.7 The quality assurance department is responsible for maintaining complete and accurate records of all customer (government) furnished material/property, devices, units, and making these records available for review upon the government's request.

CHAPTER THIRTEEN

Government Inspection

GOVERNMENT INSPECTION

QCP 7.1.1 gives the requirement of MIL-Q-9858A as it pertains to Alpha Designator - H, of 8200.1, Government Inspection at Subcontractor or Vendor Facilities.

MIL-Q-9858A, paragraph 7.1, states, "The Government reserves the right to inspect at source, supplies or services not manufactured or performed with the contractor's facility (manufactured and/or supplied by a source not within the prime contractor's facility). Government inspection (at the vendor/supplier/subcontractor's facility) shall not constitute acceptance, nor shall it, in any way, replace contractor inspection (at the vendor/supplier/subcontractor's facility) or, otherwise relieve the contractor of his responsibility to furnish an acceptable end item. The purpose of this Government Source Inspection, (GSI), is to assist the government representative at the contractor's prime facility, to determine the conformance of supplies or services with contract requirements (if it can not be easily determined at the prime facility utilizing physical, chemical, metallurgical or other inspections/tests to show that the material does in fact conform to the requirements/specifications of the contract or purchase order). Such inspection (GSI) can only be requested by or under authorization of the Government Representative."

The above bracketed statements are not in MIL-Q-9858A. They are an attempt to clarify the meaning of the requirement as stated in MIL-Q-9858A. MIL-I-45208, under Requirements for Purchases MIL-HDBK-H51, paragraph 3.11, Government Inspection At Subcontractor Or Vendor Facilities, states, "The government reserves the right to inspect at source supplies or services not manufactured or performed within the contractor's facility. Government Inspection shall not constitute acceptance; nor shall it in any way replace contractor inspection or otherwise relieve the contractor of his responsibility to furnish an acceptable end item."

Paragraph 3.11.1, Government Inspection Requirements. This paragraph is discussed in detail in the QCP to follow. The required statement is part of the quality procedure. Paragraph 3.11.2, Purchasing Documents. This paragraph is discussed in detail in the QCP that follows (QCP 7.1.1). This required statement is part of the quality procedure.

QUALITY CONTROL PUBLICATION	QCP NO. 7.1.1
	PAGE NO. 1 OF 3
	ISSUE DATE:
TITLE: GOVERNMENT INSPECTION AT SUBCONTRACTOR'S FACILITY	APPROVED BY:
	REVISION NO: 0
	REVISION DATE:

1.0 PURPOSE

This quality control publication establishes the methods and procedures for facilitating a government request for Government Source Inspection (GSI) at a supplier's, vendor's, or subcontractor's facility, and the actions to be taken by various departments within the company when such a request occurs.

2.0 INTENT

This procedure applies to government contracts and purchase orders where the government representative has requested that, Government Source Inspection (GSI), be added to the quality requirements of the company's purchase order.

3.0 APPLICABLE FORMS, PUBLICATIONS AND PROCEDURES

3.1 QCP 5.1.5

3.2 QCP 5.1.9

3.3 QCP 3.2.1

4.0 PROCEDURE

4.1 When the government representative requests that GSI be added to the quality requirements of a purchase order to a vendor/supplier/subcontractor, the following statement will be added to the purchase order and signed/stamped for on the purchase order by the government Representative.

4.1.1 "Government inspection is required prior to shipment from your plant. Upon receipt of this order, promptly notify the Government Representative who normally services your plant so that appropriate planning for government inspection can be accomplished."

QUALITY CONTROL PUBLICATION	QCP NO. 7.1.1
	PAGE NO. 2 OF 3
	ISSUE DATE:
TITLE: GOVERNMENT INSPECTION AT SUBCONTRACTOR'S FACILITY	APPROVED BY:
	REVISION NO: 0
	REVISION DATE:

4.2 When, under authorization of the government representative, copies of the purchasing document are to be furnished directly by the subcontractor or vendor to the government representative at his facility rather than through government channels, the contractor shall add to his purchasing document the statement that follows:

4.2.1 "On receipt of this order, promptly furnish a copy of this purchase order to the government representative who normally services your plant, or, if none, to the nearest Army, Navy, Air Force, or Defense Logistics Agency inspection office. In the event the representative or office cannot be located, our purchasing agent shall be notified immediately."

4.2.2 A note should be added to the purchase order (if applicable) that states the following:
"If redelegation of this request has not been approved, the Government Quality Office at the contractors facility that issued this purchase order shall be notified if the place of performance of this purchase is at a location other than that stated on the purchase order."
This is basically a note to the government office receiving the purchase order so that appropriate actions can be taken by the government to notify the prime government office for further action.

4.3 Under no circumstances will government source inspection relieve the company or its suppliers, vendors, from their responsibilities to provide for company source inspection if needed, or relieve any of the parties of the responsibility of providing a quality product and a complete and authorized quality program or inspection system, as applicable.

<table>
<tr><td rowspan="3">QUALITY CONTROL PUBLICATION</td><td>QCP NO. 7.1.1</td></tr>
<tr><td>PAGE NO. 3 OF 3</td></tr>
<tr><td>ISSUE DATE:</td></tr>
<tr><td rowspan="3">TITLE: GOVERNMENT INSPECTION AT SUBCONTRACTOR'S FACILITY</td><td>APPROVED BY:</td></tr>
<tr><td>REVISION NO: 0</td></tr>
<tr><td>REVISION DATE:</td></tr>
</table>

4.4 When Government Source Inspection is invoked on a purchase order, or any type of interplant work request, a statement will be placed in the quality requirements as follows:

4.4.1 Gauges, test equipment and other means of inspection/test will be made available to the government for determining conformance to contract/purchase order requirements and specifications.

4.4.2 MIL-Q-9858A and MIL-I-45208A state this particular requirement (see QCP 4.4.1). It is recommended that this requirement be made a part of the company's vendor/supplier quality requirements.

CHAPTER FOURTEEN

Handling, Storage and Delivery

HANDLING, STORAGE AND DELIVERY

MIL-Q-9858A and MIL-HDBK-H50, states, "The quality program shall provide for adequate work and inspection instructions for handling, storage, preservation, packaging, and shipping to protect the quality of products and prevent damage, loss, deterioration, degradation, or substitution of products." Control of supplies during handling, storage, and delivery is an important aspect of satisfactory quality programs. Manufacturers and users of products which are subject to damage and deterioration when improperly handled and stored carelessly, plan their preservation, packaging, and storage efforts. They conduct regularly scheduled inspections of all stored material. The dates of manufacture and/or receipt of the material is marked on incoming materials so that they can be used in order of receipt and thus spend minimum time in storage. This can be related to Alpha Designator - K, Material and Materials Control, (QCP 6.1.1, and QCP 6.1.2).

Shipping and storage control departments usually develop documented work and inspection instructions for handling, storing, preserving, packaging, marking, and shipping materials to prevent damage, loss, deterioration, substitution, degradation, or any other quality defects.

The control of the handling and moving of material from one work location to another is a very important aspect in the prevention of defective material. In many instances material has been damaged due to the way in which it was loaded into bins, trays and racks to be stored or moved from one location to another during the manufacturing/production cycle.

AQAP 1, states, "The contractor shall establish and maintain a system for the identification, handling, storage and packing of all material from the time of receipt through the manufacturing process until delivery.

a. *Material Handling*

   The system shall include handling procedures that prevent abuse, misuse, damage or deterioration.

b. *Storage*

   Secure storage facilities shall be provided as necessary to isolate and protect material pending use or shipment. The condition of material in stock shall be assessed periodically.

c. *Packing*

The contractor shall arrange for the protection of the quality of material and for its identification including where specified packing, preservation, marking and transit arrangements."

AQAP 4, paragraph 212, states, "The contractor shall inspect the packing, preservation and marking and the materials used in these processes to the extent necessary to ensure conformance to contract requirements."

QUALITY CONTROL PUBLICATION	QCP NO. 6.4.1
	PAGE NO. 1 OF 4
	ISSUE DATE:
TITLE: HANDLING, STORAGE AND DELIVERY	APPROVED BY:
	REVISION NO: 0
	REVISION DATE:

1.0 PURPOSE

This quality control publication establishes the procedure for the proper handling of all materials, parts, subassemblies, and assemblies, to prevent damage to the items during, transit, storage, delivery and while in the process of being handled during the manufacturing/production cycle, and to establish a Packaging Requirement Worksheet, that is to be filled out by the quality department during the planning cycle of the contract and used by the shipping department and final QC, to package all deliverable material/product as required by the contract.

2.0 INTENT

This QCP applies to all departments within the company. The objective of this QCP is to prevent damage to all material/parts due to mishandling, improper transit practices, lack of adequate storage instructions, improper storage, inadequate or the lack of adequate delivery instructions, which will result in scrap, rework, repair. Preservation, marketing and packaging as required by the contract is an important part of this QCP, and the military specifications listed in 3.0 should be obtained and read thoroughly.

3.0 APPLICABLE FORMS, PUBLICATIONS AND PROCEDURES

3.1 MIL-STD-130F - Identification Marking Of US Military Property.

3.2 MIL-P-116H - Preservation, Methods Of.

3.3 MIL-STD-647 - Packaging Standards, Preparation And Use Of.

3.4 MIL-STD-726F - Packaging Requirement Codes.

3.5 MIL-STD-794D - Parts And Equipment, Procedures For Packaging And Packing Of.

3.6 MIL-STD-834C - Packaging Data Forms - Instructions For Preparation And Use Of.

QUALITY CONTROL PUBLICATION	QCP NO. 6.4.1
	PAGE NO. 2 OF 4
	ISSUE DATE:
TITLE: HANDLING, STORAGE AND DELIVERY	APPROVED BY:
	REVISION NO: 0
	REVISION DATE:

3.7 QCP 6.4.1 - Form 6.4.1-1, Packaging Requirements Worksheet.

3.8 QCP 3.2.1 - Initial Quality Planning.

4.0 PROCEDURE

4.1 The quality assurance department is responsible for developing procedures for the handling of all material, parts and product to prevent damage during the total manufacturing/production life cycle. These procedures are to address all stages of handling material/product so as to preclude any damage due to lack of controls during the production, manufacturing, transit, and storage of all material/product. The procedures so developed will be distributed to the departments and/or locations involved, and, will become part of the *Quality Audit System*. The procedures developed will be referenced in this publication, when developed, to assure traceability to the developed procedures.

4.2 The quality assurance department is responsible for verifying that the applicable references to these procedures are referenced in all work orders and inspection/testing instructions and for the periodic auditing of the various departments/locations to verify these procedures are being followed. If any nonconformance to these procedures are found, immediate corrective action is to be obtained and verified.

4.3 Al l departments are responsible for the monitoring of the handling of any material/product within their department, and if observed, will report questionable practices of handling, storage, and delivery of all material/product to the quality department wherever it may occur.

4.4 When a contract or purchase order is received by the quality assurance department, the quality control planning function will prepare Form 6.4.1-1, Packaging Requirements Worksheet, utilizing the packaging

QUALITY CONTROL PUBLICATION	QCP NO. 6.4.1
	PAGE NO. 3 OF 4
	ISSUE DATE:
TITLE: HANDLING, STORAGE AND DELIVERY	APPROVED BY:
	REVISION NO: 0
	REVISION DATE:

requirements as stated in the contract for purchase order. MIL-STD-726F is used to interpret the packaging codes in the contract or purchase order. A sample code that will appear in a contract or purchase order is as follows:

4.4.1 3Q1106GBBBBED6WEAB9AQAQZR123

4.5 The fields this code represents are as follows:

DIGIT POSITION		CODE FIELDS	MEANING OF CODE
1 & 2	- 3Q	Method of Preservation	Method 1A-14
3	- 1	Quantity per unit measure	One per unit pkg.
4	- 1	Cleaning and drying procedure	Cleaning process C-1
5 & 6	- 06	Preservative Material	Preservative P-6 of MIL-P-116
7 & 8	- GB	Wraps	MIL-B-121 Greaseproof - Waterproof Barrier,Grade A
9 & 19	- BB	Cushioning and Dunnage	PPP-C-843, cellulosic cushioning material in PPP-B-566 or PPP-B-676 Box
11	- B	Cushioning Thickness	1/2" Thick
12 & 13	- ED	Unit Container	PPP-B-636, Type CF, Class Weather resistant, fiber box
14	- 6	Intermediate Container Qty.	6 pkgs. per intermediate container

<table>
<tr><td rowspan="6">QUALITY CONTROL PUBLICATION

TITLE: HANDLING, STORAGE AND DELIVERY</td><td>QCP NO. 6.4.1</td></tr>
<tr><td>PAGE NO. 4 OF 4</td></tr>
<tr><td>ISSUE DATE:</td></tr>
<tr><td>APPROVED BY:</td></tr>
<tr><td>REVISION NO: 0</td></tr>
<tr><td>REVISION DATE:</td></tr>
</table>

15 & 16 - WE	Intermediate Container	Kraft paper overwrap
17 - A	Level of Protection	Level A
18 & 19 - BJ	Maximum Weight	1.5 lbs.
- B9	Maximum Length	10 inches
20 & 21 - AL	Maximum Cube	.231 cubic feet
- AQ	Maximum Width	6.0 inches
22 & 23 - AQ	Maximum Depth	6.0 inches
24 - Z	A special packing/container requirement not defined herein, which is to be delineated by means of a separate enclosure.	
25 - R	Packing shall be accomplished in accordance with the requirements in the applicable commodity or procedural packaging/packing specifications for Level B.	
26 - 1	Packing is not required. The container used to effect the unit package shall also serve as the shipping container.	
27 & 28 - 23	Perishable biological, do not freeze.	

4.6 After the Packaging Requirements Worksheet, is filled in, it is forwarded to the final quality control area and to the shipping department along with all other instructions and remarks pertaining to the packaging, preservation and marking of material/product to be shipped. It is final QC's responsibility to verify that all shipping instructions and the associated documentation are correct and the applicable federal, state, and carrier regulations are being followed.

PACKAGING REQUIREMENTS WORKSHEET

CONTRACT NUMBER (1)	WORK ORDER NO. (2)	PROJECT NAME (3)	
PART NUMBER (4)	PART DESCRIPTION (5)	NATIONAL STOCK NO. (6)	DATE (7)

DIGIT POSITION (8)	RETAIL MIL-STD-726 (9)	SEE TABLE (10)	CODE (11)	REQUIREMENTS (12)
1 2	METHOD OF PRESERVATION	II. IIA, IIB. IIC		
3	QUANTITY PER UNIT PACKAGE	III		
4	CLEANING AND DRYING PROCEDURE	IV		
5 6	PRESERVATIVE MATERIAL	V		
	DESICANT TYPE & QUANTITY			
7 8	WRAPS	VI		
9 10	CUSHIONING AND DUNNAGE	VIa		
11	CUSHIONING THICKNESS	VIb		
12 13	UNIT CONTAINER	VII		
	CLOSURE TYPE OF MATERIAL			
14	INTERMEDIATE CONTAINER QUANTITY	VIII		
15 16	INTERMEDIATE CONTAINER	VII		
17	LEVEL OF PRESERVATION PKG.	IX, IXa, Xb		
18 19	MAXIMUM WEIGHT	XI		
20 21	MAXIMUM CUBE	XII		
22 23	MAXIMUM LENGTH	X, Xa, Xb		
20 21	MAXIMUM WIDTH	X, Xa, Xb		
22 23	MAXIMUM DEPTH	X, Xa, Xb		
24	LEVEL A PACKING	XIII		
25	LEVEL B PACKING	XIV		
26	LEVEL C COMMERCIAL PACKING	XV		
27 28	SPECIAL MARKINGS	XVI		

PURPOSE: The purpose of this form is to translate and/or definitize packaging requirements of orders and/or contracts which specify packaging requirments code as outline in MIL-STD-726.

NOTES: (13)

PREPARED BY (Typed Name & Signature) (14)	DATE OF PREPARATION (15)

FORM 6.4.1-1

CHAPTER FIFTEEN

Indication of Inspection Status

INDICATION OF INSPECTION STATUS

MIL-Q-9858A and MIL-HDBK-H50, paragraph 6.7, Indication of Inspection Status, states, "The contractor shall maintain a positive system for identifying the inspection status of products. Identification may be accomplished by means of stamps, tags, routing cards, move tickets, tote box cards or other normal control devices. Such controls shall be of a design distinctly different from Government inspection identification...There must be a positive way of knowing at all times whether a product has (1) not been inspected (absence of a stamp), (2) been inspected and approved (presence of an acceptance stamp), or, (3) been inspected and rejected (presence of a rejection stamp or identification number in the appropriate spot on the records). These conditions can be identified in a variety of ways (such as bracketed above). In the absence of a contractual requirement, MIL-Q-9858A permits contractors to select any method for indicating inspection status, provided only that it cannot be mistaken for government identification (such as the use of stamps that resemble the government quality stamps or inspection records that take the form of the government's inspection record, DoD Form 1711)."

MIL-I-45208A and MIL-HDBK-H52, paragraph 3.5, *Indication of Inspection Status*, states, "Manufacturers engaged in commercial production normally maintain some system for positive identification of inspection status. When such manufacturers become government contractors, it is not necessary to change the method of identifying inspection status unless it can be mistaken for that of the Government...Contractors may prefer inspection stamps in lieu of other identification methods. Contractors find serially numbered stamps assigned on an individual basis useful in achieving better quality control since they identify each inspector's work...Whatever system is used (stamps, tags, punched cards, etc.), the system should provide positive identification of inspection status in such areas as completion of work operations or processes, requirements for special handling, stage of heat treatment, Material Review Board status, etc. The reason most contractors use inspection stamps, is to aid in keeping conforming and nonconforming, inspected and uninspected products properly segregated."

AQAP 1, Paragraph 216, Indication of Inspection Status, states, "The contractor shall establish and maintain a system for identifying the inspection status of material during all stages of manufacture. The contractor shall distinguish between inspected and uninspected material by using suitable identification media such as stamps, tags, routing cards, move tickets or other control devices. Where they are used, inspection stamps shall be traceable to the individuals responsible for their use."

All of the above requirements point out the need for a means of identifying the points during the production cycle where inspections/tests occur and the means of identifying conforming or nonconforming product/material at these specific points prior to being moved to a higher level assembly point/station or prepared for shipment. These inspection and/or test points were established during the contract planning cycle and is a means utilized to prevent discrepant material from flowing from stage to stage in the production cycle thus preventing costly repairs, rework and possible scrap and most importantly, to prevent nonconforming/discrepant material from reaching the customer.

QUALITY CONTROL PUBLICATION **TITLE:** INDICATION OF INSPECTION STATUS	QCP NO. 6.7.1
	PAGE NO. 1 OF 4
	ISSUE DATE:
	APPROVED BY:
	REVISION NO: 0
	REVISION DATE:

1.0 PURPOSE

This quality control publication establishes the procedure for indicating the inspection status of all parts, materials, subassemblies, and complete items whether they are in receiving inspection, in-process inspection/testing, or in final inspection testing prior to the actual shipping of the product.

2.0 INTENT

This QCP applies to all deliverable product, whether in receiving, in-process, stock, or completed.

3.0 APPLICABLE FORMS, PROCEDURES, SPECIFICATIONS

3.1 Quality Inspection and Identification Stamps, QCP 2.2.1

3.2 Work Instructions, QCP 3.3.1

3.3 Inspection/Test Instructions, QCP 3.3.2

3.4 First Article Inspection - Procured Material, QCP 5.1.8

3.5 First Article Inspection - In-House, QCP 3.3.7

3.6 In-Process Inspection and Test, QCP 3.3.5

3.7 Rejection and Disposition Tag, Form 6.7.1-1

3.8 Acceptance Tag, Form 6.7.1-2

3.9 Source Inspection tag - Vendor/Supplier, Form 5.1.9-4

4.0 PROCEDURE

4.1 The inspection status of all parts, Materials, subassemblies, finished product will be recorded in the area prescribed for on the Work Order/ Process Routing Sheet, as described in QCP 3.3.1 and on all individual inspection/test reports and other records as required. The inspection

QUALITY CONTROL PUBLICATION	QCP NO. 6.7.1
	PAGE NO. 2 OF 4
	ISSUE DATE:
TITLE: INDICATION OF INSPECTION STATUS	APPROVED BY:
	REVISION NO: 0
	REVISION DATE:

status indicates whether or not the product or material has been accepted or rejected, the number of items inspected/tested, the lot size, the sample size (to the applicable specification), and the characteristic that passed or failed.

4.2 The quality inspection and identification stamps (see QCP 2.2.1) will be used to indicate the particular inspections completed. No inspection or test will be accomplished/started until the previous operation has been completed, unless, an internal, Engineering Change order, (in the case of non-contractual requirements), has been approved and distributed to the applicable inspection/test departments. In the case of a contractual requirement that specifies the order and the manner in which the inspections/tests are to be performed, a formal, waiver/deviation, will have to be submitted to the procuring agency for approval.

4.3 The Rejection and Disposition Tag, Form 6.7.1-1, is to be used for identifying and routing rejected parts for disposition and must remain with the material/parts until a formal disposition has been obtained. This form is to be filled out as follows:

1. The part number.
2. The date of rejection.
3. The part name (description).
4. The department, person, or vendor submitting the parts/material for disposition.
5. The work order contract number.
6. The contract or purchase order number.
7. Lot size.
8. The quantity of items rejected.
9. The quantity of material accepted.

QUALITY CONTROL PUBLICATION	QCP NO. 6.7.1
	PAGE NO. 3 OF 4
	ISSUE DATE:
TITLE: INDICATION OF INSPECTION STATUS	APPROVED BY:
	REVISION NO: 0
	REVISION DATE:

10. The reason for rejecting the material.
11. The name of the inspector originating this ticket.
12. Location of the material to be dispositioned.
13. The inspector's stamp.
14. The Tag Number, (as assigned or pre-printed).

4.4 The tag will remain with the material until an authorized disposition has been obtained and the disposition has been recorded on the Material Review Board - Disposition Report, the work order, and on all other records as required.

4.5 The Accepted tag, Form 6.7.1-2, will be used for material that has been accepted after the dispositioning of the material has been accomplished and the necessary rework or repair has been accomplished. After reinspection or retesting of the material has been accomplished and the material is found conforming. After the material has been accepted and the necessary information has been documented, the tag will be discarded unless there is a contract, purchase order, or other requirement/ specification that requires the tag to accompany the material to its destination.

1. The part/assembly number.
2. The date of acceptance of material.
3. The part name (description).
4. The work order number.
5. The contract or purchase order number.
6. The quantity of material parts assemblies accepted.
7. The quantity of items reworked/repaired.

QUALITY CONTROL PUBLICATION	QCP NO. 6.7.1
	PAGE NO. 4 OF 4
	ISSUE DATE:
TITLE: INDICATION OF INSPECTION STATUS	APPROVED BY:
	REVISION NO: 0
	REVISION DATE:

8. The quantity of items accepted.
9. Applicable remarks.
10. Inspectors stamp impression.
11. Government/customer stamp impression.
12. Accepted tag number.

REJECTION AND ACCEPTANCE TAGS

REJECTED TAG

(14) TAG NO.

PART NUMBER (1) DATE (2)
PART NAME: (3)
DEPARTMENT OR VENDOR (4)
WORK ORDER NUMBER (5)
CONTRACT/PO NUMBER (6)

LOT SIZE (7) QTY. REJECTED (8) QTY. ACCEPTED (9)
REASON (10)

NAME OF INSPECTOR (11)
LOCATION OF MATERIAL (12)

(13) STAMP

FORM 6.7.1-1

ACCEPTED TAG

(12) TAG NO.

PART NUMBER (1) DATE (2)
PART NAME: (3)
WORK ORDER NO. (4)
CONTRACT/PO NO. (5)

QTY. ACCEPTED (6) QTY. REWORK/REPAIR (7)
QTY. ITEMSACCEPTED (8)
REMARKS (9)

(10) STAMP

(11) STAMP

FORM 6.7.1-2

CHAPTER SIXTEEN

Measuring and Test Equipment

MEASURING AND TEST EQUIPMENT

The control of all measuring and test equipment is of importance to a company's ability to produce a product that meets the requirements and specifications of a government contract. If a company does not establish a means of total control over any measuring or test device that is being used as a means for the controlling of product quality, it will find that the cost of producing a quality product will increase to the point that the ability to compete in today's marketplace will be seriously jeopardized. But, more importantly, will find itself losing contracts due to discrepant/nonconforming material and product finding its way into products sold to the government. Discrepant/nonconforming material and product is of special concern to the military and NASA due to the unnecessary loss of life and mission failures that have occurred during simulated exercises, flight missions, and actual military warfare operations.

MIL-Q-9858A and its handbook, MIL-HDBK-H50, states the following concerning metrology requirements: "The contractor shall provide and maintain gauges and other measuring and testing devices necessary to assure that supplies conform to technical requirements. These devices shall be calibrated against certified measurement standards which have known valid relationships to national standards at established periods to assure continued accuracy. The objective is to assure that inspection and test equipment is adjusted, replaced or repaired before it becomes inaccurate. The calibration of measuring and testing equipment shall be in conformity with military specification MIL-STD-45662A. In addition, the contractor shall insure the use of only such subcontractor and vendor sources that depend upon calibration systems which effectively control the accuracy of measuring and test equipment."

MIL-I-45208A and its handbook MIL-HDBK-H51, paragraph 3.3 starts with the same introduction as MIL-Q-9858A and its handbook MIL-HDBK-H50. Selected paragraphs from MIL-HDBK-H51 will be presented here in order to clarify the stated requirement for a calibration system. MIL-HDBK-H51 states, "Most contractors recognize the necessity of carefully and continually checking test and inspection equipment to assure that the necessary degree of accuracy is being maintained. A comprehensive calibration system, such as that required by MIL-STD-45662A, is necessary. The system should assure the direct or indirect traceability of contractor calibration standards through an unbroken chain of calibrations to National Reference Standards. The frequency of calibration is determined on the basis of the type, purpose, usage rate, and degree of accuracy of the equipment involved...Gauge identification is also extremely important. In addition to numbering every gauge, color codes, labels and the like are frequently employed to give a quick visual indication of the gauge's accuracy and the date this accuracy was last verified...To effectively control this equipment, contractors should establish such things as gauge-wear policies and keep accurate records on each piece of equipment. Obsolete or inaccurate equipment should be carefully segregated or discarded to prevent its use."

MIL-STD-45662A and its handbook MIL-HDBK-H52A, state the requirements of a calibration system in more detail than either MIL-Q-9858A or MIL-I-45208A and their associated handbooks. The Table of Contents that follows will give a brief description of what the various topic headings are in MIL-STD-45662A.

1. Introduction
    - 1.1 Purpose
    - 1.2 Scope
2. Referenced Documents
3. Definitions
4. General Statement of Requirements
    - 4.1 General
    - 4.2 Quality Assurance Provisions
5. Detailed Statements of Requirements
    - 5.1 Description
    - 5.2 Adequacy of Standards
    - 5.3 Environmental Controls
    - 5.4 Intervals of Calibration
    - 5.5 Calibration Procedures
    - 5.6 Out of Tolerance Evaluators
        - 5.6.1 Adequacy of the Calibration System
        - 5.6.2 Notification of Out of Tolerance Conditions

5.7 Calibration Sources

5.7.1 Domestic Contracts

5.7.2 Foreign Contracts

5.8 Application and Records

5.9 Calibration Status

5.10 Control of Subcontractor Calibration

5.11 Storage and Handling

5.12 Amendments and Revisions

Appendix, Checklist for Evaluation of Contractor's Calibration System, AQAP-1, paragraph 209, Control of Inspection, Measuring and Test Equipment, states, "The contractor is responsible for providing, controlling, calibrating and maintaining inspection, measuring and test equipment including ancillary computer software suitable to demonstrate conformance of material with contract requirements. Sub-contractor-owned devices shall be subject to surveillance by the contractor to ensure their suitability for intended use, proper calibration and maintenance. Equipment shall be used in a manner to ensure measurements whose uncertainty is known and is consistent with the required measurement capability. The measurement and calibration system shall be in accordance with AQAP-6."

AQAP-4, states "The contractor shall provide, calibrate and maintain inspection, measuring and test devices suitable to demonstrate conformance of material and services with contract requirements. Equipment shall be used in a manner to ensure measurements whose uncertainty is known and is consistent with required measurement capability. As necessary such responsibility shall include the validity of sub-contractors' measurement systems. Calibration of standards and measuring equipment shall be in accordance with AQAP-6."

Following is the table of contents from the NATO calibration system requirements handbook. This table of contents could be used as a guide in formatting a calibration system.

CHAPTER 1 GENERAL

Paragraph 101 Scope

102 Applicability

CHAPTER 2	REQUIREMENTS
Paragraph 201	General
202	Review and Evaluation
203	Planning
204	Measure Limits
205	Documented Calibration Procedures
206	Records
207	Calibration Labelling
208	Sealing for Integrity
209	Intervals of Calibration
210	Invalidation of Calibration
211	Sub-Contractor Measurement and Calibration
212	Storage and Handling
213	Traceability
214	Cumulative Effect of Errors
215	Environmental Control
216	Tech. Meas. Eval.
217	Accommodation and Assistance

QUALITY CONTROL PUBLICATION	QCP NO. 4.2.1
	PAGE NO. 1 OF 7
TITLE: CALIBRATION DEFINITIONS AND SYSTEM RESPONSIBILITIES	ISSUE DATE:
	APPROVED BY:
	REVISION NO: 0
	REVISION DATE:

1.0 PURPOSE

The purpose of this quality control publication is to establish methods and procedures for the control of all measuring and test equipment used to assure that product supplied to the government is in conformance to all specifications, drawings and requirements of the contract or purchase order.

2.0 INTENT

This QCP applies to the calibration, inspection and test functions of the quality assurance department and all other departments that utilize inspection, test and computer programs and associated equipment to verify that the product conforms to the technical requirements and specifications of a contract or purchase order.

3.0 DEFINITIONS

3.1 Calibration

3.1.1 Calibration is the comparison of a measurement standard or instrument of known accuracy with another standard or instrument to detect, correlate, report, or eliminate by adjustment, any variation in the accuracy of the item being compared to the standard.

3.2 National Bureau of Standards

3.2.1 The National Bureau of Standards (NBS), is a governmental organization which maintains the ultimate national standards against which all other standards are referred through an unbroken chain of traceability from the NBS standard down to lower level standards and finally to all calibrated Measuring and Test Equipment (MTE).

QUALITY CONTROL PUBLICATION	QCP NO. 4.2.1
	PAGE NO. 2 OF 7
	ISSUE DATE:
TITLE: CALIBRATION DEFINITIONS AND SYSTEM RESPONSIBILITIES	APPROVED BY:
	REVISION NO: 0
	REVISION DATE:

3.3 Traceability

3.3.1 Traceability is the ability to trace the accuracy of an item of Measuring and Test Equipment (MTE), or a standard used by the company, vendors, suppliers or subcontractors, from the company's, suppliers, vendors subcontractors calibration laboratory, to a commercial laboratory (if utilized), through the manufacturer of the equipment (if utilized/required), ultimately, to the National Bureau of Standards.

3.4 MTE Recall System

3.4.1 A recall system establishes the method and procedure for assuring that all measuring and test equipment and standards that are being used in the various inspection, production and test areas are recalled at established intervals before the established calibration expiration dates have expired.

3.5 Calibration Interval

3.5.1 The period of time between the last calibration of MTE, and when it is due for calibration again. These periods can/may vary due to manufacturer's recommendations, stability, purpose, degree of usage, and record of failures.

3.6 Measuring and Test Equipment (MTE)

3.6.1 The standard definition of measuring and test equipment is: "All devices used to measure, gauge, test, inspect or otherwise examine item/product. This includes fixtures that are used as a media of inspection to determine compliance (accuracy, stability, range) of the product that is being offered to the Government or other customers for acceptance."

QUALITY CONTROL PUBLICATION TITLE: CALIBRATION DEFINITIONS AND SYSTEM RESPONSIBILITIES	QCP NO. 4.2.1
	PAGE NO. 3 OF 7
	ISSUE DATE:
	APPROVED BY:
	REVISION NO: 0
	REVISION DATE:

3.7 Reference Standard

3.7.1 Standards of the highest accuracy order in a calibration system, traceable to the National Bureau of Standards, which will establish the basic accuracy values for that system. System meaning, the controls established for all measuring and test equipment used to prove the quality of all product.

3.8 Transfer Standard

3.8.1 Transfer standards is that measuring and test equipment used in the calibration system for transferring the basic value of the reference standards to lower echelon transfer standards or the measuring and test equipment used to prove product quality.

3.9 Interim Standard

3.9.1 An instrument and/or measuring device that is used until an authorized standard is established (usually, an advanced metrology requirement).

4.0 APPLICABLE FORMS, PUBLICATIONS AND PROCEDURES

4.1 Calibration Control and Recall, QCP 4.2.2

4.2 Calibration/Service Specifications and Instructions, QCP 4.2.3

4.3 Certification of Measuring and Test Equipment and Test Processes, QCP 4.2.4

4.4 Calibration and Control of Dimensional Working Instruments, QCP 4.2.5

4.5 Subcontracting of Calibration and MTE Instruments, QCP 4.2.6

4.6 Employee-Owned Measuring Equipment, QCP 4.2.7

QUALITY CONTROL PUBLICATION	QCP NO. 4.2.1
	PAGE NO. 4 OF 7
	ISSUE DATE:
TITLE: CALIBRATION DEFINITIONS AND SYSTEM RESPONSIBILITIES	APPROVED BY:
	REVISION NO: 0
	REVISION DATE:

5.0 PROCEDURE

5.1 All measuring and test equipment, instruments and gauges that control process, recording instruments, devices that indicate temperature, stress, environmental conditions and devices that are used in conjunction with these devices, such as thermocouples, laboratory control devices, shall be calibrated and maintained to the recommended procedures of the manufacturer who produced or supplied these devices, or to published requirements and/or contract/purchase order requirements/specifications. This equipment will be calibrated at intervals or as recommended/prescribed by original manufacturers recommendation, contract/purchase order requirements, purpose, degree of usage, or if it is proven by measurement or test records that indicate inconsistencies, and nonconformances exist that is affecting product/material conformance to the contract or purchase order requirements and/or specifications.

5.2 All equipment that is used for measuring, testing, process control will be calibrated to reference standards or transfer standards that can be traced in their calibration to the National Bureau of Standards, Standards Laboratory, through certifications and test reports if this equipment is to be calibrated by an outside/contracted for calibration laboratory, either government or commercial, see QCP 4.2.6.

5.3 A record is to be established and maintained that identifies each item of measuring and test equipment, reference standards, transfer standards as to the date of calibration, when the next calibration is due, what reference and/or transfer standard was used in the calibration, who did the calibration, the date of calibration, and traceability or certification(s), reference/transfer standards traceability to the National Bureau of Standards.

5.4 All calibrated equipment including all MTE whether calibrated in-house or at an outside (contracted) laboratory, shall have a calibration

QUALITY CONTROL PUBLICATION	QCP NO. 4.2.1
	PAGE NO. 5 OF 7
	ISSUE DATE:
TITLE: CALIBRATION DEFINITIONS AND SYSTEM RESPONSIBILITIES	APPROVED BY:
	REVISION NO: 0
	REVISION DATE:

sticker, tag, or other type of marking on it (color code marking if the item is too small for a sticker to tag), indicating who did the calibration (employee or contracted laboratory), the date the equipment was calibrated, identifying number traceable to records (that are available to the quality assurance department and the government) maintained by the calibration department and the date when the next calibration of the equipment is due.

5.5 If a color coded dot system is incorporated into the calibration system, a master file shall be kept by the calibration department identifying the color code as to the items themselves by use of a number on the item which is traceable to the applicable records and the color code itself, identifying the required calibration and recalibration dates.

5.6 The calibration recall system is used to notify all department supervisors and hourly employees prior to the expiration of the calibration due date that the equipment is due for calibration and must be turned into the calibration department. Technical assistance will be requested, if the equipment to be calibrated can not be easily moved or is impractical to move due to weight, etc. This does not relieve the department supervisors or individual employees from notifying the calibration department if out of calibration or out of tolerance conditions exist.

5.7 If any employee fails to turn in equipment as in paragraph 5.6, any material and/or tests that have been performed by that individual will be returned for re-inspection and/or testing, and that individual and/or department will be charged for the time of re-inspection/testing or could be charged for any scrap resulting from non adherence to policy. If such actions are taken, they will impact on employee and/or department performance records.

No employee can accept a measurement or test value using MTE that has exceeded its calibration due date or where there are no calibration controls.

QUALITY CONTROL PUBLICATION	QCP NO. 4.2.1
	PAGE NO. 6 OF 7
	ISSUE DATE:
TITLE: CALIBRATION DEFINITIONS AND SYSTEM RESPONSIBILITIES	APPROVED BY:
	REVISION NO: 0
	REVISION DATE:

5.8 Measuring and test equipment and other instruments or devices that control product quality cannot be calibrated with measurement/test standards that have exceeded their calibration due dates whether the calibrations are to take place in-house or at an outside calibration laboratory.

5.9 Employee-owned measuring equipment (such as micrometers, verniers, or any other type of MTE) cannot be used as a measurement device for the acceptance of any product/material unless the device has been included into the calibration system, and is calibrated by the company's calibration laboratory or other accepted calibration source. Failure to adhere to this policy will result in a negative report in the employee's personnel history record and possible confiscation of such devices. If any employee has any doubts as to this policy, or does not wish to have their personnel MTE under the control of company policy, *Leave It Home.*

5.10 The environment where measuring and test equipment, instruments, and devices are to be either calibrated and/or used, must be controlled to the extent necessary to assure required accuracy (this includes process controls), with consideration given to temperature, humidity, vibration, noise (from whatever source), cleanliness and manufacturers recommendations, published procedures for inspection, testing, process controls, etc., and from experience and records of scrap, nonconformances and customer complaints.

5.11 All new, reworked, repaired or modified MTE, instruments and other devices will be examined and calibrated (certifications required and test results will be obtained if calibrations are accomplished outside), and when proven acceptable, certified by a calibration sticker, tag, or color code affixed to the equipment, as complying to all calibration requirements as depicted in these, Quality Control Publications (QCP) and as required by the contract or purchase order.

QUALITY CONTROL PUBLICATION	QCP NO. 4.2.1
	PAGE NO. 7 OF 7
	ISSUE DATE:
TITLE: CALIBRATION DEFINITIONS AND SYSTEM RESPONSIBILITIES	APPROVED BY:
	REVISION NO: 0
	REVISION DATE:

5.12 The engineering design group is responsible for providing the calibration department with instructions for the calibration of company-designed MTE. The quality assurance engineering function is responsible for assuring that this equipment is put into the calibration control system.

5.13 The purchasing department is responsible for securing calibration job instructions for all commercial MTE that has been procured, and will provide this information to quality engineering for inclusion into the calibration control system.

5.14 The calibration department is responsible for compiling, maintaining and publishing a listing of all MTE and other devices including employee owned MTE that is part of the established calibration system. This listing will include equipment location, number assigned to equipment, name of equipment, manufacturer, type of model number, a short description as to use, equipment measurement and test limits (including multiple ranges - if applicable), accuracy requirements/limits, and frequency of calibration/recalibration. This listing will be the basis for determining the recall schedule and for recording inaccuracies.

5.15 Any MTE that does not have a calibration sticker, tag, color code or other means of assuring that it is calibrated and within the calibration system will be tagged with a red tag, with a clear warning on it stating "DO NOT USE."

5.16 The engineering design department, calibration department and quality engineering will be responsible for developing interim measuring and test standards in those instances where measurement standards are not yet established.

QUALITY CONTROL PUBLICATION	QCP NO. 4.2.2
	PAGE NO. 1 OF 5
	ISSUE DATE:
TITLE: CALIBRATION CONTROL AND RECALL PROCEDURES	APPROVED BY:
	REVISION NO: 0
	REVISION DATE:

1.0 PURPOSE

As part of the total calibration system this quality control publication establishes the method and procedures for an MTE locater/recall system and a method for the recording of all calibrations accomplished, as part of the calibration system.

2.0 INTENT

This QCP applies to the calibration department and to those employees and departments within the company who utilize measuring and test equipment and process control equipment.

3.0 DEFINITIONS

3.1 Calibration Control

3.1.1 Calibration control is a method used to control the accuracy of all MTE and process control/measuring equipment that is used to either verify the quality of all material product or to control the actual manufacturing/production processes.

3.2 Calibration Recall

3.2.1 The calibration recall system assures that all MTE and process control equipment, devices, and calibration standards are recalibrated at established intervals to assure their continuing accuracy. This is to prevent nonconforming/discrepant material, due to the lack of calibration controls from being presented to the government for acceptance.

4.0 APPLICABLE FORMS, PROCEDURES AND PUBLICATIONS

4.1 Calibration System Responsibilities, QCP 4.2.1

4.2 Equipment location and Recall Record, Form 4.2.2-1

QUALITY CONTROL PUBLICATION	QCP NO. 4.2.2
	PAGE NO. 2 OF 5
	ISSUE DATE:
TITLE: CALIBRATION CONTROL AND RECALL PROCEDURES	APPROVED BY:
	REVISION NO: 0
	REVISION DATE:

4.3 Calibration Record, Form 4.2.2-2

4.4 Calibration Decal, Form 4.2.2-3

4.5 Not Calibrated/Out-Of-Service Tag, Form 4.2.2-4

4.6 Calibration Specifications and Instructions QCP 4.2.3

5.0 PROCEDURE

5.1 The calibration department is responsible for the identification of MTE, the calibration and repair (repair if feasible in-house), the associated record keeping (calibration records, calibration certifications - that show traceability to NBS, lists of MTE, other devices, measurement standards - (reference, transfer, or interim).

5.2 All departments and personnel using MTE, controlled jigs or fixtures, process control instrumentation, Automatic Test Equipment (ATE), are responsible for making sure that none of the above equipment is used to prove or control product quality if the equipment in question has exceeded its calibration expiration date. The calibration department is to be notified so that immediate disposition of this equipment can be obtained. If outside calibration laboratories are to be used, the Purchasing Department is to be notified. The purchasing department is to make arrangements with the contracted laboratory for the calibration of this equipment and for the making out of the purchase requisitions. The quality assurance department is to make sure that all quality requirements are included in the purchase document.

5.3 An Equipment Location and Recall Record, Form 4.2.2-1 is a computerized listing by item number (assigned by the calibration department) that has been created and maintained as a master locater file and calibration record. The computer run depicted below is used and filled out as follows:

QUALITY CONTROL PUBLICATION	QCP NO. 4.2.2
	PAGE NO. 3 OF 5
	ISSUE DATE:
TITLE: CALIBRATION CONTROL AND RECALL PROCEDURES	APPROVED BY:
	REVISION NO: 0
	REVISION DATE:

1. The item number (as assigned) to the particular MTE.
2. The name (designation) of that particular item of MTE.
3. The location code (as assigned to all areas of use and storage) of the particular item of MTE.
4. The calibration instruction or specification number that was either assigned to the MTE in-house or by the manufacturer.
5. The date of last calibration.
6. The individual in-house or contracted that calibrated the MTE. If the calibration was contracted, insert the name of the calibration laboratory that did the calibration.
7. The date the next calibration is to be accomplished.

5.4 A Calibration data Record, Form 4.2.2-2, which is a computerized form, is to be used to record the calibration results and other applicable information as follows:

1. The year of this calibration data record.
2. Is this record being used as a weekly record of calibrations that have been accomplished.
3. The item number of the particular MTE.
4. The name (description) of the MTE to be, or is, calibrated.
5. The location code of the MTE, whether being used or in storage.
6. The calibration specification or instructions used in the calibration of the particular MTE.
7. The assigned part number of manufacturers part number of the calibration standards used to calibrate the particular item.

QUALITY CONTROL PUBLICATION	QCP NO. 4.2.2
	PAGE NO. 4 OF 5
	ISSUE DATE:
TITLE: CALIBRATION CONTROL AND RECALL PROCEDURES	APPROVED BY:
	REVISION NO: 0
	REVISION DATE:

8. The parameters that the particular MTE is to be calibrated to.
9. The maximum limit of tolerance of the particular MTE, as per specification/instruction.
10. The minimum limit of tolerance of the particular MTE, as per specification/instruction.
11. The tolerance required by the specification/instruction.
12. The actual readings obtained - Maximum (as required).
13. The actual readings obtained - Minimum (as required).
14. The actual date of calibration.
15. The name of the person and stamp of the person conducting the calibration.
16. The date when the next calibration of the particular MTE is due.

5.5 A calibration status label/tag/color code is to be affixed to the particular item of MTE. Where space allows, a calibration label as pictured in Form 4.2.2-3 is to be filled out and affixed to the MTE at the time of its calibration. This label is filled out as follows:

1. Date of Calibration.
2. Name of the person who accomplished the calibration.
3. If calibrated at an outside source - The name of the Source.
4. The date when the next calibration is due.
5. The designated number of the MTE.

5.6 If due to environmental, size, or other limitations it is inappropriate to place a label directly on the calibrate item, a calibration tag or a color coding system may be used to identify the item that has/will be calibrated.

QUALITY CONTROL PUBLICATION	QCP NO. 4.2.2
	PAGE NO. 5 OF 5
	ISSUE DATE:
TITLE: CALIBRATION CONTROL AND RECALL PROCEDURES	APPROVED BY:
	REVISION NO: 0
	REVISION DATE:

If a tag is used it will contain the same information on it as the label. If a color coding system is utilized, a master listing of all color codes will be kept in the calibration department and will also identify the particular item of MTE.

5.7 If there is an item of MTE, jig/fixture, test chamber, or other items that is/could/would be used to prove product quality in any area of the company that has/is - not to be calibrated at once, a tag will be placed on it, as pictured in Form 4.2.2-4. This tag will be of the color red and read DO NOT USE - THIS ITEM MUST BE CALIBRATED/ REPAIRED PRIOR TO USE.

5.8 The quality assurance department is responsible for auditing the calibration department to verify that calibration intervals are being adjusted as required, for verifying that the recall system is working, for verifying that there is no uncalibrated equipment in the plant that has not be tagged as DO NOT USE.

5.9 If during a Quality Audit, there are any violations of the calibration control and recall system, these violations will be written up and appropriate corrective action will be pursued.

EQUIPMENT LOCATION AND RECALL RECORD

ITEM NO.	EQUIP. NAME	LOCATION OF EQUIP.	CALIB. INST. NO.	DATE OF CAL.	CAL. BY	CAL. DUE
(1)	(2)	(3)	(4)	(5)	(6)	(7)

FORM 4.2.2-1

CALIBRATION DATA RECORD

CALIBRATION YEAR OF THIS RECORD: ___(1)___

WEEKLY CALIBRATION RECORD: YES ______ NO___(2)___

ITEM NUMBER OF EQUIP	EQUIP. CALIB. (NAME)	LOC. OF EQUIP. (NO.)	CALIB. SPEC. NO.	NUMBER OF STANDARD(s) USED	REQ. PARA.	MAX.	MIN. LIMIT	TOLERANCE REQUIRED	ACTUAL READINGS MAX.	MIN.	DATE OF CALIB.	CALIB. BY	NEXT CALIB DUE DATE
(3)	(4)	(5)	(6)	(7)	(8)	(9)	(10)	(11)	(12)	(13)	(14)	(15)	(16)

FORM 4.2.2-2

FORM 4.2.2-3

DATE OF CALIBRATION

____

CALIBRATED BY: ____________________

NAME OF COMPANY: ____________________

DATE NEXT CALIB. DUE: ____________________

MTE NUMBER: ____________________

FORM NO. 4.2.2-4

DO NOT USE

THIS ITEM MUST
BE CALIBRATED
PRIOR TO USE

QUALITY CONTROL PUBLICATION	QCP NO. 4.2.3
	PAGE NO. 1 OF 4
	ISSUE DATE:
TITLE: CALIBRATION SPECIFICATIONS AND INSTRUCTIONS	APPROVED BY:
	REVISION NO: 0
	REVISION DATE:

1.0 PURPOSE

The purpose of this Quality Control Publication is to establish a method for the preparation, use, and control of calibration specifications and instructions, and, the use of the specifications and instructions in the calibration of test standards and actual test equipment.

2.0 INTENT

The intent of this QCP is to assign the responsibility for the writing, and control of all calibration specifications and instructions.

3.0 APPLICABLE FORMS, PUBLICATIONS AND PROCEDURES

3.1 Calibration Definitions and System Responsibilities, QCP 4.2.1

3.2 Calibration Control and Recall System, QCP 4.2.2

3.3 Calibration/Repair Instruction, Form 4.2.3-1

3.4 Automated Test Equipment, QCP 3.3.3

4.0 PROCEDURE

4.1 The calibration department will coordinate with the purchasing department all requests, for the purchasing, calibration (if not accomplished in-house) and repair (if not accomplished in-house) (with design engineering if the MTE has been developed in-house) of all MTE. This includes jigs, fixtures, automated test equipment calibration standards, and all other devices used to prove product quality.

4.2 A system will be developed for the control, serialization and identification of all specifications and calibration instructions used, and for the maintaining of a revision control system.

QUALITY CONTROL PUBLICATION	QCP NO. 4.2.3
	PAGE NO. 2 OF 4
	ISSUE DATE:
TITLE: CALIBRATION SPECIFICATIONS AND INSTRUCTIONS	APPROVED BY:
	REVISION NO: 0
	REVISION DATE:

4.3 The purchasing department (when purchasing MTE) is responsible for the acquisition of all calibration/service specifications and instructions at the time of procurement of the applicable MTE, and will provide these instructions/specifications/manuals, etc. to the calibration department upon receipt. Receiving inspection will be given instructions to hold all MTE if the applicable instruction manuals, etc. are not received with the equipment and will notify the purchasing department if such is the case.

4.4 The test equipment designer is responsible for the preparation (in conjunction with quality engineering) of all calibration/service specifications/instructions for the use of MTE, jigs, fixtures, automated test equipment and other devices that have been/are designed internally.

4.5 The calibration department in conjunction with quality engineering and the equipment designer is responsible for developing calibration specifications and instructions for MTE, standards, Automated Test Equipment (ATE), and other devices when no other sources are available or exist.

4.6 The Calibration/Repair Instruction, Form 4.2.3-1, is to be utilized by the design function, calibration function and quality engineering in writing the calibration/repair instructions to be utilized for the calibration/ repair of all MTE and other devices, including ATE. This form will be filled out as follows:

1. Item Number - The number assigned by the calibration department to that particular MTE, ATE, jigs/fixtures, or other devices as a means of identifying that particular item.
2. Item Name - Name (Description) of the item to be calibrated.
3. The name of the Manufacturer of the MTE, standard, etc. If the item was made in house, the name of department.
4. Type of equipment and model number (as appropriate).

QUALITY CONTROL PUBLICATION	QCP NO. 4.2.3
	PAGE NO. 3 OF 4
	ISSUE DATE:
TITLE: CALIBRATION SPECIFICATIONS AND INSTRUCTIONS	APPROVED BY:
	REVISION NO: 0
	REVISION DATE:

5. Serial number of the item.

6. A short description of the use of the item.

7. The environmental conditions required with the use of the item.

8. If this a Qualified Product Item, indicate the specification number.

9. Indicate whether there is a maximum interval required prior to recalibration. (This will appear in the manufacturer's specifications).

Items 1 through 9 are for the items to be calibrated. Items 10 through 17 are for the calibration standards to be used for the calibration of items.

10. The number assigned to the calibration standard. (Crossed referenced to the manufacturer's part number).

11. Name (description) of the calibration standard.

12. The known (published) accuracy of the calibration standard.

13. The published required frequency of calibration of the standard.

14. The serial number of the calibration standard.

15. The published requirements for the environmental conditions for which the standard are to be used.

16. Date of last calibration of the standard.

17. The date that the standard is due for recalibration.

Items 18 through 24 refer to the items to be calibrated (continuation and results for numbers 1 through 9).

18. The characteristic and/or range the items is to be calibrated to.

19. The tolerance of the calibrated items.

QUALITY CONTROL PUBLICATION	QCP NO. 4.2.3
	PAGE NO. 4 OF 4
	ISSUE DATE:
TITLE: CALIBRATION SPECIFICATIONS AND INSTRUCTIONS	APPROVED BY:
	REVISION NO: 0
	REVISION DATE:

20. The set point or median of the range to be calibrated to.
21. The actual variation from the median that is required.
22. The variation readings required. (set limits).
23. The expected average median reading. (if applicable).
24. Notes regarding any observations to be made.
25. The name of the individual approving the calibration instructions.
26. The title of that individual and department number.
27. Date of approval of instruction.

CALIBRATION/REPAIR INSTRUCTIONS

ITEM NUMBER	ITEM NAME	MANUFACTURER	TYPE OR MODEL NO.	SERIAL NO.	DESCRIPTION OF USE	ENVIRONMENTAL REQUIREMENTS	QUALIFIED PRODUCT SPECIFICATION NO.	MAXIMUM INTERVAL OF CALIBRATION
(1)	(2)	(3)	(4)	(5)	(6)	(7)	(8)	(9)

CALIBRATION STANDARD NO.	REQUIRED FREQUENCY OF CALIBRATION	ACCURACY OF STANDARD	CALIBRATION STANDARD NAME (DESCRIPTION)	SERIAL NUMBER OF STANDARD	ENVIRONMENTAL REQUIREMENTS OF STANDARD	DATE CALIBRATED	DATE DUE FOR CALIBRATION
(10)	(11)	(12)	(13)	(14)	(15)	(16)	(17)

CHARACTERISTIC/ RANGE	TOLERANCE	SET POINT	VARIATION + VARIATION -	READING + READING -	EXPECTED AVERAGE READING	NOTES
(18)	(19)	(20)	(21)	(22)	(23)	(24)

NAME OF PERSON APPROVING INSTRUCTIONS	TITLE OF PERSON APPROVING INSTRUCTIONS	DATE
(25)	(26)	(27)

FORM 4.2.3-1

QUALITY CONTROL PUBLICATION	QCP NO. 4.2.4
	PAGE NO. 1 OF 4
	ISSUE DATE:
TITLE: CERTIFICATION OF MEASURING AND TEST EQUIPMENT	APPROVED BY:
	REVISION NO: 0
	REVISION DATE:

1.0 PURPOSE

The purpose of this quality control publication is to establish the method for certifying the use of MTE, devices, processes, and their applicable specifications and instructions.

2.0 INTENT

This QCP applies to all MTE, etc., used to make the determination as to whether or not all deliverable products conform to the contract or purchase order requirements/specifications.

3.0 DEFINITION

3.1 Certification:

3.1.1 The approval given by project engineering management and quality assurance management for the use of newly acquired, reworked or modified MTE, test equipment devices, or processes that have been verified acceptable and are compatible with other devices or processes in the system and when calibrated according to specifications and the documented procedures are accurate and capable of fulfilling all intended functions and Government requirements and specifications. The accuracy of all MTE, etc., will be traceable to the National Bureau of Standards, and to the actual number of the NBS equipment/standards.

4.0 APPLICABLE FORMS, PROCEDURES AND PUBLICATIONS

4.1 Calibration System Responsibilities, QCP 4.2.1

4.2 Notice of Certification, Form 4.2.4-1

4.3 Certification Decal/Tag, Form 4.2.2-2

QUALITY CONTROL PUBLICATION	QCP NO. 4.2.4
	PAGE NO. 2 OF 4
	ISSUE DATE:
TITLE: CERTIFICATION OF MEASURING AND TEST EQUIPMENT	APPROVED BY:
	REVISION NO: 0
	REVISION DATE:

5.0 PROCEDURE

5.1 The calibration department is responsible for examining and testing all newly purchased, repaired, reworked or modified MTE, jigs, fixtures, or process control equipment to determine if they meet the applicable in-house or other manufacturers specifications as to accuracy and functional use. The calibration, design engineering, production engineering and quality assurance departments are responsible for determining if the above equipment is capable of meeting the requirements and specifications of the contract or purchase order.

5.2 After each device has been accepted by the various engineering departments, a, Notice of Certification, as depicted in Form 4.2.4-1 will be prepared as follows:

1. The item number of the device being certified (as assigned).
2. The name of the device.
3. The manufacturers name.
4. The manufacturers part number (as applicable).
5. The manufacturers model number (as applicable).
6. The manufacturers serial number (as applicable).
7. A brief description as to the intended use of the device.
8. The date of certification of the device.
9. The device's specification number (if different from the devices item number or manufacturers part number).
10. The applicable job number assigned to this project.
11. The recommended environmental and physical conditions under which the devices is to be used.

QUALITY CONTROL PUBLICATION	QCP NO. 4.2.4
	PAGE NO. 3 OF 4
	ISSUE DATE:
TITLE: CERTIFICATION OF MEASURING AND TEST EQUIPMENT	APPROVED BY:
	REVISION NO: 0
	REVISION DATE:

12. The name and title of the person preparing this form.

13. The names of the individuals approving this certification.

5.3 For each device found acceptable, a Certification Decal, Form 4.2.2-3, will be filled out as explained in QCP 4.2.2, paragraph 5.5, and placed on the device/equipment that has been certified. If it is impractical to put the decal on the device/equipment due to size, environmental conditions, etc., the instruction in paragraph 5.6 of QCP 4.2.2 will be followed.

5.4 A master listing of all certified devices and equipment will be kept in the calibration department. This listing as depicted in Form 4.2.4-1, will be used to identify all certified MTE utilized by the company.

5.5 It is the responsibility of each department supervisor and/or operator of this equipment, to return the equipment/device to the calibration department for re-certification prior to the applicable calibration expiration date.

5.6 The test equipment designer is responsible for providing the calibration department advance notice when a company fabricated MTE, device, etc. is scheduled for completion and is in need of calibration and certification.

5.7 The purchasing, receiving, quality and manufacturing departments are responsible for submitting to the calibration department for calibration and certification all newly acquired commercial MTE.

5.8 If any purchased MTE is found to be not acceptable by the calibration department, the purchasing department is to be notified and all appropriate corrective action will be obtained from the vendor, manufacturer, etc., or arrangements will be made by the purchasing department to return the MTE to the vendors/manufacturers involved.

<table>
<tr><td rowspan="6">QUALITY CONTROL PUBLICATION

TITLE: CERTIFICATION OF MEASURING AND TEST EQUIPMENT</td><td>QCP NO. 4.2.4</td></tr>
<tr><td>PAGE NO. 4 OF 4</td></tr>
<tr><td>ISSUE DATE:</td></tr>
<tr><td>APPROVED BY:</td></tr>
<tr><td>REVISION NO: 0</td></tr>
<tr><td>REVISION DATE:</td></tr>
</table>

5.9 The quality assurance and calibration departments have the authority to de-certify any MTE when conditions occur that affect product quality.

NOTICE OF CERTIFICATION

NAME OF INDIV. PREPARING FORM ______ (12)

NAME OF INDIV. APPROV. CERT. ______ (13)

Date of Report: ______ (month) ______ (day) ______ (year)

ITEM NO.	ITEM NAME	MANUFACTURER'S PART NO.	MODEL NO.
(1)	(2)	(4)	(5)

MANUFACTURER ______ (3)

SERIAL NO.	SPECIFICATION NO.	DESCRIPTION OF USE
(6)	(9)	(7)

JOB NO.	RECOM. ENVIR. COND.	DATE OF CERTIFICATION
(10)	(11)	(8)

FORM 4.2.4-1

QUALITY CONTROL PUBLICATION	QCP NO. 4.2.5
	PAGE NO. 1 OF 3
TITLE: CALIBRATION AND CONTROL OF DIMENSIONAL WORKING INSTRUMENTS	ISSUE DATE:
	APPROVED BY:
	REVISION NO: 0
	REVISION DATE:

1.0 PURPOSE

This quality control publication establishes the method and procedures for the control of dimensional working instruments.

2.0 INTENT

This QCP applies to the calibration and control of dimensional working instruments such as limit gauges, measurement hand tools, gauge blocks tri-rolls, crimpers, pitch gauges and measurement amplifiers.

3.0 DEFINITIONS

3.1 Limit Gauges

3.1.1 Limit gauges are measurement devices that have fixed sizes and measure the limits of a part tolerance on a "GO-NO-GO" basis.

3.2 Measurement Hand Tools

3.2.1 Measurement hand tools are portable, hand operated measurement devices such as micrometers, height gauges, depth gauges, vernier calipers, etc.

3.3 Standards Kits

3.3.1 Standards kits are sets of precision machine steel blocks such as gauge blocks, rods, balls, cylinders, rings and flats that are used for checking measurement accuracy.

3.4 Electronic Measurement Amplifiers

3.4.1 Electronic measurement amplifiers are solid state devices that are bench or pedestal mounted, or self contained, such as limit indication scales that are digital, or electromechanical, or both,

QUALITY CONTROL PUBLICATION	QCP NO. 4.2.5
	PAGE NO. 2 OF 3
TITLE: CALIBRATION AND CONTROL OF DIMENSIONAL WORKING INSTRUMENTS	ISSUE DATE:
	APPROVED BY:
	REVISION NO: 0
	REVISION DATE:

contour projectors, optical comparators, optical height gauges, laser and video measurement devices.

5.0 PROCEDURE

5.1 All dimensional working instruments are to be certified to their accuracy upon purchase, and the certifications are to be traceable to the National Bureau of Standards. The calibration and certification of these devices are the responsibility of the calibration department under the direction of the quality assurance department.

5.2 A tool crib has been established which has the responsibility for the custody, issuance and return of all dimensional working instruments throughout the facility. The equipment is to be signed out by either a department supervisor or by the individual who is going to use the equipment/device.

5.3 The calibration department will create and maintain an Equipment Location and Recall Record, Form 4.2.2-1, and a Calibration/Service Data Record, Form 4.2.2-2, for each dimensional working instrument (see the detailed instructions in QCP 4.2.2).

5.4 The tool crib is responsible for forwarding all measuring devices to the calibration department prior to the calibration due date for those devices, and when the tool crib receives the monthly calibration due date listing.

5.5 Each dimensional working instrument is to be marked as follows:

1. The date of last calibration.
2. The date when re-calibration is due.
3. The stamp of the individual who last calibrated the item/device.
4. The assigned part number (used for system recall).

QUALITY CONTROL PUBLICATION	QCP NO. 4.2.5
	PAGE NO. 3 OF 3
	ISSUE DATE:
TITLE: CALIBRATION AND CONTROL OF DIMENSIONAL WORKING INSTRUMENTS	APPROVED BY:
	REVISION NO: 0
	REVISION DATE:

See QCP 4.2.2 - If the item is too small or is an environmentally unsuitable area, a color code, serial number or other identification is to be assigned to and stamped into the device, and is to be keyed into the Identification Control Record System.

QUALITY CONTROL PUBLICATION	QCP NO. 4.2.6
	PAGE NO. 1 OF 4
	ISSUE DATE:
TITLE: SUBCONTRACTING OF CALIBRATION AND REPAIR WORK	APPROVED BY:
	REVISION NO: 0
	REVISION DATE:

1.0 PURPOSE

This quality control publication establishes the method and procedures for the selection and for the monitoring of the performance of subcontractors who will be picked to calibrate and repair the company's MTE.

2.0 INTENT

This QCP establishes the responsibilities related to the purchasing and the monitoring of vendors and outside calibration laboratories who have been chosen to calibrate and/or repair the company's MTE.

3.0 APPLICABLE FORMS, PROCEDURES AND PUBLICATIONS

3.1 Calibration System Responsibilities, QCP No. 4.2.1.

3.2 Subcontractor Facility-Calibration/Repair Survey, Form 4.2.6-1.

3.3 Subcontractor Equipment Survey, Form 4.2.6-2.

4.0 PROCEDURE

4.1 When MTE calibration or repair/rework of the MTE is to be accomplished at a contracted for calibration laboratory, there must be objective evidence that the outside laboratory's calibration equipment can be traced to the National Bureau of Standards. The outside laboratory's calibration system must also meet the requirements of MIL-STD-45662A.

4.2 The calibration, quality assurance and purchasing departments have the responsibility for assuring through objective evidence that the contracted for laboratory's calibration system can be systematically traced to MIL-STD-45662A and the National Bureau of Standards through the use of quality surveys. The quality assurance department will perform the actual survey. The purchasing department is the main point of contact

<table>
<tr><td rowspan="6">QUALITY CONTROL PUBLICATION

TITLE: SUBCONTRACTING OF CALIBRATION AND REPAIR WORK</td><td>QCP NO. 4.2.6</td></tr>
<tr><td>PAGE NO. 2 OF 4</td></tr>
<tr><td>ISSUE DATE:</td></tr>
<tr><td>APPROVED BY:</td></tr>
<tr><td>REVISION NO: 0</td></tr>
<tr><td>REVISION DATE:</td></tr>
</table>

with the laboratory and will also determine the outside laboratory's financial capabilities. The purchasing department will make all of the necessary arrangements for the Quality Review, to be held at the outside laboratory.

4.3 In conducting a Calibration Survey the quality assurance person assigned to the survey will prepare the Subcontractor Facility Calibration/Report Survey Form 4.2.6-1. This form will be filled out as follows:

1. The proposed subcontractor's name.
2. The proposed date of the survey.
3. The subcontractor's location (address).
4. The name of the subcontractor's employee who will serve as the liaison with the quality assurance auditor for this survey.
5. A general description of the subcontractors MTE calibration/ repair capabilities.
6. The number of subcontractor's employees who will be engaged in the calibrations/repairs.
7. A diagram of the subcontractor's facility, including the calibration/repair locations.
8. A statement of warranty policy for calibration and repair work.
9. A list of on-file calibration instructions, manuals and procedures, test equipment and standards to be used in the applicable calibrations and/or repairs.
10. Documentation as to the traceability of calibration equipment and standards used in the calibrations/repairs to the National Bureau of Standards.

QUALITY CONTROL PUBLICATION	QCP NO. 4.2.6
	PAGE NO. 3 OF 4
	ISSUE DATE:
TITLE: SUBCONTRACTING OF CALIBRATION AND REPAIR WORK	APPROVED BY:
	REVISION NO: 0
	REVISION DATE:

11. The name of two companies who have done business with the subcontractor/laboratory previously (if no previous business was transacted with the subcontractor/laboratory).

4.4 In the process of conducting a calibration/repair survey the quality assurance auditor is to prepare a Subcontractor Equipment Survey, Form 4.2.6-2. This form is to be filled out as follows:

1. The proposed subcontractor's name and address.
2. The date of the survey.
3. A listing of the equipment to be used to calibrate/repair the subcontracted items.
4. The manufacturer of the equipment to be used.
5. The model and serial number of the equipment to be used.
6. Verification of the traceability of all equipment to be used for calibration to the National Bureau of Standards.
7. Auditor's findings as to the capability of the subcontractor to perform the required calibrations/repairs.
8. Auditor's comments and recommendations regarding the survey.
9. Name of the auditor and title.

4.5 The above report is to be attached to the report in Form 4.2.6-1 and submitted to the approving quality assurance official, the manager/supervisor of the calibration department and to the manager of purchasing. If all of the above approve the subcontractor as a qualified calibration/repair station, the purchasing department will take the necessary steps to secure an agreement from the subcontractor/laboratory.

<table>
<tr><td rowspan="6">QUALITY CONTROL PUBLICATION

TITLE: SUBCONTRACTING OF CALIBRATION AND REPAIR WORK</td><td>QCP NO. 4.2.6</td></tr>
<tr><td>PAGE NO. 4 OF 4</td></tr>
<tr><td>ISSUE DATE:</td></tr>
<tr><td>APPROVED BY:</td></tr>
<tr><td>REVISION NO: 0</td></tr>
<tr><td>REVISION DATE:</td></tr>
</table>

4.6 The quality assurance department will create and maintain a list of qualified subcontractors/laboratories for MTE and will distribute this list to the calibration and purchasing departments.

4.7 The quality assurance department is responsible for maintaining a surveillance system of all approved subcontractors/laboratories, reporting on their workmanship, accuracy, record keeping, their continuing ability to comply with schedule requirements and the applicable standards and regulations. A monthly summary will be established and reviewed to verify the status of corrective actions and completion dates, the status of nonconformances and their completion status and all other quality status reviews. This monthly review is one of the basis on whether or not a particular subcontractor/laboratory will be kept or dropped from the list of approved calibration subcontractors/laboratories.

SUBCONTRACTOR FACILITY - CALIBRATION/REPORT SURVEY

Date Survey Filled In: ______ ____ ______
(month) (day) (year)

Name of Auditor ____________________

Name of Conractor	Address of Contractor/Laboratory	Name of Contractor's Representative	Telephone Number
(1)	(3)	(4)	

Number of Employees	Facility Diagram Attached	Warranty Policy	Traceability to NBS	Traceability Deficiencies
(6)	YES ____ NO ____	(8)	(10)	
Date of Survey (2)	(7) Will Obtain Date: ____			

Description of Capabilities: (5)

List of Calibration Instructions/Procedures/Manuals: (9)

Reference No. 1: ______ (11) ______ Reference No. 2: ____________

FORM 4.2.6-1

SUBCONTRACTOR EQUIPMENT SURVEY

Date of Survey : ______ (month) ____ (day) ______ (year) (2)

Name of Auditor ______ ( )

Name of Subcontractor (Organization)	Address of Subcontractor (Organization)	Auditor's Comments
(1)	(1)	(8)

Item/Device To Be Used	Manufacturer	Model No.	Serial No.	Traceability	Findings
(3)	(4)	(5)	(5)	(6)	(7)

FORM 4.2.6-2

QUALITY CONTROL PUBLICATION	QCP NO. 4.2.7
	PAGE NO. 1 OF 3
	ISSUE DATE:
TITLE: EMPLOYEE-OWNED MEASURING EQUIPMENT	APPROVED BY:
	REVISION NO: 0
	REVISION DATE:

1.0 PURPOSE

This quality control publication establishes the method and procedures for the control and use of employee-owned measuring, testing, or other devices that may be used as a means for controlling product quality.

2.0 INTENT

This QCP applies to all employee-owned measuring and test devices that could be used in any measurements and tests where the measurements and tests are to be used as a means for controlling product quality, or verifying contract/purchase order requirement and specifications.

3.0 DEFINITION

3.1 Employee-owned measuring and testing devices are defined in this QCP as any devices used in the production and test cycle that are used or could be used to verify any measurements and/or tests that are specified by the company's or contract/purchase order requirements or specifications, throughout the complete manufacturing, production and test cycle of any deliverable product. This includes all types of micrometers, gauges, rulers, measurement calipers of all types and other measuring and test devices including measurement types and rulers of all types.

4.0 APPLICABLE FORMS, PROCEDURES AND PUBLICATIONS

4.1 Calibration System Responsibilities, QCP 4.2.1.

4.2 Employee-owned Measuring Equipment Calibration Record, Form 4.2.7-1.

5.0 PROCEDURE

5.1 All employee-owned measuring and test devices that may, could, or is being used to verify material, items or product delivered to this facility

QUALITY CONTROL PUBLICATION	QCP NO. 4.2.7
	PAGE NO. 2 OF 3
TITLE: EMPLOYEE-OWNED MEASURING EQUIPMENT	ISSUE DATE:
	APPROVED BY:
	REVISION NO: 0
	REVISION DATE:

by suppliers, vendors, etc., or used in any part of the manufacturing, production, inspection, test, process control or in the final measurement and/or test of a deliverable product must be included in the established calibration system.

5.2 All employees are required to submit personally owned measurement or test devices to their supervisor. It is the responsibility of the supervisor to submit these inspection and/or test devices to the calibration department or to the quality assurance department (if all MTE is calibrated or repaired outside) so that this equipment can be included into the calibration system and calibrated. There will be no exceptions to this policy.

5.3 If any of these employee-owned devices are found in this facility they will either be subject to the company's calibration control system, or the employee will remove them from the facility.

5.4 If there is any reason to believe that any employee-owned device, that is not part of the calibration system, was used to measure, test, or otherwise to accept deliverable product at any stage of the manufacturing, test, inspection cycle of the material, items finished goods, the items will be recalled, and all inspections or tests will be verified using known calibrated MTE.

5.5 The calibration department is to create and maintain an Employee-Owned MTE-Calibration Record, for each piece of employee owned MTE and this record is to become part of the total calibration system.

5.6 The Employee-Owned MTE-Calibration Record, Form 4.2.7-1 is to be filled out as follows:

1. The initial date of this record.
2. The number or color code assigned to the device.
3. The name of the device.

QUALITY CONTROL PUBLICATION	QCP NO. 4.2.7
	PAGE NO. 3 OF 3
	ISSUE DATE:
TITLE: EMPLOYEE-OWNED MEASURING EQUIPMENT	APPROVED BY:
	REVISION NO: 0
	REVISION DATE:

4. The manufacturer of the device.
5. The model number of the device.
6. The serial number of the device.
7. The employee's name.
8. The employee's identification number.
9. The department or work location of the employee.
10. Calibration frequency assigned to the device.
11. The date of calibration of the device.
12. The date next calibration of the device is due.
13. The identification number of the person who did the calibration.

5.6 Each device is to be identified with the date of the most recent calibration. The stamp of the technician who performed the calibration, and the date when the next calibration is due. If the item is too small for this type of marking, the color code system or other identifying number will be inscribed on the device according to the established procedures of the Calibration Department. The device is to be keyed into the established calibration and recall system.

5.7 Failure to follow these requirements could/will be recorded in the employee's personnel record and disciplinary action may be taken according to the severity of each case. The department and the department supervisors performance records could/will be anecdoted with the applicable remarks (as required).

EMPLOYEE-OWNED MTE-CALIBRATION RECORD

INITIAL DATE OF ______ (month) ______ (day) ______ (year) (1)

DEVICE NO.	NAME OF DEVICE	MANUF.. OF DEVICE	MODEL NO.	SERIAL NO.	EMPLOYEE NAME	EMPLOYEE NO.	DEPARTMENT	CAL. FREQ.	DATE CAL.	NEXT CAL. DUE	ID. OF TECH.
(2)	(3)	(4)	(5)	(6)	(7)	(8)	(9)	(10)	(11)	(12)	(13)

FORM 4.2.7-1

PRODUCTION TOOLING USED AS A MEDIA OF INSPECTION

The topic of *production tooling used as media of inspection*, as presented in paragraph 4.3 of MIL-Q-9858A, and paragraph 3.3 of MIL-I-45208A, is the method required to control all jigs, fixtures, templates, and patterns that are being utilized to form, cut, assemble, or any other production or assembly operation whereby that particular device is to be used as a method for making the determination as to the correctness of the completed operation. Contractors who have or are using these devices, have found through experience, that it is cost effective to control the accuracy of these types of devices prior to a production/manufacturing operation rather than finding inaccuracies that could lead to expensive rework or costly scrap. The government in order to prevent nonconforming material from getting into completed items it purchases, requires a contractor system that will prevent such material from being incorporated into the finished product, no matter what that finished product/item may be.

The requirement as stated in paragraph 4.3 of MIL-Q-9858A, states, "When production jigs, fixtures, tooling masters, templates, patterns and such devices are used as a media of inspection, they shall be proved for accuracy prior to release for use. These devices shall be proved again for accuracy at intervals formally established in a manner to cause their timely adjustment, replacement or repair prior to becoming inaccurate." Here again, is a requirement for a calibration and recall/recalibration system to be established and maintained by the contractor.

The requirement as stated in paragraph 3.3 of MIL-I-45208A, states, "In the event contractors elect to use production tooling for inspection and gauging, special precautions must be taken to assure accuracy. This involves both proof of accuracy before release for use as well as checking at a regular, formally established interval thereafter to prevent inaccuracy."

AQAP 1, paragraph 209 states, "Jigs, fixtures, templates, patterns or other devices used as media of inspection shall be proven capable of verifying the acceptability of material prior to release for use during manufacture. Jigs, fixtures and tooling masters shall be reproven at established periods. The contractor shall establish the extent and frequency of such trials and maintain records as evidence of control. Design data for tools and gauges and performance data for measuring and test equipment shall be made available when required by the government QAR."

AQAP 4, paragraph 204, references AQAP 6, NATO Measurement and Calibration System Requirements for Industry. AQAP 6 states, "Procedures shall contain sufficient instruction to provide data adequate to ensure valid measurement when the equipment is used for measurement of product or process characteristics or calibration." (This is in paragraph 205 of AQAP 6). Paragraph

206 states, "Functionally simple and rugged measuring equipment shall be the subject of records (individual or collective) or other means of showing that they are within their calibration interval and designated limits."

QUALITY CONTROL PUBLICATION **TITLE:** PRODUCTION TOOLING USED AS A MEDIA OF INSPECTION	QCP NO. 4.3.1
	PAGE NO. 1 OF 2
	ISSUE DATE:
	APPROVED BY:
	REVISION NO: 0
	REVISION DATE:

1.0 PURPOSE

This quality control publication establishes the method and procedure for controlling the accuracy of all production tooling, templates, jigs or fixtures, etc. that, through its use, controls product quality.

2.0 INTENT

This QCP applies to all departments that utilize these types of devices to control the size, shape, etc., of items, units, material, to be incorporated into a finished product or the finished product itself.

3.0 APPLICABLE FORMS, PROCEDURES, PUBLICATIONS

3.1 Calibration Control and Recall, QCP No. 4.2.2.

3.2 Calibration location and Recall Record, Form 4.2.2-1.

3.3 Calibration Data Record, Form 4.2.2-2.

3.4 Calibration/Repair Instructions, Form 4.2.3-1.

3.5 Calibration Decal, Form 4.2.2-3.

3.6 Notice of Certification, Form 4.2.4-1.

4.0 PROCEDURE

4.1 The quality assurance department is responsible for coordinating the identification, inspection, and calibration of jigs, fixtures, templates, patterns, etc. with the calibration, design engineering and the applicable manufacturing/production departments.

4.2 Prior to the use of the above items, these items will be identified and submitted to the calibration department for inspection and the initial calibration.

QUALITY CONTROL PUBLICATION	QCP NO. 4.3.1
	PAGE NO. 2 OF 2
	ISSUE DATE:
TITLE: PRODUCTION TOOLING USED AS A MEDIA OF INSPECTION	APPROVED BY:
	REVISION NO: 0
	REVISION DATE:

4.3 Every item identified above will be inspected and calibrated (as required), utilizing the items engineering drawings and specifications as reference documents. These documents will include a detailed drawing of the specific item as part of the documentation of the items.

4.4 A Calibration/Repair Instruction Form 4.2.3-1, and a Calibration Location and Recall record, Form 4.2.2-1, are to be prepared for each item (refer to QCP's 4.2.2 and 4.2.3).

4.5 Once calibrated, each tool, jig, fixture, etc., is to be identified with a Calibration Due Decal, Form 4.2.2-3, or a color code and/or identification number is to be etched into the item, and will be traceable to the calibration/recall system (as required by QCP 4.2.2).

4.6 All tools, jigs, fixtures, templates, etc., will not be used if their calibration due date has expired (see QCP 4.2.2).

4.7 If it is suspected or there has been an occurrence of such a nature as to place the accuracy of these devices in question, they are to be identified with an OUT-OF-SERVICE DECAL, Form 4.2.2-4, which carried the following message, DO NOT USE - THIS ITEM MUST BE CALIBRATED PRIOR TO USE.

4.8 This equipment is to be periodically inspected/recalibrated at the intervals as specified on the Equipment Location and Recall Record, Form 4.2.2-1.

GOVERNMENT USE OF CONTRACTOR'S INSPECTION EQUIPMENT

MIL-Q-9858A states "The contractor's gauges, measuring and testing devices shall be made available for use by the government when required to determine conformance with contract requirements. If conditions warrant, contractor's personnel shall be made available for the operation of such devices, and for the verification and traceability to the NBS in respect to their accuracy and condition...Contractors rightfully expect government QA representatives to avoid unnecessary production delays because of Government inspection and testing. Thus, government QA representatives sometimes accomplish their inspection by witnessing a company inspection rather than conducting a separate one. However, this is not always required and often is not *practical* or *desirable*." The next statement of MIL-Q-9858A addresses this statement and sometimes common practice. "Many contractors choose to protect the performance of their complex and specialized equipment by offering to operate it for the government. In some cases, however, *the manner of operating such testing equipment can give false results. Under these conditions the government QA representative may wish to operate the equipment himself.* When this occurs, the contractor may wish to instruct the government QA representative in the operation of the more specialized testing and measuring equipment."

MIL-I-45208A and MIL-HDBK-H51 state "When required, the contractor's measuring and testing equipment shall be made available to the government representative to determine conformance of product with contract requirements." The rest of the statements are essentially the same as MIL-Q-9858A.

QUALITY CONTROL PUBLICATION	QCP NO. 4.4.1
	PAGE NO. 1 OF 1
	ISSUE DATE:
TITLE: GOVERNMENT USE OF CONTRACTORS INSPECTION EQUIPMENT	APPROVED BY:
	REVISION NO: 0
	REVISION DATE:

1.0 PURPOSE

This quality control publication establishes the procedure for the use of the company's measuring and test equipment by the government QAR. This procedure also establishes the policy and procedure for the use of the company's MTE by customers other than the government.

2.0 INTENT

This QCP is applicable to all departments and areas in the facility where measuring and test equipment is being used to prove product quality. This procedure is to be used to facilitate requests by customers to use the company's MTE.

3.0 PROCEDURE

3.1 All gauges, inspection and measurement devices will be made available to the government upon request. If the government representative requests company personnel to conduct any inspection/ test the quality assurance department will make the necessary arrangements to facilitate the request. If the government requests verification of the accuracy of any MTE, the quality assurance department is responsible for providing the necessary verification to the government or other customer's representatives.

3.2 If the equipment is of such a nature as to require instruction in its use, the assigned quality engineer will accomplish the instruction in its use, or if mutually agreed upon, will assign an inspector/technician to

CHAPTER SEVENTEEN

Nonconforming Material

NONCONFORMING MATERIAL

MIL-Q-9858A and MIL-HDBK-50, section 6.5, state the *requirements* for the *control and disposition of* nonconforming material. "The contractor shall establish and maintain an effective and positive system for controlling nonconforming material, *including procedures for its identification, segregation, and disposition.* Repair or rework of nonconforming material shall be in accordance with documented procedures acceptable to the government. The acceptance of nonconforming supplies is a prerogative of and shall be as prescribed by the government and may involve a monetary adjustment." The subject of monetary adjustments is discussed in detail in 8200.10. This is a publication of the Defense Logistics Agency guiding the various levels of DLA in the actions to be taken regarding the possible recoupment of money from the contractor due to excessive levels of nonconforming material incorporated into the finished product shipped to the government. *All nonconforming supplies shall be positively identified to prevent unauthorized use, shipment and intermingling with conforming supplies.* Systems have been developed by many contractors that would preclude the possibility of nonconforming material from finding its way into the finished product. This includes the identification of all nonconformances at the very start, and various methods used to keep all nonconformances out of the finished and deliverable product. This usually entails establishing an area in the contractor's facility which is secure and tightly controlled, and will prevent unauthorized personnel from gaining access to this material and incorporating it into items/product that are to be delivered to the government. These areas are generally referred to as MRB *bond rooms.*

The next six lines of MIL-Q-9858A and MIL-HDBK-H50 relate to the Costs Related to Quality, paragraph 3.6 of MIL-Q-9858A. *Here is another indication of the relationship between nonconforming material and the costs associated with the rework, repair and scrap, due to the lack of system controls.* "The contractor shall make known to the Government upon request the data associated with the costs and losses in connection with scrap and with rework necessary to reprocess nonconforming material to make it conform completely." In the Review of Requirement, the following statements are made: "Since most production processes inevitably yield some defective products, methods for preventing further regular processing, completion or delivery of such products are essential and must be established by the contractor." Each quality control publication in this chapter relates to one of the statements in 6.5 of MIL-Q-9858A. MIL-I-45208A, section 3.7, the requirements for the control of nonconforming material, has the same intent and paraphrases MIL-Q-9858A. Read both requirements and note the sameness of intent.

MIL-STD-1520B is used by many contractors in establishing a Material Review Board (MRB) to control nonconforming material, and, a Corrective Action Board (CAB) to determine the causes of nonconformances. The CAB has the authority to investigate and assure positive and timely implementation of the necessary corrective actions to prevent the recurrence of the nonconformances.

AQAP-1 states the requirement for the control of nonconforming material in a slightly different way. The following statement is a quote from the text of AQAP-1, NATO Requirements For An Industrial Quality Control System. "The contractor's procedures for controlling material which does not conform to technical data shall include provisions for identification, segregation and acceptance, rework or disposal, as appropriate, taking into account that the acceptance of nonconforming material is the *prerogative of the purchaser*. All nonconforming material shall be *clearly identified to prevent unauthorized use, shipment, or mixing with conforming material.* Holding areas or procedures mutually agreed to by the contractor and the QAR shall be provided by the contractor. Procedures for rejecting, processing and dispositioning of nonconforming material shall be documented, and *are subject to disapproval by the QAR* when it can be shown that they do not provide the necessary controls. *All repair and use-as-is dispositions must be acceptable to the QAR*. The procedures shall provide for reinspection and retest of characteristics affected by repair, rework or replacement. Adequate records, clearly identifying the material, the nature and extent of nonconformance and disposition, shall be maintained and form part of the contractor's records."

AQAP-4 is a scaled down version with the same meaning as AQAP-1. AQAP-4 states, "The contractor shall maintain procedures that ensure the identification of all nonconforming materials, parts, work or articles, and prevent use, shipment or intermingling with conforming material or work. Repairs shall be in accordance with procedures acceptable to the Quality Assurance Representative."

DLAR 8200.10 presents the government's view of nonconforming material and the steps it intends to take to receive monetary consideration in return for accepting nonconforming material. "By continually accepting this vast amount of minor nonconformances, the government is sending the wrong message to the contractors. What it did was indicate *Business As Usual*, which resulted in the contractors not taking corrective action to change their processes and procedures when nonconforming material was produced. In addition, little, if any, effort was expended in making changes to specifications/drawings when they were unrealistic or not practical for manufacturing."

QUALITY CONTROL PUBLICATION	QCP NO. 6.5.1
	PAGE NO. 1 OF 6
	ISSUE DATE:
TITLE: FAILURE REPORTING	APPROVED BY:
	REVISION NO: 0
	REVISION DATE:

1.0 PURPOSE

The purpose of this quality control publication is to establish the method and procedure for the accumulation of data that will accurately report nonconformances in product characteristics during the entire production life cycle of the product. This includes receiving inspection, production/ manufacturing, inspection and testing, laboratory analysis, raw material inspection and testing, assembly areas, purchasing, internal and external auditing, and all other process control areas within the facility including the auditing functions.

2.0 INTENT

All departments within the facility will adhere to the failure/nonconforming material and disposition reporting system as prescribed in this QCP.

3.0 APPLICABLE FORMS, PROCEDURES AND PUBLICATIONS

3.1 Failure/Nonconforming Material and Disposition Report, Form 6.5.1-1.

4.0 PROCEDURE

4.1 All failures, nonconformances, discrepancies are to be entered into the failure reporting system format via the appropriate computer terminals strategically located throughout the plant. The input code for each type of failure, nonconformance and discrepancy has been distributed to all departments and inspection/testing areas within the plant.

4.2 Form 6.5.1-1 is the format of a typical Failure Report you will see when this form is keyed into any terminal. The following instructions will be used to key the appropriate data into the terminal located in your area.

QUALITY CONTROL PUBLICATION	QCP NO. 6.5.1
	PAGE NO. 2 OF 6
	ISSUE DATE:
TITLE: FAILURE REPORTING	APPROVED BY:
	REVISION NO: 0
	REVISION DATE:

1. *The Product Code.* This is the code that appears on the individual Work Order and is keyed to the various product produced by the company (by product line).
2. *The Work Order Number.* This is assigned by production planning.
3. *The Operation Number.* The sequential operation code number as assigned on the work order.
4. *The Part Number.* This is the number of the part/assembly found to be discrepant/nonconforming.
5. *The Part Name.* Description.
6. *The Serial Number.* This is the number of the part, assembly, etc. (as required).
7. *The Defect Code.* This is assigned to each defect that can or is found based on the knowledge of the product and as assigned by the joint design manufacturing quality engineering department panel that has been established during the planning cycle of the product.
8. *The Department Code.* The code assigned to every department within the company where the discrepancy/nonconformance was found. This is the cost center code assigned to each department within the company.
9. *The Vendor or Subcontractor Code Testing Facility.* This is the cost center code assigned to every vendor, subcontractor, supplier, testing facility or laboratory.
10. *The Contract or Purchase Order Number.* This is the number assigned by the government purchasing office, or other customer purchase order number.

QUALITY CONTROL PUBLICATION	QCP NO. 6.5.1
	PAGE NO. 3 OF 6
	ISSUE DATE:
TITLE: FAILURE REPORTING	APPROVED BY:
	REVISION NO: 0
	REVISION DATE:

11. *The Specification Number*. The number that appears on the work order that refers to the applicable specification to be used by production, manufacturing, inspection or testing in the performance of the applicable operation.

12. *The Function Code*. The code assigned to each functional inspection, test, etc. For example, unit inspection, unit test, system inspection, system test, field inspection, field test, acceptance inspection, acceptance test, production, or special process (such as, soldering, welding, plating, etc.)

13. *System Run Time*. The amount of time the system ran prior to a failure.

14. *System Down Time*. The amount of time the system was down during repair and/or rework.

15. *System Retest Time*. The amount of time it took to re-run that characteristic that failed.

16. *Total System Run Time*. The amount of time it took to run the entire test.

17. *Failure/Nonconformance Description*.

18. *Cause of Failure/Nonconformance*.

19. Description of rework or repair necessary to fix part, assembly, unit, system, etc.

20. Corrective action required to prevent recurrence.

21. Date corrective action to be completed.

22. Actual date corrective action was *completed*.

23. *Disposition Code*. The code assigned to each possible type of disposition of material, part, assembly, unit, system, etc. Code

QUALITY CONTROL PUBLICATION	QCP NO. 6.5.1
	PAGE NO. 4 OF 6
	ISSUE DATE:
TITLE: FAILURE REPORTING	APPROVED BY:
	REVISION NO: 0
	REVISION DATE:

(01) - Scrap, Code (02) - Return to Vendor, Code (03) - Return-To-Stock, Code (04) - Use As Is, Code (05) - Rework To Print - This requires a documented and approved rework procedure (may require government acceptance), Code (06) - Repair Contrary To Print - (Check the contract requirements - This type of disposition may require a Waiver or Deviation).

24. Reworked or repaired to procedure no. XXXX.
25. The identification number of the employee that reported the failure, discrepancy or nonconformance.
26. The date the discrepancy, etc. was found.
27. The lot size.
28. The sample size.
29. The number of parts rejected.
30. The number of parts accepted.

If parts have been removed from an assembly and replaced with known conforming parts or subassembly(ies), the following will be filled in:

31. The part or assembly number of the part/subassembly replaced.
32. The serial number (if applicable).
33. Manufacturer or vendor code.
34. Description of defect.
35. Identification number of employee who replaced part or subassembly.
36. Serial number (if applicable) of the replacement part/subassembly.
37. Total time required to accomplish replacement.

<table>
<tr><td rowspan="6">QUALITY CONTROL PUBLICATION

TITLE: FAILURE REPORTING</td><td>QCP NO. 6.5.1</td></tr>
<tr><td>PAGE NO. 5 OF 6</td></tr>
<tr><td>ISSUE DATE:</td></tr>
<tr><td>APPROVED BY:</td></tr>
<tr><td>REVISION NO: 0</td></tr>
<tr><td>REVISION DATE:</td></tr>
</table>

Signatures of authorized personnel (members of the MRB board).

38. Design engineering signature.
39. Date of signature.
40. Manufacturing engineering signature.
41. Date of signature.
42. Quality engineering signature.
43. Date of signature.
44. Reliability engineering signature.
45. Date of signature.
46. Department supervisor/manager signature.
47. Date of signature.
48. Government quality assurance concurrence - signature.
49. Date of signature.
50. *Hard copy of report required.* As mentioned previously DLAH 8200.10 requires the government representative to write a report delineating the contractor's nonconforming material actions monthly. This will necessitate the contractor having the ability in the system to make a hard copy of this report, if the report involves material/items that could be, or is known to be, incorporated into product to be delivered to the government.
51. The report number.

4.3 The part of the Failure/nonconforming Material and Disposition Report (FNMDR) that is to be filled out by the inspector/technician production

QUALITY CONTROL PUBLICATION	QCP NO. 6.5.1
	PAGE NO. 6 OF 6
	ISSUE DATE:
TITLE: FAILURE REPORTING	APPROVED BY:
	REVISION NO: 0
	REVISION DATE:

person when a discrepancy/nonconformance to the drawing specification is found, is as follows:

4.3.1 Item Nos. 1, 2, 3, 4, 5, 6, 7, 8, 11, 12, 25, 27, 28, 29, and 30.

4.4 The department supervisor is to sign the FNMDR item No 47.

FAILURE/NONCONFORMING MATERIAL AND DISPOSITION REPORT

Hard Copy Required ____ (YES) ____ (NO) (50) Report Number ______ (51) ______

Product Code	W.O. Number	OP. No.	Part Number	Part Name	Serial No.	Defect Code	Dept. No.	Vendor No.
(1)	(2)	(3)	(4)	(5)	(6)	(7)	(8)	(9)

Contract/P.O. No.	Spec. No.	Function Code	Disposition Code	Employee I.D. Number	Rework/repair Procedure No.	Date Found MM/DD/YY
(10)	(11)	(12)	(23)	(25)	(24)	(26)

Lot Size	Sample Size	QTY Rej.	QTY Accept	Description of Failure/Nonconformance	Cause of Failure
(27)	(28)	(29)	(30)	(17)	(18)

Description of Rework/Repair	Corrective Action Required	Date C/A Due	Actual C/A Completed Date
(19)	(20)	(21)	(22)

Part/Assembly Replacement Record

Part Number Replaced	Serial Number	Vendor Code	Description of Defect	I.D. No. of Employee	Serial No. of Replacement	Total Time to Replace	Date of Replacement
(31)	(32)	(33)	(34)	(35)	(36)	(37)	(37A)

Test Failure Record

Run Time ______ (13) ______ Down Time ______ (14) ______ Retest Time ______ (15) ______ Total Run Time ______ (16) ______

Authorized Signatures (NAMES) (38)

Design Engineer	(39) Date	(42) Quality Engineer	(43) Date	(46) Department Manager	(47) Date
(40) Manuf./Prod. Engineer	(41) Date	(44) Reliability Engineer	(45) Date	(48) Goverment Rep.	(49) Date

FORM 6.5.1-1

QUALITY CONTROL PUBLICATION	QCP NO. 6.5.2
	PAGE NO. 1 OF 9
	ISSUE DATE:
TITLE: MATERIAL REVIEW PROCESS	APPROVED BY:
	REVISION NO: 0
	REVISION DATE:

1.0 PURPOSE

This quality control publication establishes the method and procedures for reviewing materials that have been found to be nonconforming to the applicable drawing, specification or work order, and the methods in which the appropriate disposition of this material will be obtained.

2.0 INTENT

The material review process is to be applied to all nonconforming materials, except to those materials where there is a documented and approved rework procedure available (see standard rework - QCP 3.3.6).

3.0 DEFINITIONS

3.1 Use-as-is Material

3.1.1 Material that is found to be nonconforming to print due to tightened tolerances, or the nonconformance is such that it will not affect the form, fit or function in this part or assembly, or the next assembly/production level, and is accepted on a limited basis so that the necessary corrective action can be taken to eliminate that type of nonconformance. The government QAR's concurrence with this decision will be obtained prior to using this classification of material in product that is to be presented to the government for acceptance.

3.2 Repair Contrary To Print

3.2.1 Material found to be nonconforming, but a decision has been made to repair the material even through there will be minor nonconformances that will not affect the form, fit or function of the material, part, assembly or end-product. As in use-as-is decisions, this decision to repair contrary to print will require the government QAR's concurrence.

QUALITY CONTROL PUBLICATION	QCP NO. 6.5.2
	PAGE NO. 2 OF 9
	ISSUE DATE:
TITLE: MATERIAL REVIEW PROCESS	APPROVED BY:
	REVISION NO: 0
	REVISION DATE:

3.3 Return To Vendor

3.3.1 This type of decision is to be made when it has been determined that the material can not be repaired in-house, or a decision to use-as-is would jeopardize the quality of the end product.

3.4 Return To Stock

3.4.1 This type of decision is to be made when it has been determined that the alleged discrepancy or nonconformance has no basis for any other type of actions.

3.5 Rework To Print

3.5.1 This type of decision is to be made when it has been determined that the material can be reworked completely to the applicable requirements, specifications, and drawings and all discrepancies/nonconformances will be removed due to this rework. A document and accepted rework procedure is required prior to the start of any rework.

3.6 Scrap Material

3.6.1 Nonconforming/discrepant material that cannot be reworked/ repaired to any acceptable condition.

3.7 Deviation

See QCP 4.1.2, paragraph 4.1.1, for the definition of a *Deviation*.

3.8 Waiver

See QCP 4.1.2, paragraph 4.2.1, for the definition of a *Waiver*.

QUALITY CONTROL PUBLICATION	QCP NO. 6.5.2
	PAGE NO. 3 OF 9
	ISSUE DATE:
TITLE: MATERIAL REVIEW PROCESS	APPROVED BY:
	REVISION NO: 0
	REVISION DATE:

4.0 APPLICABLE FORMS, PROCEDURES AND PUBLICATIONS

4.1 Rejection and Disposition Tag, Form 6.7.1-1.

4.2 Failure/Nonconforming Material and Disposition Report, Form 6.5.1-1.

4.3 Failure/Nonconforming Material and Disposition Log Sheet, Form 6.5.2-1. (FNMDR).

4.4 Corrective Action, see QCP's 3.5.1 and 3.5.2.

5.0 PROCEDURE

5.1 Material received for action by the Material Review Board (MRB), is to be first examined by the board's quality assurance representative to determine if the material and accompanying documentation are in order, and that the material has been properly tagged with a Rejection and Disposition Tag, Form 6.7.1-1 and the items in the Failure/ Nonconforming Material and Disposition Report, Form 6.5.1-1, that were to be filled in by the department/area involved with the reporting of the failure/nonconformance were filled in and accurately describe the information required. If the material and documentation is not in order, the quality assurance representative is responsible for initiating the appropriate corrective action.

5.2 The MRB's quality assurance representative is responsible for filling out the following blocks in the FNMDR (Form 6.5.1-1) when the material and/or documentation is received in the MRB area.

1. *Block 9* Vendor number (if applicable).
2. *Block 10* Contract/Purchase order number.
3. *Block 12* The Function code (as assigned).
4. *Block 17* Verify description of failure/nonconformance.
5. *Block 18* Cause of failure.
6. *Block 51* A report number is to be assigned to each FNMDR in numerical order as received. The Log Sheet, Form

QUALITY CONTROL PUBLICATION	QCP NO. 6.5.2
	PAGE NO. 4 OF 9
	ISSUE DATE:
TITLE: MATERIAL REVIEW PROCESS	APPROVED BY:
	REVISION NO: 0
	REVISION DATE:

6.5.2-1, on page 303 will be used to track the previous FNMDR number sequences.

5.3 After the previous sections of the FNMDR have been filled out, the FNMDR is to be logged into the FNMDR Log Sheet, Form 6.5.2-1 as follows:

1. The FNMDR number (as assigned).
2. The date when the FNMDR was initiated.
3. The date when all actions on the FNMDR are due.
4. Completion date of the FNMDR.
5. If any follow-ups to the FNMDR are due, the due date.
6. Name of the company quality assurance representative initiating log entry.
7. The defect code, as assigned from list of product/supplies defects listing.

5.4 When any material product is found to be nonconforming to the applicable drawings, specifications, or procedures, it will be examined first by members of the preliminary review board assisted by manufacturing and/or production engineering, or by other technical disciplines as needed/required. It will be determined by the preliminary review board, if the failure or nonconformance can be dispositioned as follows:

1. The nonconformances can be eliminated by rework.
2. The nonconformance requires scrapping due to the nature of the nonconformance and repair or rework will not make the material fit for use.

QUALITY CONTROL PUBLICATION	QCP NO. 6.5.2
	PAGE NO. 5 OF 9
	ISSUE DATE:
TITLE: MATERIAL REVIEW PROCESS	APPROVED BY:
	REVISION NO: 0
	REVISION DATE:

3. The materal/product can be repaired by standard Repair Processes which have been approved by the MRB and the government representative. (If Class II nonconformance dispositions have not been withheld by the contract requirements/specifications).

4. The nonconformance is of such a nature that the material/product, has to be returned to the supplier.

5. The material/product meets none of the above criteria, it will be referred to the MRB.

The preliminary review board actions must be reported and documented on the FNMDR and the associated corrective actions be taken to eliminate the cause of the associated Failures and/or Nonconformances. These actions are taken if it is determined that the nonconformance can be handled more economically at the location of the identification of the failure/nonconformance. The appropriate signatures (or in the case of a computer generated system - the appropriate approval identification code) must be inserted into blocks 38 through 49 on the FNMDR's, as in Form 6.2.1-1.

5.5 To document the dispositions and corrective actions to be taken after the preliminary review board has met, the board's quality representative will document the results and corrective action to be taken on the FNMDR, Form 6.5.1-1 as follows:

1. *Block 23* The disposition code will be entered. These codes will as discussed in 11 through 5 of page 537 of this QCP.
2. *Block 18* The determined cause of failure/nonconformance.
3. *Block 19* A brief description of the rework to print to be accomplished, the number of the documented and approved procedure, (approved by the government representative) along with members of the preliminary review board.

QUALITY CONTROL PUBLICATION	QCP NO. 6.5.2
	PAGE NO. 6 OF 9
	ISSUE DATE:
TITLE: MATERIAL REVIEW PROCESS	APPROVED BY:
	REVISION NO: 0
	REVISION DATE:

4. *Block 20* The corrective action to be taken to eliminate those failures/nonconformances.
5. *Block 21* The date corrective action is due, (C/A may, in certain circumstances by required before the material/product can be either integrated into the next or final assembly or be presented to the government for acceptance).
6. *Block 22* Actual C/A completion date. The date when all C/A has been accomplished and approved.

If part/sub-assembly replacements were required, Blocks 31 through 37 are to be completed. If these actions were due to test failures, Blocks 13 through 15 are to be filled in. The FNMDR shown in Form 6.5.2-1 is to be filled in for every preliminary review board action. This will be a separate log entry system used that identifies all preliminary review board actions.

5.6 If none of the conditions in 1 through 5 of paragraph 5.4 can be met when a failure/nonconformance is found, the FNMDR, material, parts or sub-assemblies are to be forwarded to the MRB area along with all other documentation including the failure tag attached to the material, parts, etc., for a formal material review board review.

5.7 The membership of the material review board will be discussed in quality control publication 6.5.3.

5.8 All applicable drawings, specifications, and contract/purchase order requirements will be used to determine the nature, extent of impact on higher level assemblies or on purchased parts, the disposition of the material, parts, sub-assemblies or on purchased parts, the disposition of the material, parts, sub-assemblies or finished product, the extent of repair contrary to print, use-as-is, or scrapping of the nonconformances, and the necessary corrective action required to prevent these type of

QUALITY CONTROL PUBLICATION	QCP NO. 6.5.2
	PAGE NO. 7 OF 9
	ISSUE DATE:
TITLE: MATERIAL REVIEW PROCESS	APPROVED BY:
	REVISION NO: 0
	REVISION DATE:

occurrences from occurring again. All of the above decisions will require the acceptance of the government quality assurance representative.

5.9 The company quality assurance representative on the MRB is to fill in the applicable blocks of the FNMDR as follows:

1. *Block 23* The disposition code.
2. *Block 24* Repair procedure number.
3. *Block 17* Brief description of the failure/nonconformance.
4. *Block 18* The defect code, or a brief description of the reason for the failure/nonconformance.
5. *Block 19* A brief description of the repairs necessary to bring the material, parts etc., to an acceptable condition.
6. *Block 20* The corrective action required to eliminate the nonconformances.
7. *Block 21* The date when corrective action is due. This date will be arrived at mutually by QC and the government quality assurance representative.
8. *Block 22* When all corrective action is competed, that date will be inserted into this block.
9. *Block 31 through 37A* If parts, sub-assemblies, etc. needed replacement due to the applicable MRB decisions, these blocks are to be filled in.
10. *Blocks 13 through 16* These will be filled in if nonconformances were found during any testing. This documents the system running and down time.

QUALITY CONTROL PUBLICATION	QCP NO. 6.5.2
	PAGE NO. 8 OF 9
	ISSUE DATE:
TITLE: MATERIAL REVIEW PROCESS	APPROVED BY:
	REVISION NO: 0
	REVISION DATE:

11. *Blocks 38 through 47* The appropriate signatures or employee code numbers and date of these actions will be inserted into these blocks.

12. The acceptance signature and printed name of the government quality assurance representative will be obtained on a hard copy of this report. And an acceptance code will be inserted into this block on the computer system (if used).

5.10 When all MRB actions are completed, the Rejection and Disposition Tag that accompanied the material to the MRB will be marked with either the material review acceptance stamp or with the material review rejection stamp (see QCP 2.2.1 - Quality Inspection and Identification Stamps). This is to be accomplished by the QC member the material review board.

5.11 All materials that have been dispositioned by the MRB team will now be forwarded to the appropriate departments/locations for dispositioning as required by the MRB. If the circumstances are warranted, the dispositioned material will not be moved to these areas until the appropriate corrective actions have been completed and approved (this is where the government requires the completion of C/A prior to the materials being processed further).

5.12 The FNMDR Log Sheet is to be filled out (or inserted into the computer base for MRB actions. This is to be accomplished by the QC member of the MRB team.

5.13 When all the required corrective actions have been completed, the QC member will insert that date of completion into Block 22 of the FNMDR.

5.14 As the FNMDR's are received t the MRB area, a serialized sequential number will be assigned to each FNMDR by the QC member of the MRB and inserted into Block 51 of the FNMDR.

QUALITY CONTROL PUBLICATION	QCP NO.
	PAGE NO. 9 OF 9
	ISSUE DATE:
TITLE: MATERIAL REVIEW PROCESS	APPROVED BY:
	REVISION NO: 0
	REVISION DATE:

5.15 A copy of all FNMDR's that required government acceptance will be given to the government quality assurance representative.

FAILURE/NONCONFORMING MATERIAL AND DISPOSITION LOG

FNMDR NO.	DATE FNMDR INITIATED	DATE DUE	COMPLETION DATE	FOLLOW/ UP DUE	NAME OF QA REP.	DEFECT CODE
(1)	(2)	(3)	(4)	(5)	(6)	(7)

FORM 6.5.2-1

QUALITY CONTROL PUBLICATION	QCP NO. 6.5.3
	PAGE NO. 1 OF 3
	ISSUE DATE:
TITLE: MATERIAL REVIEW BOARD	APPROVED BY:
	REVISION NO: 0
	REVISION DATE:

1.0 PURPOSE

This quality control publication establishes the organization and organizational responsibilities of the Material Review Board (MRB). This organization within the company operates due to the consent of the government. If the government decides that there are too many nonconformances accepted by the company, the material review board could be disbanded by direction of the government and all nonconformances would then have to be processed through the Purchasing and Contract Officer (PCO) at the prime purchasing facility of the government.

2.0 INTENT

This QCP applies to the make up of a material review board that is authorized to disposition Type II Minor nonconforming material, no matter where it is discovered in the manufacturing cycle, and the formation of a Corrective Action Board (CAB), that will have the authority to assure the implementation of all recommended corrective actions (see QCP's 3.5.1 and 3.5.2). CAB activity is subject (as is MRB) to reviews and acceptance by the government quality assurance representative.

3.0 APPLICABLE DOCUMENTS, PROCEDURES AND PUBLICATIONS

3.1 Failure Reporting, QCP 6.5.1.

3.2 The Material Review Process, QCP 6.5.2 which includes the use of the FNMDR, Form 6.5.1-1.

3.3 Corrective Actions, QCP's 3.5.1 and 3.5.2.

3.4 FNMDR Report Log, Form 6.5.2-1.

3.5 Rework Procedures, QCP 3.3.6.

QUALITY CONTROL PUBLICATION	QCP NO. 6.5.3
	PAGE NO. 2 OF 3
	ISSUE DATE:
TITLE: MATERIAL REVIEW BOARD	APPROVED BY:
	REVISION NO: 0
	REVISION DATE:

4.0 PROCEDURE

4.1 Members of the material review board are selected from the design engineering, production/manufacturing engineering, material control and the quality engineering function of the quality assurance departments. Quality engineering will chair the material review board operations. All decisions of the MRB are subject to the approval or disapproval of any or all procedures, activities, reports and decisions of the MRB by the government quality assurance representative. The dispositioning of Type II Minor nonconformances is given to the company at the government's discretion. In no cases will Type I nonconformances be dispositioned by the company. These type of nonconformances have to be submitted to the government prime purchasing office through the use of formal requests for deviations or waivers. All requests for deviations and waivers are to be submitted through the government quality assurance representative to the PCO. An advance copy is to be sent directly to the PCO to expedite the requests. This does not mean that formal acceptance by the government is given until the formal proposal has been routed and accepted through normal government channels. To proceed with production is to do so at the company's risk.

4.2 The primary responsibility of the MRB is to decide on the disposition of nonconforming/discrepant materials. This includes raw materials, purchased parts/material/sub-assemblies, material and goods produced/manufactured in-house, nonconformances found during inspection and testing whether in-process or final. Final acceptance of all dispositions still remains the prerogative of the government representative.

4.3 When appropriate and necessary, MRB members will call upon the services of other company employees and/or departments to serve on the board in an advisory capacity.

4.4 The quality assurance department is responsible for providing a secured holding area for all nonconforming material to prevent this material

QUALITY CONTROL PUBLICATION	QCP NO. 6.5.3
	PAGE NO. 3 OF 3
	ISSUE DATE:
TITLE: MATERIAL REVIEW BOARD	APPROVED BY:
	REVISION NO: 0
	REVISION DATE:

from being used in normal production until the appropriate MRB actions have been accomplished, and will provide a suitable area for holding of MRB meetings.

4.5 Nonconforming materials that are covered by a Standard Rework Procedure (see QCP 3.3.5), do not require MRB action, but all rework decisions must be documented on a Failure/Nonconforming Material Disposition report, Form 6.5.1-1, and the appropriate and approved corrective actions must be accomplished and documented on the FNMDR. The rework procedures must have the approval of the government quality assurance representative.

4.6 The recording of the number of occurrences by defect code will be recorded on the applicable FNMDR. This is the responsibility of quality engineer chairing the MRB.

4.7 The collection of the costs associated with nonconforming material will be identified on the associated FNMDR report. These costs will include the following:

4.7.1 If reworked as a result of an MRB decision, the cost associated with the rework.

4.7.2 If scrapped, the cost of replacing the item.

4.7.3 If repaired, the costs associated with the repair.

QUALITY CONTROL PUBLICATION	QCP NO. 6.5.4
	PAGE NO. 1 OF 2
	ISSUE DATE:
TITLE: MATERIAL REVIEW BOARD DOCUMENTATION	APPROVED BY:
	REVISION NO: 0
	REVISION DATE:

1.0 PURPOSE

This quality control publication provides the list and description of the documents used in the material review board system.

2.0 INTENT

This QCP applies to all activities related to the rejection of nonconforming materials, their review, the applicable dispositions, and the applicable corrective actions taken to prevent recurrence of the nonconformances.

3.0 APPLICABLE FORMS, PUBLICATIONS AND PROCEDURES

3.1 Failure Reporting, QCP 6.5.1.

3.2 Material Review Process, QCP 6.5.2.

3.3 Material Review Board Organization, QCP 6.5.3.

3.4 Rejection and Disposition Tag, QCP 6.7.1.

3.5 Failure/Nonconforming Material and Disposition Report, Form 6.5.1-1.

3.6 Failure/Nonconforming Material and Disposition Log, Form 6.5.2-1.

3.7 Corrective Action Request, QCP 3.5.1 and 3.5.2.

3.8 Request for Deviations and Waivers, QCP 4.1.2.

3.9 Scrap Control, QCP 6.5.5.

4.0 PROCEDURE

4.1 Material received for MRB action at the MRB hold area, arrives with a Rejection and Disposition Tag attached to the material (See QCP 6.7.1). The applicable drawings and other documentation including the FNMDR with the section described in QCP 6.5.1 filled out.

QUALITY CONTROL PUBLICATION	QCP NO. 6.5.4
	PAGE NO. 2 OF 2
	ISSUE DATE:
TITLE: MATERIAL REVIEW BOARD DOCUMENTATION	APPROVED BY:
	REVISION NO: 0
	REVISION DATE:

4.2 When the material arrives at the MRB hold and disposition area the quality engineer will fill in those blocks as described in QCP 6.5.2, paragraph 5.2.

4.3 The FNMDR Log will then be filled in as per paragraph 5.3 by the quality engineer.

4.4 When the applicable disposition(s) have been made by the MRB group the quality engineer will then secure the required corrective actions and disposition approvals and document the same on the FNMDR as described in paragraph 5.9 thru 5.15 of QCP 6.5.2.

4.5 The quality engineer will then obtain the acceptance of the government quality assurance representative for all dispositions recommended by the MRB group. If approval for Class II, Minor Nonconformances, can not be obtained from the government QAR, a formal request for a deviation/waiver may have to be obtained from the purchasing and contracting officer at the prime government purchasing office as described in Waivers and Deviations, QCP 4.2.1. These actions are to be recorded on the FNMDR and in the FNMDR log.

4.6 After all actions and acceptances have been obtained pertaining to the FNMDR, the quality engineer is to close out the FNMDR and the applicable FNMDR Log entries that show completion are to be made.

4.7 When the necessary acceptances have been obtained the materials are to be forwarded to their designated locations according to the approved dispositions (see QCP 6.5.2).

4.8 Materials to be scrapped are processed as required in QCP 6.5.5.

QUALITY CONTROL PUBLICATION	QCP NO. 6.5.5
	PAGE NO. 1 OF 2
	ISSUE DATE:
TITLE: SCRAP CONTROL	APPROVED BY:
	REVISION NO: 0
	REVISION DATE:

1.0 PURPOSE

This quality control publication establishes the method and procedures for the processing of materials, parts, sub-assemblies that have been determined to be scrap.

2.0 INTENT

This QCP applies to all materials designated as scrap, except government/customer property which is discussed in QCP 7.2.1.

3.0 DEFINITION

3.1 Scrap - Parts, material, sub-assemblies that have been found to be unfit for further processing or delivery.

4.0 APPLICABLE FORMS, PUBLICATIONS OR PROCEDURES

4.1 Quality Control Publications 6.5.2, 6.5.4, 6.1.2.

5.0 PROCEDURE

5.1 Material that has been determined to be scrap, is to be painted or defaced so that there can be no possibility of it getting back into the production process.

5.2 Material that has been clearly marked, stamped or defaced and has been determined to be scrap, is to be delivered to the scrap material holding area promptly.

5.3 The quality assurance department is responsible for verifying that the material has been correctly and completely identified as scrap.

5.4 In those cases where vendor/supplier responsibility has been established for a scrap condition, and an authorization has not been received from the

QUALITY CONTROL PUBLICATION	QCP NO. 6.5.5
	PAGE NO. 2 OF 2
	ISSUE DATE:
TITLE: SCRAP CONTROL	APPROVED BY:
	REVISION NO: 0
	REVISION DATE:

vendor/supplier to scrap the material in-house, the material is to be returned to the vendor/supplier as requested and credit or replacement of the material will be obtained.

5.5 Scrap material that is not the property of the government or any other customer can be analyzed to determine if all or part of it can be used for display or instructional purposes. Any material so used must be clearly and prominently identified, so as it cannot under any circumstance be confused or used as acceptable material for any production or manufacturing operation.

5.6 Materials for which no practical alternative uses can be found is/are to be disposed of in an efficient, cost-effective manner.

5.7 The quality assurance department is to maintain complete and accurate records of all transactions, and is to supply cost accounting with the appropriate record of transactions.

5.8 The quality assurance department is to establish and operate a system to educate all employees as to the company policy regarding scrap prevention and conservation of resources.

CHAPTER EIGHTEEN

Process Control

PROCESS CONTROL

The similarities in Alpha Designators P and R of DLAM 8200.1, P-Process Controls, and R-Production Processing and Fabrication, will be discussed as it applies to MIL-Q-9858A, MIL-I-45208A, AQAP-1 and AQAP-6, the military quality and inspections systems of both the United States and the NATO Alliance.

MIL-Q-9858A and MIL-HDBK-H50, Section 6.2, relates to both, 1. The Control of Processes, and 2. Production Processing and Fabrication. Using selective quotations from MIL-HDBK-H50 the correlation will make itself clear.

Paragraph 6.2, states, "The contractor's quality program must assure that all machining, wiring, batching, shaping and all basic *production operations* of any type together with all *processing and fabrication* of any type is accomplished under controlled conditions."

The next quotation relates to the methods that are to be used to control the process and production of all material. "Controlled conditions include *documented work instructions, adequate production equipment* (controlling of the means of production), and *any special working environment* (climatically controlled environment as necessary to control the processes, inspections or tests required and control of processes)...*Documented work instructions* are considered to be the criteria for much of the production, processing and fabrication work. *These instructions are the criteria for acceptable or unacceptable workmanship*....Production and manufacturing operations must be systematically controlled and documented in appropriate work instructions. Only the manner of doing the work specified in these instructions, without deviation, is acceptable." Repeatability of production without nonconformances is the key to acceptable workmanship.

Another useful quotation from MIL-HDBK-H50 that sheds a little more insight into the world of process control is, "Producers of complex products are generally aware that production control must be highly disciplined to be effective. Omission of any operations or processes from control invites inferior quality. Ineffective, incomplete or intermittent control is almost as bad and usually leads to costly and unnecessary defects." And, "Even so-called basic work operations may be prone to defects. For example, in chemical cleaning, too short an immersion time may leave parts dirty (if the next operation is an electrochemical plating bath, poor adhesion, no adhesion of the plating medium to the base part could and does occur), while too long a time can cause corrosion or erosion damage, (which is reason enough to scrap the parts - higher costs and lower production)." The next statement in MIL-HDBK-H50 brings to light the need for reliable comparison methods that show production and inspection personnel what is, and what is not, an acceptable product. "Blindly following prescribed instructions is not enough to guarantee acceptable results. The results must be examined critically and compared with satisfactory standard samples," (accept/ reject criteria in the form of graphic representations are extensively used). Many references are made in paragraph 6.2 of MIL-HDBK-H50 in relation to inspection as a method of control. In-process and final inspection and test is dealt with in Chapter 22.

Statistical process control is being used more extensively by manufacturers who realize the need for more effective control of production processes. A few definitions of what is meant by statistical process control is included in this chapter.

1. *Statistical Quality Control* — The process of maintaining an acceptable level of product quality by means of statistical methods.

2. *Statistical Process Control* — A process is said to be in a state of statistical control when it exhibits only random variations which can be tracked, and effective corrective actions will eliminate the cause of variations considering the state of the art of the process at any given time.

3. *Stability of a Process* — A process is said to be stable if it exhibits no recognizable pattern of change. As processes become increasingly complex the notion of no recognizable pattern of change will also change.

4. *Statistical Inference* — The process of drawing conclusions on the basis of statistics. The statistics of change.

5. *Feedback Loop* — Using the results of a process controller or other device that feeds back process information (such as a measurement or test) to an operator or computer in order to control the process itself.

There are many useful books on the market that go into great detail on the many methods of statistical process control. Interested readers should consult some of these books.

MIL-I-45208 and MIL-HDBK-H51 deals with the method of controlling what is considered *Special Processes*. The following quotations from MIL-HDBK-H51 will shed some light on what is considered special processes. "Process control procedures shall be an integral part of the inspection system when such inspections are a part of the specification or contract...The detailed requirements pertaining to the co*ntrols for some manufacturing processes,* such as welding, plating, soldering, painting, molding/encapsulation or non-destructive inspection and test methods, such as radiography, zyglo, liquid penetrant, and magnetic particle, appear in federal or military specifications. Process control requirements also may be set forth in the contract or its references. However specified, the contractor is required to incorporate these process controls into the inspection system ... Every manufacturing operation affects product quality and, therefore, requires some kind of quality assurance action. The required action, however, may not necessarily involve an examination or test of the product. The quality of a welded or heat-treated part, for example, may be impossible to determine without destroying the part. In such cases the quality assurance requirements include some form of process control to be applied when performing the work. To meet the objective of requirements in this paragraph, *the contractor must identify and integrate into the inspection system all process controls applicable to his product.* In compliance with paragraph 3.4, contractors make all operations or process control procedures a part of the inspection system when such procedures are cited in the contract or referenced specifications. These operations are then controlled and inspected to all of the applicable requirements of MIL-I-45208A."

AQAP-1, paragraph 211, states the requirements of this chapter in similar terms. Under Manufacturing Control, it states "The contractor shall ensure that manufacturing and inspection and test operations are carried out under controlled conditions. Controlled conditions include *documented work instructions* defining the manner of manufacturing or processing, criteria for workmanship, suitable manufacturing equipment, and when required, any special working environment. Workmanship including *accept* and *reject criteria* shall be defined to the greatest practical extent by written standard, or by samples inspected and accepted by the contractor and the QAR (Quality Assurance Representative - Government). When process control is appropriate, or when physical inspection of the product is not practical, control by monitoring work operations, process methods, equipment, and personnel shall be provided. Both inspection and monitoring shall be provided when both are essential. Inspection methods or controls selected by the contractor shall be corrected whenever their unsuitability is demonstrated." Under Control of Special Processes, AQAP-1, states "The contractor shall establish and maintain control of all special processes (here again is that term) which form part of the manufacturing or inspection operations, or required safety precautions."

AQAP-6, paragraph 206, In-Process Inspection, will be discussed in a later chapter of this book.

Paragraph 207, of AQAP-6, is more in line with the requirements of this chapter. It states, "Unless standards are stipulated in the contract, the contractor shall establish criteria for acceptable workmanship through written standards or representative samples."

QUALITY CONTROL PUBLICATION	QCP NO. 6.2.1
	PAGE NO. 1 OF 3
	ISSUE DATE:
TITLE: PROCESS CONTROL	APPROVED BY:
	REVISION NO: 0
	REVISION DATE:

1.0 PURPOSE

The purpose of this quality control publication is to establish the method and procedures for controlling all production operations. This includes documented work instructions for machining, soldering, welding (arc and resistance), painting, molding and encapsulation, non-destructive inspection and testing, and the control of production and manufacturing equipment and their associated logs.

2.0 INTENT

This QCP applies to all production and process operations that occur during the entire life cycle of producing a finished product that meets the requirements and specifications of a contract or purchase order.

3.0 APPLICABLE FORMS, PROCEDURES AND PUBLICATIONS

3.1 QCP 3.3.5 - In-Process Inspection

3.2 QCP 6.2.2 - Soldering Procedure

3.3 QCP 6.2.3 - Welding Procedure

3.4 QCP 4.2.8 - Inspection of Jigs and Fixtures

3.5 QCP 3.3.4 - Testing Procedure

3.6 QCP 6.5.1 - Failure/Nonconforming material Dispositioning

3.7 Chapter 7 - Initial Quality Planning

4.0 PROCEDURE

4.1 During the planning cycle the quality assurance department, and the design/manufacturing/production engineering departments participated in contract planning and design reviews. At that time the baseline of the product was established. Planning was then accomplished in which

QUALITY CONTROL PUBLICATION	QCP NO. 6.2.1
	PAGE NO. 2 OF 3
	ISSUE DATE:
TITLE: PROCESS CONTROL	APPROVED BY:
	REVISION NO: 0
	REVISION DATE:

drawings, prototypes, and production models of the product were planned and developed. These same departments are responsible for the establishment of all manufacturing and process controls and in developing the written procedures applicable to the specific manufacturing, production, special process and inspection/test operations. This group of disciplines will also develop the applicable accept/reject criteria as it applies to a specific operation.

4.2 The sample procedures in this chapter outlines a broad method for the development of other procedures that pertain to the complete production cycle of a product.

4.3 Once the applicable procedures and process controls are in place, the quality assurance department will be responsible for auditing the procedures, processes and process controls used in the actual manufacturing/production operations to verify that the procedures, processes, and process controls, are in fact, controlling those processes and operations, and that the procedures are being followed by all personnel. The applicable accept/reject criteria used in the different areas will be used to determine if the controls are adequate in protecting product quality and whether or not the personnel involved are following the applicable procedures and using the accept/reject criteria correctly and as prescribed.

4.4 The Production/Process Survey, Form 6.2.1-1, will be used to record the results of each survey. This form will be filled out as follows:

1. The survey number.
2. The date of the survey.
3. The name of the person accomplishing the survey.
4. The process or operation being surveyed.
5. The department name/number or area being surveyed.

QUALITY CONTROL PUBLICATION	QCP NO. 6.2.1
	PAGE NO. 3 OF 3
	ISSUE DATE:
TITLE: PROCESS CONTROL	APPROVED BY:
	REVISION NO: 0
	REVISION DATE:

6. The contract or purchase order number.
7. The operation sheet number (as assigned for the particular production run).
8. The number of the operation (as designated on the operation sheet.
9. The applicable drawing number.
10. The applicable procedure or specification number.
11. The part/sub-assembly/assembly number (the identification number of the part/sub-assembly/assembly).
12. Calibration labels evident on inspection and test equipment. Yes _____ , No____.
13. Do the drawing revisions match the associated documentation? Yes _____ , No____.
14. Are the process or production/inspection procedures being followed? Yes_____ , No ____.
15. Upon inspection of the material, parts, sub-assemblies, etc. using the applicable production/inspection procedures, drawings and the applicable accept/reject criteria, have any defective and/or nonconforming items, drawings or procedures been found? Yes _____ , No ____.
16. Briefly describe the nature of the defects found.
17. List the applicable defect codes.
18. Briefly describe the nature of the corrective action that needs to be taken to eliminate any defect.
19. Insert the due date for the completion of the applicable corrective action.
20. Insert the actual completion date of all corrective actions.

PRODUCTION/PROCESS SURVEY FORM

SURVEY NUMBER ___(1)___ DATE OF SURVEY ___(2)___

NAME OF AUDITOR ___(3)___ PROCESS/OPERATION SURVEYED ___(4)___

Department No. ___(5)___ Contract/P.O. No. ___(6)___ Operation Sheet No. ___(7)___ Operation No. ___(8)___

Drawing Number ___(9)___ Procedure/Spec. No. ___(10)___ Defect Code ___(17)___ Part Number ___(11)___

Calibration Labels: Yes ___ No ___ (12) Revision(s) Same: Yes ___ No ___ (13) Procedure/Spec. Followed: Yes ___ No ___ (14)

Defective/Nonconforming Items, Procedures, Processes: ___(15)___

Brief Description of Defects: ___(16)___

Corrective Action To Be Taken: ___(18)___

Due Date For C/A ___(19)___ Actual Completion Date ___(20)___

FORM 6.2.1-1

QUALITY CONTROL PUBLICATION	QCP NO. 6.2.2
	PAGE NO. 1 OF 4
	ISSUE DATE:
TITLE: SOLDERING	APPROVED BY:
	REVISION NO: 0
	REVISION DATE:

1.0 PURPOSE

This quality control publication establishes the methods and procedures for communication between the design engineering, production/manufacturing engineering, quality engineering departments and those personnel and employees within the company who are responsible for production soldering and for the inspection of all soldering operations.

2.0 INTENT

It is the intent of this procedure to set the standards for all soldering operations and the related inspections thereof. This procedure when called out in a purchase requisition, will be used, or the referenced soldering standards will be used, to control all vendors/subcontractors soldering activities.

3.0 APPLICABLE FORMS, PROCEDURES, PUBLICATIONS AND STANDARDS

3.1 MIL-STD-454G, Requirement 5, - Soldering.

3.2 MIL-S-45743E, INT. AMENDMENT 4, Soldering, Manual Type, High Reliability.

3.3 DOD-STD-2000-1B - Soldering Technology, High Quality/high Reliability.

3.4 DOD-STD-2000-2A - Part and Component Mounting for High Quality/ High Reliability Soldered Electrical and Electronic Assemblies.

3.5 DOD-STD-2000-3 - Criteria for High Quality High Reliability Soldering Technology.

3.6 DOD-STD-2000-4 - General Purpose Soldering Requirements for Electrical and Electronic Equipment.

3.7 MIL-STD-1460(MU) - Soldering of Electrical Connections and Printed Wiring Assemblies.

QUALITY CONTROL PUBLICATION	QCP NO. 6.2.2
	PAGE NO. 2 OF 4
	ISSUE DATE:
TITLE: SOLDERING	APPROVED BY:
	REVISION NO: 0
	REVISION DATE:

4.0 SPECIFICATIONS

4.1 FEDERAL

4.1.1 O-E-760 - Ethyl Alcohol (Ethanol) Denatured Alcohol.

4.1.2 QQ-S-571 - Solder, Tin Alloy, Lead Tin Alloy and Lead Alloy.

4.1.3 TT-I-735 - Isopropyl Alcohol.

4.2 MILITARY

4.2.1 MIL-F-14256 - Flux, Soldering, Liquid (Rosin Base).

4.2.2 MIL-P-28809 - Printed Wiring Assemblies.

4.2.3 MIL-P-50884 - Printed Wiring, Flexible and Rigid-Flex.

4.2.4 MIL-P-46843 - Printed Wiring Assemblies.

4.2.5 MIL-P-81728 - Plating, Tin Lead (Electrodeposited).

4.3 STANDARDS

4.3.1 MIL-STD-202 - Test Methods for Electronic and Electrical Component Parts.

4.3.2 MIL-STD-429 - Printed-Wiring and Printed Circuit Terms and Definitions.

4.3.3 MIL-STD-275 - Printed Wiring for Electronic Equipment.

4.3.4 MIL-STD-750 - Test Methods for Semiconductor Devices.

4.3.5 MIL-STD-883 - Test Methods and Procedures for Microelectronics.

4.3.6 ANSI/IPC-T-50/ - Terms and Definitions for Interconnecting.

5.0 DEFINITIONS

5.1 ALLOY - Mixture of two or more metals melting together.

5.2 AWG - American Wire Gauge - The term used to describe the diameter of the wire.

QUALITY CONTROL PUBLICATION	QCP NO. 6.2.2
	PAGE NO. 3 OF 4
	ISSUE DATE:
TITLE: SOLDERING	APPROVED BY:
	REVISION NO: 0
	REVISION DATE:

5.3 AXIAL - A component in which the electrical leads exit from the body of the part parallel to the major axis and at opposite ends of the component.

5.4 CERTIFICATION - The training and qualification of soldering examiners, instructors, inspectors, operators, by a certified instructor who has been certified to a specific soldering specification that is required by a contract or purchase order.

6.0 PROCEDURE

6.1 All soldering operations are to be accomplished to DOD-STD-2000-1B throughout this facility/plant.

6.2 The quality assurance department is responsible for the training and qualification of certified instructors to the requirements of DOD-STD-2000-1B, paragraph 5.4.3.3.

6.3 The quality assurance department is responsible for the training and certification of all quality assurance inspectors whose job is that of a quality assurance soldering inspector, as required in paragraph 5.4.3.4 of the above standard.

6.4 The quality assurance department is responsible for the training of Category E Operators (those personnel who will be authorized to perform the applicable soldering operations), as required in paragraph 5.4.3.5 of the above standard.

6.5 All personnel who are involved in soldering operations are to be instructed as the applicable accept/reject criteria of DOD-STD-2000-3.

6.6 All instructors, inspectors, operators shall be recertified at the intervals required in DOD-STD-2000-1B.

6.7 The quality assurance department will be responsible for the keeping of all records as applicable to certification and recertification of all personnel.

QUALITY CONTROL PUBLICATION	QCP NO. 6.2.2
	PAGE NO. 4 OF 4
	ISSUE DATE:
TITLE: SOLDERING	APPROVED BY:
	REVISION NO: 0
	REVISION DATE:

6.8 The production planning department assisted by the quality engineering group, will, in the process of making out the work order/process routing sheet (see QCP 3.3.1), will insert the applicable soldering specification number, and this publication number into the operation number line that applies to any soldering operation, which includes the actual soldering operation and the following soldering inspection operation. The accept/reject criteria of DOD-STD-2000-3 will also be referenced in the work order/process routing sheets at the specified soldering operations operation line number.

6.9 The soldering operation that is to be carried out is prescribed by the operation line number on the work order/process routing sheet and will make reference to DOD-STD-2000-1B as the requirement specification for production soldering operations.

6.10 The soldering inspection operation that is to be accomplished as required in the Work order/Process Routing Sheet, will reference paragraph 5.1 of DOD-STD-2000-1B, (or if in the future the company makes the decision to design its own Soldering Specification Manual that makes the necessary references to the DOD-STD-2000 series for all production and inspection operations then the manual will be referenced in the work order/process routing sheets for the soldering operations, which in turn will reference these DOD Standards.

6.11 All nonconformances found will be dispositioned as specified in quality control publications 6.5.1 thru 6.5.4 and to the requirements of paragraphs 5.2 and 5.3 of DOD-STD-2000-3.

6.12 The quality engineering group will audit the appropriate departments to verify these requirements as set forth are being followed.

QUALITY CONTROL PUBLICATION	QCP NO. 6.2.3
	PAGE NO. 1 OF 6
	ISSUE DATE:
TITLE: WELDING	APPROVED BY:
	REVISION NO: 0
	REVISION DATE:

1.0 PURPOSE

This quality control publication establishes the method and procedures for the welding of all material to be used in the fabrication of a deliverable product.

2.0 INTENT

This procedure is to be used in the qualification of all welding personnel, the establishment of a welding procedure, the establishment of workmanship standards and the establishment of the accept/reject criteria to be used in the company that will meet the requirements of a contract or purchase order received from a particular government purchasing agency or other customers.

3.0 APPLICABLE DOCUMENTS, PUBLICATIONS AND STANDARDS

3.1 MIL-R-5632 - Rods, Steel, Welding for Aircraft Applications.

3.2 MIL-I-6866 - Inspection, Penetrant Method of.

3.3 MIL-E-8697 - Electrodes, Welding, Coated, Low Hydrogen, Heat-Treatable Steel.

3.4 MIL-W-8611 - Welding, Metal-Arc and Gas, Steels.

3.5 MIL-E-18193 - Electrode, Welding, Carbon Steel and Alloy Bare.

3.6 MIL-E-22200/1 - Electrode, Welding, Mineral Covered, Iron-Powder, Low-Hydrogen, Medium and High Tensile Steel.

3.7 MIL-E-22200/2 - Electrode, Welding, Covered (Austenitic Chromium-Nickel Steel for Corrosive and High Temp. services.

3.8 MIL-I-6868 - Inspection Process, Magnetic Particle.

3.9 MIL-E-22200/7 - Electrode, Welding, Covered, Moly. Alloy Steel.

3.10 MIL-E-23765/1 - Electrodes and Rods-Welding, Bare, Solid, Mild and Alloy Steel.

QUALITY CONTROL PUBLICATION	QCP NO. 6.2.3
	PAGE NO. 2 OF 6
	ISSUE DATE:
TITLE: WELDING	APPROVED BY:
	REVISION NO: 0
	REVISION DATE:

3.11 MILITARY

3.11.1 DOD-STD-100 - Engineering Drawing Practices.

3.11.2 MIL-STD-410 - Nondestructive Testing Personnel Certification.

3.11.3 MIL-STD-1595 - Qualification of Fusion Welders.

4.0 DEFINITIONS

4.1 WELDING - A materials joining process used in making welds. The process of thermally joining of two similar or dissimilar materials.

4.2 ACCEPTABLE WELD - A weld that meets all the requirements and the acceptance criteria prescribed by the welding specification.

4.3 COALESCENCE - The growing together or growth into one body of the materials being welded.

4.4 COMPLETE JOINT PENETRATION - Joint penetration in which the weld metal completely fills the groove and is fused to the base metal throughout its total thickness.

4.5 JOINT - The junction of members or the edges of members which are to be joined or have been joined.

4.6 COMPLETE FUSION - Fusion which has occurred over the entire base material surfaces intended for welding, and between all layers and passes.

4.7 PASS - A single progression of a welding or surfacing operation along a joint, weld deposit, or substrate. The result of a pass is a weld bead that is formed through the application of heat to two surfaces and the resulting melting and fusion of the two surfaces.

4.8 ROOT SURFACE - The exposed surface of a weld on the side other than that from which welding was done.

QUALITY CONTROL PUBLICATION	QCP NO. 6.2.3
	PAGE NO. 3 OF 6
	ISSUE DATE:
TITLE: WELDING	APPROVED BY:
	REVISION NO: 0
	REVISION DATE:

5.0 PROCEDURE

5.1 The welding that is to be accomplished utilizing this publication will meet the requirements of the contract and MIL-STD-1261B as required in the contract.

5.2 The following classification of metal-arc welding procedures as is prescribed in the 1261B specification:

Class 1. Constructional steels, readily weldable, for low stressed joints.
Class 2. Constructional steels, readily weldable for highly stressed joints.
Class 3. Constructional steels requiring special welding procedures, excluding corrosion resistant steels.

5.3 The following classification of welding processes are as prescribed by the 1261B specification:

a. Shielded metal arc (SMAW) - manual.
b. Gas tungsten arc (GTAW) - manual or automatic.
c. Gas metal arc (GMAW) - semi-automatic or automatic.
d. Submerged arc (SAW) - semi-automatic or automatic.
e. Flux cored arc (FCAW) - semi-automatic or automatic.
f. Plasma arc (PAW) - manual or automatic.
g. Stud arc (SW) - manual or semi-automatic.
h. Electrogas (EGW) - automatic.

5.4 The design engineering, production/manufacturing engineering and quality engineering departments will at the time of the design review, will review the requirement of each contract or purchase order to determine and prepare the detailed methods and techniques that will be used to document and detail the engineering and production/manufacturing drawings that will be used to produce the end product.

QUALITY CONTROL PUBLICATION	QCP NO. 6.2.3
	PAGE NO. 4 OF 6
	ISSUE DATE:
TITLE: WELDING	APPROVED BY:
	REVISION NO: 0
	REVISION DATE:

5.5 The welding drawings that will include the factors as depicted in Table I of MIL-STD-1261B, and as described in paragraph 4.1 of the Standard. The quality engineering section will obtain the required government approvals are specified in paragraphs 4.1, 5.1.1, 5.2.1 and 5.3.1 of the Standard.

5.6 All steels that do not fall within the limits of paragraph 3.3, Readily Weldable steels, of the Standard, will require special process controls.

5.7 For steels requiring heat-input controls, the heat input, expressed in joules per inch (per mm), (the formula for which is found in paragraph 6.2 of the Standard), shall be made part of the drawing and used as required by the welder, and is hereby made a part of this procedure.

5.8 Also included in the drawing will be the following characteristics below:

1. Joint description.
2. The appropriate welding symbols.
3. The specific type of metal to be used in the weld operation and its thickness (Gauge).
4. The amperage to be used.
5. The voltage to be used.
6. The travel speed of the welding head.
7. The welding process used by the weld operator.
8. The preheat temperature (if required).
9. The interpass temperature (if required).
10. The filler wire identification, part number, diameter (AWG) of filler wire.

QUALITY CONTROL PUBLICATION	QCP NO. 6.2.3
	PAGE NO. 5 OF 6
	ISSUE DATE:
TITLE: WELDING	APPROVED BY:
	REVISION NO: 0
	REVISION DATE:

11. The manufacturers recommended maximum heat input to the filler wire for each different welding condition.

5.9 If nonconformances/discrepancies are found on any weldments the repair/rework procedure of QCP 3.3.6 will be followed, with the following exceptions due to the specific requirements of MIL-STD-1261B(MR).

5.9.1 If the contract allows MRB rework/repair for Type II-nonconformances, a rework welding procedure will be prepared detailing the factors listed in Table II of the MIL-STD. The information as required in paragraph 4.1 of the Standard will be used as a format for the repair procedures, and where heat input controls are required, paragraph 4.1.1 will be included into the appropriate repair procedures.

5.10 The factors to be detailed in a repair procedure are as follows:

1. The method to be used (grinding or other way) to remove the defects.

2. The method to be used to inspect the repaired welds to ensure the removal of defects.

3. The contour of the cavity prior to welding (such as minimum root dimensions and included angle).

5.11 All welding repair procedures will be submitted to the government QAR and/or the procuring activity (as specified by the contract), prior to the commencement of repair operations.

5.12 All welders and welding equipment operators who will be welding Class 2 and Class 3 welds are to be qualified in accordance with the American Welding Society (AWS) Specification-AWS B2.1 and this quality publication. This procedure and the qualification results will be made available to the government upon request.

QUALITY CONTROL PUBLICATION	QCP NO. 6.2.3
	PAGE NO. 6 OF 6
	ISSUE DATE:
TITLE: WELDING	APPROVED BY:
	REVISION NO: 0
	REVISION DATE:

5.13 The government at its option may require recertification of the applicable welders or welding equipment.

5.14 All welds will be inspected to the criteria as established in MIL-STD-1261B, paragraphs 5.5 (if applicable as a contract requirement), 4.5, 5.1.3 thru 5.1.6.2 and pages 1 thru 18 of the Standard.

5.15 The filler metal to be used in the welding of materials as required by the Standard shall be as detailed in paragraph 5.1.2 of the standard.

5.16 Periodic audits shall be accomplished by the quality assurance department to verify that the procedures are meeting the criteria of MIL-STD-1261B, and that the welders and equipment are performing to this publication and 1261B. The quality assurance department is to establish a system for the periodic recertification of all welders and welding equipment, or cause to be recertified immediately, any welders or welding equipment, if the welds do not meet the requirements and criteria of this publication and/or that of MIL-STD-1261B. If a contract or purchase order specifies MIL-STD-1261B the MIL-STD will take precedence over this procedure.

CHAPTER NINETEEN

Records and Record Control

RECORDS

Alpha Designator T, Records, as required by MIL-Q-9858A, in paragraph 3.4 states, "The contractor shall maintain and use any records or data essential to the economical and effective operation of his quality program. These records shall be available for review by the government representative and copies of individual records shall be furnished him upon request." Further it states, "Management by intuition, rather than by analysis of tabulated records, is not acceptable." There are actually two requirements in the above sentences:

1. *Records of a Contractor:* a. Planning records. b. Records of tests/ inspections. c. Records of nonconformances and associated corrective actions. d. Records of purchases. e. Records of special process operations. f. Calibration records. g. Design and drawing records. h. Engineering actions. i. Waiver/deviation action records. j. Cost of quality records. k. Records of logbooks. l. Work operation records.

2. *Making Records Available to the Government:* "Government Representatives ordinarily review and use records at the places where the contractor keeps them. If test records are maintained in a laboratory office, for example, the government should expect to use them there...Financial audits are used to verify the accuracy and completeness of fiscal records, and assure their validity as a basis for financial management. Quality management can obtain the same assurance by carefully validating the records used to make decisions, report achievements and identify problems. Contractor inspection alone does not suffice. The Government also needs to sample contractor record keeping practices." The government will require a contractor to show all records (as required by various agencies within the government).

MIL-I-45208A and MIL-HDBK-H51, states, "The contractor shall maintain adequate records of all inspections and tests. The records shall indicate the nature and number of observations made, the number and type of deficiencies found, the quantities approved and rejected and the nature of corrective action taken as appropriate...Records are considered one of the principal aspects of objective evidence in quality." On the subject of deficiencies, refer to DLAR 8200.10. All contractors should be aware of the nature of this publication, it applies to MIL-Q-9858A and MIL-I-45208A contractors alike. It is one of the many good reasons why top management of a company (board chairmen, company presidents and comptrollers) should know where every expense that is incurred and every profit that is realized, comes from.

AQAP-1, states, "The contractor shall develop and maintain records that demonstrate the effective operation of the System. These records shall be analyzed and used by the contractor in managing the System. Pertinent subcontractor records are an element of this data. Records shall as appropriate include explicit identification of material, part, sub-assembly, assembly, equipment sub-system or system; the nature and number of observations made, the number and type of deficiencies found, the quantities approved or rejected, and the nature of the corrective action taken. records shall be made available to the QAR." (Government Quality Assurance Representative).

AQAP-4 states approximately the same requirements as AQAP-1 and therefore will not be repeated.

QUALITY CONTROL PUBLICATION	QCP NO. 3.4.1
	PAGE NO. 1 OF 2
	ISSUE DATE:
TITLE: RECORD CONTROL	APPROVED BY:
	REVISION NO: 0
	REVISION DATE:

1.0 PURPOSE

The purpose of this quality control publication is to establish a procedure for the maintenance of all records that have been accumulated during the complete work/production cycle, and storage of the applicable records.

2.0 INTENT

This QCP is applicable to all purchasing, inspection/test, process, assembly, production/manufacturing, calibration, MRB, engineering and all other records pertaining to the total work cycle.

3.0 APPLICABLE FORMS, PUBLICATIONS, PROCEDURES AND RECORDS

3.1 Inspection Stamp Records, QCP 2.2.1.

3.2 Quality Audit Records, Chapter 5.

3.3 Quality Workshop Records, Chapter 5.

3.4 Training and Certification Records, Chapter 5.

3.5 Quality Planning Records, Chapter 7.

3.6 Inspection/Test Records, Chapters 8, 13, 16, 20, 21, 22, and 23.

3.7 Nonconforming material and C/A Records, Chapters 9 and 17.

3.8 Purchasing Records, Chapter 20.

3.9 Cost of Quality Records, Chapter 10.

3.10 Drawing Change Control Records, Chapter 10.

3.11 Handling, Storage and Delivery Records, Chapter 14.

3.12 Process and Production Records, Chapter 18.

3.13 Materials: Company and Government Control Records, Chapters 18 and 20.

QUALITY CONTROL PUBLICATION	QCP NO. 3.4.1
	PAGE NO. 2 OF 2
	ISSUE DATE:
TITLE: RECORD CONTROL	APPROVED BY:
	REVISION NO: 0
	REVISION DATE:

3.14 MIRR Records, Appendix I.

3.15 Scrap Records, Chapters 17 and 23.

3.16 Raw Material Control Records, Chapter 23.

4.0 PROCEDURE

4.1 A records and document storage department that is operated under the direction of the comptrollers office has been established in order to control and maintain all company records.

4.2 Access to these records by approved personnel is to be documented by personnel in control (as assigned) of the records department.

4.3 The data to be included in this system will include, but is not limited to: 1. Financial records 2. All cost records 3. All inspection/test records 4. Records of all engineering documentation, including, ECO's, ECP's drawings, waivers/deviations. 5. Material and calibration control records 6. Failure records 7. Purchasing records 8. Warranty records 9. Customer records And any other records that are requred to be kept due to contract and/or purchase order requirements/specifications and by the various government auditors.

4.4 Unless otherwise specified, all records are to be kept in its original form for a period of five years. Financial records are to be kept in their original form for a period of ten years.

4.5 After the original time period has elapsed, the records are to be micro-fiched and stored in the climatically controlled vault.

4.6 The records that are kept in the records and documentment storage area, are to be clearly marked as to contents, retention dates and the departments responsible for the contents.

CHAPTER TWENTY

Control of Purchases

CONTROL OF PURCHASES

The requirements of MIL-Q-9858A in regards to subcontractor/vendor *purchasing data* and the *responsibility for the control of purchases,* complement each other in assuring that subcontractor and vendor supplies and services are meeting the requirements of the contract. The prime contractor has to be assured it is receiving supplies and material that will, when integrated into a finished product, meet the requirements and specifications of the contract. It has been found that these requirements can not be met, unless effective controls have been established.

MIL-HDBK-H50 of MIL-Q-9858A, paragraph 5.2, states, "The contractor's quality program shall not be acceptable to the government unless the contractor requires of his subcontractors a quality effort achieving control of the quality of the services and supplies which they provide." Paragraph 5.1 states, "The contractor is responsible for assuring that all supplies and services procured from his suppliers (subcontractors and vendors) conform to the contract requirements." Many contractors have had their quality system turned down due to the lack of understanding of this basic requirement. One word of warning is appropriate here. If the contractor's system is found unacceptable by the government due to incomplete and nonconforming procedures and the ability to perform to the requirements of a contract are in serious doubt, then at the discretion of the government the proposed contract could be terminated. Usually, contract negotiations, pre-award and post-award surveys and conferences will give the contractor the time needed to straighten out the quality system deficiencies. It must be remembered, *the system must be in place prior to the start of production.* Various methods are used by contractors to assure adequate supplier control of quality. A few of the most frequently used methods are:

a. *Contractor evaluation of supplier past performance for the type of purchases involved (vendor rating system).* Do you have a documented rating system, by vendors, to qualify them?

b. *Contractor inspection (and audits) at subcontractor's and vendor's plants.*

c. *Review of supplier's test and inspection records.* Do you require inspection and/or test records from your suppliers/vendors? Do you require actual physical and/or chemical analysis records for the material you are purchasing? Do you require certifications and traceability to NBS for the inspection/test equipment you are purchasing?

d. *Receiving inspection of supplier's products.* What inspections/tests can only be accomplished at the subcontractors/suppliers facility? What inspections/tests can be accomplished at the contractor's facility? Is the subcontractor inspecting/testing to the applicable characteristics and using an acceptable inspection plan?

Subcontracts and purchase orders of many contractors require suppliers to maintain quality records such as inspection and test results. The contractor also may require information about inspections and tests made by the supplier during manufacturing. Actions which the prime contractor cannot duplicate. Often the contractor will require delivery of such records along with the material they cover. When such records accompany shipments, the contractor knows more about the quality of the purchases. In defense industries, the relationships between contractors and suppliers consist mainly of practices intended to meet the objectives and requirements of the contracts with DOD.

MIL-I-45208A and MIL-HDBK-H51 state the requirements for purchasing control and data in a manner related to an inspection system. In MIL-HDBK-H51, paragraph 3.11.3, Referenced data, states, "A prime contractor is solely and exclusively responsible for the quality of all material delivered to the government regardless of the source of the product...Contractors who obtain materials from subcontractors must establish effective controls to assure the quality of these supplies. Such controls may be either in the contractor's plant (if the characteristics of the material can be readily inspected/tested) or in the subcontractor's plant (if the characteristics to be inspected/tested can not be readily checked at the contractor's plant, such as soldering, part material conformance, etc.) In either event the contractor is equally responsible for the quality of the supplies and must be able to provide to the Government QAR, objective evidence which will demonstrate the quality of the supplies...All documents and referenced data for purchases applying to a government contract shall be available for review by the government representative to determine compliance with the requirements for the control of such purchases." Is the contractor passing down to subcontractors, vendors or suppliers, the quality requirements of the contract? If the prime contract has the MIL-Q-9858A requirement in it, the contractor might not want to pass the full requirement down to its suppliers. Selected paragraphs from MIL-Q-9858A, that would assure the contractor its supplier's product control, could be passed to the suppliers. Many of the requirements in the MIL-Q-9858A program, may not be applicable to a particular supplier due to the material the contractor is purchasing. The same holds true for some of the requirements of the MIL-I-45208A inspection requirements. No matter what the contractor may choose to do, it is still the contractor's responsibility to make sure that all supplies and services conform to the contract.

AQAP-1, paragraph 210, states, "The contractor is responsible for ensuring that all purchased material and services conform to contract requirements. The subcontractor's control of quality shall be reviewed by the contractor at intervals consistent with the nature of the product and the subcontractor's demonstrated performance. This responsibility shall include, if need be, monitoring by the contractor's staff at the subcontractor's plant. The selection sources, and the type and extent of controls exercised by the contractor, shall be dependent upon the type of material and services and the subcontractor's demonstrated capability. The contractor shall provide objective evidence that his controls and those of his subcontractors are effective." Following, is the NATO requirement under Purchasing: "The purchasing document shall contain a complete and clear description of the material and services ordered with adequate direction for ensuring its quality control/inspection. The document shall include, as applicable:

1. The type, class, style, grade or other precise identification.
2. The title or other positive identification and applicable issue of specifications, drawings, process requirements or other relevant technical data. (This part refers to revision control).
3. The quality control/inspection requirements. For example, the appropriate AQAP or other quality requirements. (Or portions of the applicable requirement, as discussed previously). Other quality requirements could be, example: electrostatic controls, purchasing of a qualified product or specifications prefixed parts/material.
4. Change control instructions. (Engineering change control or requests for Deviations/Waivers).
5. Provision for government quality assurance at the subcontractor's plant as referenced in paragraph 210(d)." This was discussed in Chapter 13.

The AQAP-4 requirement is similar to the AQAP-1 requirement and as such will not be shown in this chapter. Some of the requirements, such as *Receiving Inspection* and *Verification of Purchased Material* are discussed in other chapters of this book. Paragraph 205 of AQAP-4 states the requirement.

QUALITY CONTROL PUBLICATION	QCP NO. 5.1.1
	PAGE NO. 1 OF 5
	ISSUE DATE:
TITLE: REQUEST FOR SUPPLIER/ VENDOR EVALUATION	APPROVED BY:
	REVISION NO: 0
	REVISION DATE:

1.0 PURPOSE

This quality control publication establishes the method and procedures for the requesting of an evaluation of a vendor or supplier to determine if the supplier has the continued ability to supply the necessary material, parts, subassemblies, assemblies that have been purchased previously.

2.0 INTENT

This QCP is to be used by those organizational elements of the company that are responsible for the purchase of material, parts, etc., and by those organizational elements responsible for confirming the quality of those parts, material, subassemblies, assemblies or completed end items that is to be delivered to the government directly due to an in-house contract or indirectly through another prime contractor through a purchase order.

3.0 APPLICABLE FORMS, PUBLICATIONS AND PROCEDURES

3.1 Request For Supplier/Vendor Evaluation, Form 5.1.1-1.

3.2 Supplier/Vendor Evaluation report, Form 5.1.1-2.

4.0 PROCEDURE

4.1 When a new vendor, supplier, subcontractor is being considered as a source of raw material, other material, parts, subassemblies or assemblies, a request for supplier/vendor evaluation will be initiated and forwarded to the quality assurance department for action. This also applies to vendors and suppliers where there has been a request for re-evaluation.

4.2 The quality assurance department will notify the purchasing department that a request for evaluation has been received.

4.3 If due to a reliability study by the reliability engineering function it has been decided that an evaluation and/or review of a proposed or an

QUALITY CONTROL PUBLICATION	QCP NO. 5.1.1
	PAGE NO. 2 OF 5
	ISSUE DATE:
TITLE: REQUEST FOR SUPPLIER/ VENDOR EVALUATION	APPROVED BY:
	REVISION NO: 0
	REVISION DATE:

existing supplier or vendor has to be accomplished, the reliability engineering function will forward the Request for Supplier/Vendor Evaluation to the quality engineering manager for action.

4.4 It is the responsibility of the department and/or person requesting a vendor evaluation to be familiar with the applicable contract and/or purchase order requirements, specifications, and where applicable, be reasonably sure that the proposed vendor (in the case of new suppliers/ vendors) is capable of meeting the applicable requirements and specifications.

4.5 A request for an evaluation of a vendor or supplier is to be made utilizing the Request for Supplier/Vendor Evaluation, Form 5.1.1-1. This form will be filled out as follows:

1. This block is pre-adressed to the quality assurance dept.
2. The request number.
3. The name of the person requesting the evaluation.
4. The date of the request.
5. The department/department number requesting the evaluation.
6. The telephone number and/or extension of the person making the request.
7. The contract/purchase order.
8. The name and address of the vendor or supplier where the proposed evaluation would take place or vendor/supplier being evaluated (if a visit is not planned to the vendor/supplier facility).
9. The parts number of the items that are to be included in the evaluation.
10. The parts description.

QUALITY CONTROL PUBLICATION	QCP NO.
	PAGE NO. 3 OF 5
	ISSUE DATE:
TITLE: REQUEST FOR SUPPLIER/ VENDOR EVALUATION	APPROVED BY:
	REVISION NO: 0
	REVISION DATE:

11. The drawing number.
12. The specification number.
13. The defect code (as applicable).
14. The reason for the evaluation or re-evaluation. (comments)
15. The name of the vendor's personnel contacted.
16. The date contacted.
17. Vendor comments.

4.6 All requests for vendor/supplier evaluation are to be forwarded to the quality assurance department for evaluation and approval. Blocks 18 and 19 will then be filled in as follows:

18. Evaluation approved by: Name __________, Title __________, Department __________ .
19. Name of company personnel assigned to accomplish the evaluation.

4.7 The request is then forwarded to the purchasing department, if a vendor/supplier facility evaluation is to be performed. The purchasing department is responsible for contacting the vendor/supplier in order to make the necessary arrangements for the site evaluation. The following blocks in the request will then be completed and returned to the quality assurance department.

20. Scheduled date of the evaluation.
21. Names of the personnel to be contacted.

4.8 The quality assurance department will obtain from finance the necessary funds as required, and will make the arrangements for the needed travel and lodging.

QUALITY CONTROL PUBLICATION	QCP NO. 5.1.1
	PAGE NO. 4 OF 5
	ISSUE DATE:
TITLE: REQUEST FOR SUPPLIER/ VENDOR EVALUATION	APPROVED BY:
	REVISION NO: 0
	REVISION DATE:

4.9 When the supplier/vendor evaluation is completed, Form 5.1.1-2 will then be filled out as follows:

1. Supplier/vendor name and address.
2. Original request number. This is the number to be assigned to both the request and evaluation report.
3. A written evaluation of the supplier/vendor.
4. Recommended disposition. The recommended disposition will address the specific reasons for the evaluation as stated on Form 5.1.1-1 and will include an indication as to approval, disapproval or conditional approval (as required).
5. Reasons for an approval or disapproval.
6. If conditional approval has been given and approved by the manager of the Quality Assurance Department. What are the conditions, limitations, corrective action, etc. to be taken.
7. If the evaluation was a system evaluation, describe the recommendations made, and if required the corrective action to be accomplished by the supplier/vendor.
8. Names of the personnel who conducted the evaluation.
9. Department name/number. (The quality assurance department personnel will head all evaluations).
10. Date all corrective actions are to be completed.
11. Date of completion and final disposition.

4.10 The original request and the associated report will be returned to the initiator. Copies will be retained by Purchasing.

QUALITY CONTROL PUBLICATION TITLE:	QCP NO.
	PAGE NO. 5 OF 5
	ISSUE DATE:
	APPROVED BY:
	REVISION NO: 0
	REVISION DATE:

4.11 The quality assurance department will initiate and follow-up all corrective actions, and will make the necessary recommendations to the purchasing department as to the recommended status and/or reliability of the supplier/vendor.

REQUEST FOR SUPPLIER/VENDOR EVALUATION

QUALITY ASSURANCE DEPARTMENT (1)

REQUEST NUMBER (2)

PERSON REQUESTING EVALUATION (3)

DATE OF REQUEST (4)

REQUESTING DEPARTMENT (5)

TELEPHONE NO. (6)

CONTRACT/PURCHASE ORDER NO. (7)

NAME AND ADDRESS OF SUPPLIER (8)

PART NUMBER (9)

PART DESCRIPTION (10)

DRAWING NUMBER (11)

SPECIFICATION NO. (12)

DEFECT CODE (13)

EVALUATION/RE-EVALUATION REASONS: (14)

VENDOR'S PERSONNEL CONTACTED (15)

DATE CONTACTED (16)

VENDOR COMMENTS: (17)

EVALUATION APPROVED BY: (18)

ASSIGNED PERSONNEL (19)

SCHEDULED DATE (20)

NAME OF SUPPLIERS/ VENDORS PERSONNEL TO BE CONTACTED (21)

1. ______

2. ______

FORM 5.1.1-1

SUPPLIER/VENDOR EVALUATION REPORT	
REPORT NUMBER (2) ______ SUPPLIER/VENDOR NAME/ADDRESS AND TELEPHONE NO. (1) ______	
WRITTEN EVALUATION: (3)	
RECOMMENDED DISPOSITION: (4)	
REASON FOR APPROVAL/DISAPPROVAL: (5)	
CONDITIONAL APPROVAL CONDITIONS: (6)	
SYSTEM EVALUATION FINDINGS AND RECOMMENDATIONS: (7)	
NAME OF EVALUATOR: (8)	DEPARTMENT: (9)
DATE CORRECTIVE ACTION COMP. (10)	DATE OF FINAL DISPOSITION: (11)
FORM 5.1.1-2	

QUALITY CONTROL PUBLICATION	QCP NO. 5.1.2
	PAGE NO. 1 OF 2
	ISSUE DATE:
TITLE: QUALITY SURVEY OF NEW SUPPLIER/VENDOR	APPROVED BY:
	REVISION NO: 0
	REVISION DATE:

1.0 PURPOSE

This quality control publication establishes the method and procedures for surveying new suppliers, vendors and subcontractors, to determine if they have the capabilities of fulfilling the requirements, specifications and terms of the applicable contract and/or purchase order.

2.0 INTENT

This QCP is to be used by those organizational elements of the company that are responsible for the purchase of material, parts, subassemblies, assemblies, and by those organizational elements responsible for determining and confirming that the vendors, suppliers, subcontractors operations and supplies conforms to the terms and conditions of the contract and/or purchase order.

3.0 APPLICABLE FORMS, PROCEDURES AND PUBLICATIONS

3.1 Request For Supplier/Vendor Quality Evaluation - QCP 5.1.1.

3.2 Supplier/Vendor Evaluation Report, Form 5.1.2-1.

3.3 Supplier/Vendor Survey, Form 5.1.2-2.

3.4 Supplier/Vendor Evaluation Report, Form 5.1.1-2.

4.0 PROCEDURE

4.1 Requests for quality surveys will be initiated by the quality assurance department in conjunction with the purchasing department, the contract manager and the design engineering department.

4.2 All surveys are to be conducted by the quality assurance department. If the survey is to be a team survey, the QA member will act as the team leader. The other members of the survey team will be selected from the purchasing department, the project engineer, design engineering, and the contract manager for the particular contract and/or purchase order.

QUALITY CONTROL PUBLICATION	QCP NO. 5.1.2
	PAGE NO. 2 OF 2
	ISSUE DATE:
TITLE: QUALITY SURVEY OF NEW SUPPLIER/VENDOR	APPROVED BY:
	REVISION NO: 0
	REVISION DATE:

4.3 The purchasing department is responsible for making the formal survey arrangements with the supplier, vendor, subcontractor. This will include explaining the purpose of the survey, and, for scheduling the applicable survey time and dates. Arrangements will be made for the appropriate interfacing of the company's personnel with those of the vendor/supplier.

4.4 The Quality Survey Form, Form 5.1.2-1, will be initiated prior to performing the actual survey. Blocks 1 through 6 will be filled out at this time. Blocks 7 through 12 will be filled out during the survey and block 13 will be filled out by the Director of Quality Assurance after the evaluation of the survey has been completed.

4.5 At the time the survey begins at the vendor/supplier facility, an initial meeting will be held with the appropriate vendor/supplier management personnel, and any other personnel the vendor/supplier management representatives need at the meeting.

4.6 At the conclusion of the survey, an outbriefing will be held with the vendor/supplier management personnel. The interim findings of the survey will be discussed at this time, and interim recommendations will be made prior to the issuance of an official survey result report. All discussions and recommendations will be documented at the meeting. If it has been mutually agreed upon, minutes of the meeting will be recorded, and a copy will be distributed to the personnel at the meeting. The official survey results will be transmitted by letter after the visit.

4.7 The quality assurance department is to evaluate the survey findings in conjunction with other members of the survey team, and, is then to generate the Supplier/Vendor Evaluation Report, refer to QCP 5.1.1, Form 5.1.1-2.

SUPPLIER/VENDOR EVALUATION REPORT

DATE ________

SUPPLIER/VENDOR (NAME & ADDRESS) ①	PRODUCT LINE ②
	NO. OF PROD. PERSONNEL ③
	NO. OF QUAL. PERSONNEL ④

SUPPLIES/ITEMS TO BE PURCHASED ⑤

LIST APPLICABLE SPECIFICATIONS ⑥

SPECIAL REQUIREMENTS AND PROCESSES USED BY SUPPLIER/VENDOR ⑦

☐ SOLDERING	☐ PLATING	☐ HEAT TREAT
☐ CHARPY TEST	☐ X-RAY	☐ MAG. PARTICLE LIQUID PENETRANT
☐ WELDING BRAZING	☐ ROCKWELL TESTS	☐ POTTING MOLDING
☐ SHELF LIFE AGE CONTROL	☐ ADVANCED METROLOGY	☐ CALIBRATION
☐ AUTOMATED TEST EQUIPMENT	☐ COMPUTER SOFTWARE	☐ RELIABILITY MAINTAINABILITY
☐ CONFIGURATION MANAGEMENT	☐ FLIGHT RISK	☐ NUCLEAR

INSPECTION AND TEST EQUIPMENT TRACEABLE TO NBS: Yes ___ ⑧ No ___

ACCEPTABLE INSPECTION/QUALITY MANUAL: Yes ___ No ___ ⑨

CONTRACT OR PURCHASE ORDER NUMBER ⑩

SURVEY LEADERS NAME (signature) ⑪	QUALITY DIRRECTOR (signature) ⑫

FORM 5.1.2-1

SUPPLIER/VENDOR SURVEY Page 1 of 10
QUALITY ASSURANCE EVALUATION
FORM 5.1.2-2

SUPPLIER ______________________ DATE OF SURVEY/EVALUATION
ADDRESS ______________________
______________________ TELEPHONE NUMBER ______________
______________________ NAME OF QC DIRECTOR ______________
______________________ Name of Team Leader ______________

1.0 QUALITY ASSURANCE PROCEDURES	YES	NO
1.1 The Quality Assurance Department's authority and responsibility is documented and approved by top management, ie. (President, Vice-President, owner, Plant Manager).		
1.2 The Quality Assurance Departments Director/Manager reports directly to top management, as in 1.1.		
1.3 The Quality Assurance Department has an employee training and development system.		
1.4 There is a Quality Assurance Manual that has been accepted by the Government.		
1.5 There is a system for the updating of the QA Manual.		
1.6 The QA Department has the authority to withhold discrepant and/or nonconforming material from the production cycle.		
1.7 The QA Department has the authority to withhold material until the proper and approved corrective action has been obtained.		
1.8 Is there a procedure for the qualification of all automatic test equipment, including the verification of the software used. QA department verification of software.		
1.9 Does the QA Department have procedures for the control of all inspection, test and identification stamps.		
1.10 Are there acceptable procedures for the dispositioning and documentation of nonconforming materials/supplies and Material Review Board Actions. Do these procedures include the transmittal of this information in the form of Cost of		

SUPPLIER/VENDOR SURVEY Page 2 of 10
QUALITY ASSURANCE EVALUATION
FORM 5.1.2-2

SUPPLIER ____________________ DATE OF SURVEY/EVALUATION
ADDRESS ____________________
____________________ TELEPHONE NUMBER ____________________
____________________ NAME OF QC DIRECTOR ____________________
____________________ Name of Team Leader ____________________

1.0 QUALITY ASSURANCE PROCEDURES	YES	NO
Quality reporting to the top levels of management. This is a MIL-Q-9858A requirement.		
1.11 Is there an adequate system for the reporting and documentation of all inspections and tests.		

COMMENTS:

2.0 CONTROL OF PURCHASES	YES	NO
2.1 There is a system for the evaluation of suppliers, vendors and subcontractors.		
2.2 There is a vendor rating system.		
2.3 Purchase orders state the necessary requirements for all purchases of material, parts and other goods.		
2.4 Purchase orders contain the necessary accept/reject criteria. This includes the necessary levels of acceptance as required by the specification requirements as stated on our purchase orders, drawings.		
2.5 The purchase orders clearly describe the work to be accomplished.		
2.6 The purchase orders specify the necessary documentation that is required.		
2.7 Quality Assurance systems requirements are stated on the purchase orders.		

SUPPLIER/VENDOR SURVEY Page 3 of 10
QUALITY ASSURANCE EVALUATION
FORM 5.1.2-2

SUPPLIER ______________________ DATE OF SURVEY/EVALUATION
ADDRESS ______________________
______________________ TELEPHONE NUMBER ______________
______________________ NAME OF QC DIRECTOR ______________
______________________ Name of Team Leader ______________

2.0 CONTROL OF PURCHASES	YES	NO
2.8 The purchase order specify the necessary material certifications when required.		
2.9 The purchase orders require the necessary physical and/or chemical analysis be transmitted with the raw material.		
2.10 The purchase orders require source inspection when the material and/or product to be delivered can not be adequately verified in receiving inspection.		
2.11 Source inspectors have ready access to the appropriate drawings, specifications, and inspection and/or test equipment as required to prove product quality.		
2.12 If there are requirements for shelf life and/or age control of materials, these requirements are passed down.		

COMMENTS:

3.0 CONTROL OF PURCHASED MATERIAL/GOODS		
3.1 The Receiving Inspection Department is being provided with the necessary drawings, specifications and other documentation in order to verify the quality of the received materials, parts, subsystems.		
3.2 Receiving Inspection is verifying the status of material received. Does the material received conform to the chemical and/or physical analysis as required by the		

SUPPLIER/VENDOR SURVEY Page 4 of 10
QUALITY ASSURANCE EVALUATION
FORM 5.1.2-2

SUPPLIER ____________________ DATE OF SURVEY/EVALUATION
ADDRESS ____________________
____________________ TELEPHONE NUMBER ____________
____________________ NAME OF QC DIRECTOR ____________
____________________ Name of Team Leader ____________

3.0 CONTROL OF PURCHASED MATERIAL/GOODS	YES	NO
purchase Order. Are the required chemical and/or physical analysis being transmitted with the material.		
3.3 If any nonconformances and/or discrepancies are found, is the required nonconforming dispositions being accomplished. Are the correct corrective actions being requested and obtained.		
3.4 Is the inspection and/or test equipment that is being used in receiving inspection calibrated and traceable to the National Bureau of Standards (NBS).		
3.5 If source inspection was required at a supplier/vendor facility, are the required source inspection reports accompanying the material, goods.		
3.6 If Government Source Inspection was required on purchased material, is the Government Quality Assurance Representative being notified when the material and/or goods are received.		
3.7 Are the indication(s) (stamps, signatures, dates, reports) of either company source inspection or Government Source Inspection on or with (as required) the received material and/or goods. If not, is this discrepancy being reported to the Quality Assurance Department and the Government representative.		
3.8 Is the material and/or goods received being protected from damage. If there are any special handling requirements for the material/goods, are these requirements being followed.		

SUPPLIER/VENDOR SURVEY Page 5 of 10
QUALITY ASSURANCE EVALUATION
FORM 5.1.2-2

SUPPLIER ____________ DATE OF SURVEY/EVALUATION
ADDRESS ____________
____________ TELEPHONE NUMBER ____________
____________ NAME OF QC DIRECTOR ____________
____________ Name of Team Leader ____________

3.0 CONTROL OF PURCHASED MATERIAL/GOODS		
COMMENTS:		

4.0 IN-PROCESS INSPECTION/TESTS, WORK INSTRUCTIONS, PROCESS CONTROL	YES	NO
4.1 Are all work instructions, including, inspection, test, production, assembly, special processes, approved, documented and to the latest revision(s).		
4.2 Are all work instructions and drawings clear, concise, not marked up, and reflect the latest accept reject criteria.		
4.3 Are all nonconformances/discrepancies being reported and the material/parts associated with these discrepancies being segregated from conforming material/parts.		
4.4 Are acceptable and approved dispositions being accomplished by the MRB, and acceptable corrective actions being obtained.		
4.5 Are all processes being controlled to the requirement(s) of the specifications and contract/purchase order.		
4.6 Are there adequate procedures for the handling and storage of all material/goods.		
4.7 If machine and/or operator certifications are required, are the necessary certifications documented and provisions being		

SUPPLIER/VENDOR SURVEY Page 6 of 10
QUALITY ASSURANCE EVALUATION
FORM 5.1.2-2

SUPPLIER ______________ DATE OF SURVEY/EVALUATION
ADDRESS ______________
______________ TELEPHONE NUMBER ______________
______________ NAME OF QC DIRECTOR ______________
______________ Name of Team Leader ______________

4.0 IN-PROCESS INSPECTION/TESTS, WORK INSTRUCTIONS, PROCESS CONTROL	YES	NO
made for the recertification of these machines and operators as required by established and approved procedures.		
4.8 Are all inspection/test, production, and special process work instructions being used by the applicable personnel.		
4.9 Are the appropriate accept/reject criteria available to all personnel. Are the personnel using these criteria.		
4.10 Is all inspection/test and process control instrumentation calibrated and traceable to the National Bureau of Standards.		
4.11 Is all work being accomplished and documented as required.		
4.12 Does the supplier/vendor maintain a system that prevents uninspected material/goods from being incorporated into the next level of assembly.		
4.13 If company or Government furnished units of material are either being used or are to be incorporated into the finished product, are these units/material being adequately protected to prevent damage. Are there approved procedures for the control of such material/equipment.		

COMMENTS:

SUPPLIER/VENDOR SURVEY Page 7 of 10
QUALITY ASSURANCE EVALUATION
FORM 5.1.2-2

SUPPLIER ______________________ DATE OF SURVEY/EVALUATION
ADDRESS ______________________
______________________ TELEPHONE NUMBER ______________
______________________ NAME OF QC DIRECTOR ______________
______________________ Name of Team Leader ______________

5.0 MEASURING AND TEST EQUIPMENT AND DEVICES, JIGS, FIXTURES	YES	NO
5.1 Are there adequate and accepted procedures for the control and maintenance of all measuring, test, special process instrumentation, jigs and fixtures used as a media of inspection, and all other equipment that is used to control product quality.		
5.2 Is all calibrated equipment including the standards used to calibrate such equipment, traceable to the National Bureau of Standards.		
5.3 Is there a documented and approved system for the recall and recalibration of all the above equipment.		
5.4 Is there a procedure to prevent personal equipment from being used in the production cycle unless such equipment is put into the calibration system.		
5.5 Is there a procedure that provides for the calibration of any equipment, that is used to prove the quality of the final product, that have been reworked or repaired.		
5.6 Does the calibration system provide for the identification of all of the above equipment.		
5.7 Does the calibration system provide for the labeling or if not practical, the color coding of all the above equipment, that indicates when the equipment was last calibrated, when the next calibration date is due.		

COMMENTS:

SUPPLIER/VENDOR SURVEY Page 8 of 10
QUALITY ASSURANCE EVALUATION
FORM 5.1.2-2

SUPPLIER ______________________ DATE OF SURVEY/EVALUATION
ADDRESS ______________________
______________________ TELEPHONE NUMBER ______________
______________________ NAME OF QC DIRECTOR ______________
______________________ Name of Team Leader ______________

6.0 REVIEW AND CONTROL OF NONCONFORMING MATERIAL	YES	NO
6.1 Does the supplier/vendor maintain a documented and approved system for the handling, dispositioning, and obtaining the appropriate corrective action for nonconforming material.		
6.2 Does the system include provisions for the segregation of nonconforming and conforming material. (Even at the work station).		
6.3 Is there provisions for a controlled holding area (locked) that will prevent nonconforming material from getting into the next assembly and/or finished product.		
6.4 Does the system make provisions for the readily identifiable identification of finished product that contains nonconforming material, parts, subassemblies.		
6.5 Does the system provide for the prompt disposition and corrective action in relation to nonconforming material.		
6.6 Does the system include acceptable methods and procedures for the reporting of costs associated with nonconforming material.		
6.7 Does the system include a method for the identification of nonconforming material to a particular Government contract or purchase order.		
6.8 Does the system include methods and procedures for the notification of the prime contractor and Government when nonconforming material is found.		

SUPPLIER/VENDOR SURVEY Page 9 of 10
QUALITY ASSURANCE EVALUATION
FORM 5.1.2-2

SUPPLIER ____________________ DATE OF SURVEY/EVALUATION
ADDRESS ____________________
____________________ TELEPHONE NUMBER ____________
____________________ NAME OF QC DIRECTOR ____________
____________________ Name of Team Leader ____________

6.0 REVIEW AND CONTROL OF NONCONFORMING MATERIAL	YES	NO
6.9 Does the system provide for prime contractor or Government approval of all dispositions that involve Government contracts and/or purchase orders. 6.10 Have any dispositions been made in relation to Government contracts and/or purchase orders where the Government had not been notified that such conditions exist.		

COMMENTS:

7.0 FINAL QC INSPECTION/TEST AND SHIPPING CONTROLS		
7.1 Does the supplier/vendor maintain a documented and approved system for the final inspection and test of all deliverable product prior to the packaging and shipping of such product. 7.2 Does the system include provisions for the verification of the completion of all work and inspection/test operations prior to the supplier/vendor final acceptance, and prior to seeking final acceptance of the product by the prime contractor or the Government. 7.3 Does the system provide for the reporting and dispositioning of nonconforming product prior to final QC acceptance.		

SUPPLIER/VENDOR SURVEY Page 10 of 10
QUALITY ASSURANCE EVALUATION
FORM 5.1.2-2

SUPPLIER ____________ DATE OF SURVEY/EVALUATION
ADDRESS ____________
____________ TELEPHONE NUMBER ____________
____________ NAME OF QC DIRECTOR ____________
____________ Name of Team Leader ____________

7.0 FINAL QC INSPECTION/TEST AND SHIPPING CONTROLS	YES	NO
7.4 Does the system provide for the finalizing of all discrepancies prior to final acceptance of product.		
7.5 Does the system provide for the formal acceptance of the completed product at final QC prior to requesting customer and/or Government acceptance.		
7.6 Does the system provide for a documented and accepted procedure for the acceptance of all required documentation and computer software, manuals, source inspection reports, and other contractually required documentation prior to seeking acceptance of such by the prime contractor or Government.		
7.7 Does the system provide for the acceptance of the packaging requirements and inspection of such upon completion, prior to requesting prime contractor of Government acceptance.		
7.8 Are there written and accurate instructions for the preservation and packaging of completed product.		
7.9 Are these instructions as required by the contract or purchase order. Have they been accepted and approved by		

COMMENTS:

QUALITY CONTROL PUBLICATION	QCP NO. 5.1.3
	PAGE NO. 1 OF 2
	ISSUE DATE:
TITLE: SUPPLIER/VENDOR QUALITY EVALUATION REPORT	APPROVED BY:
	REVISION NO: 0
	REVISION DATE:

1.0 PURPOSE

This quality control publication establishes the procedure for reporting of the results of supplier, vendor, subcontractor surveys.

2.0 INTENT

This QCP applies to all surveys of suppliers, vendors, subcontractors, and the responsibility of the quality assurance department in evaluating and reporting the results of surveys, evaluations and re-evaluations.

3.0 APPLICABLE FORMS, PROCEDURES AND PUBLICATIONS

3.1 Supplier/Vendor Evaluation Report, Form 5.1.1-2.

3.2 Supplier/Vendor Evaluation Report, Form 5.1.2-1.

3.3 Supplier/Vendor Survey, Form 5.1.2-2.

4.0 PROCEDURE

4.1 All quality surveys are to be reviewed and evaluated by the Quality Assurance Department.

4.2 The quality assurance department in conjunction with the purchasing department is to review the supplier/vendor history records to determine, if the particular supplier or vendor has been utilized previously, whether or not the suppliers or vendors past history of performance will make the supplier or vendor eligible for further material acquisitions.

4.3 There are three possible recommended dispositions for any supplier/vendor evaluation, they are as follows:

1. Approved.
2. Disapproval.
3. Conditional approval.

QUALITY CONTROL PUBLICATION	QCP NO. 5.1.3
	PAGE NO. 2 OF 2
	ISSUE DATE:
TITLE: SUPPLIER/VENDOR QUALITY EVALUATION REPORT	APPROVED BY:
	REVISION NO: 0
	REVISION DATE:

Conditional approval is given on the basis that the supplier, vendor or subcontractor will take the required corrective action to eliminate all nonconformances, problems and/or discrepancies found during the survey that were minor in nature. The corrective action will be reviewed by the quality assurance department, including the quality engineering and reliability engineering functions of QA, and the appropriate recommendations will be made based on the adequacy of the corrective actions taken. The recommendations made will be either to approve or disapprove the supplier, vendor or subcontractor.

4.4 The Supplier/Vendor Evaluation Report, Form 5.1.1-2, QCP 5.1.1 will be filled out by the quality assurance department as described in QCP 5.1.1, paragraph 4.9.

4.5 A copy of every Supplier/Vendor Evaluation Report, with a copy of the survey report attached, will be transmitted to the purchasing department for the appropriate actions. The master copies are to be maintained by the quality assurance department. If the reports are computer generated or the reporting system is part of a database, all of the necessary data will be recorded into the database for present and future determinations as to the adequacy of all vendors, suppliers and subcontractors.

QUALITY CONTROL PUBLICATION	QCP NO. 5.1.4
	PAGE NO. 1 OF 3
	ISSUE DATE:
TITLE: SUPPLIER/VENDOR PROCESS CERTIFICATION	APPROVED BY:
	REVISION NO: 0
	REVISION DATE:

1.0 PURPOSE

This quality control publication establishes the method and procedure for requesting an evaluation of a suppliers vendors, subcontractors specific process controls that is required by a contract or purchase order, to determine if the supplier, vendor, subcontractor is in fact controlling a specific process where the highest quality of a deliverable product is of importance due to the critical nature of the finished material, parts, subassemblies, assemblies that are to be delivered.

2.0 INTENT

This QCP applies to specific special processes that have been determined to be of the latest state of the art, and that they need special controls to prevent nonconformances and discrepancies from being infused into the final product, which would result in a mission failure or loss of life.

3.0 APPLICABLE FORMS, PROCEDURES AND PUBLICATIONS

3.1 Request For Supplier/Vendor Evaluation, Form 5.1.1-1.

3.2 Supplier/Vendor Evaluation Report, Form 5.1.2-1.

3.3 Supplier/Vendor Evaluation Report, Form 5.1.1-2.

3.4 Supplier/Vendor Process Certification, Form 5.1.4-1.

4.0 PROCEDURE

4.1 All requests for supplier, vendor evaluations and certifications are processed by the quality assurance department. These requests are generated by the project engineer, manufacturing/production engineering, design engineering, quality engineering and reliability engineering.

4.2 The quality assurance department is responsible for the planning and implementation of the requested evaluations and certifications.

QUALITY CONTROL PUBLICATION	QCP NO. 5.1.4
	PAGE NO. 2 OF 3
	ISSUE DATE:
TITLE: SUPPIER/VENDOR PROCESS CERTIFICATION	APPROVED BY:
	REVISION NO: 0
	REVISION DATE:

4.3 The request will be made out utilizing Form 5.1.1-1, QCP 5.1.1.

4.4 The evaluation and survey results will be documented on the forms pictured in Forms 5.1.2-1 and 5.1.1-2. Form 5.1.1-2 will be used to document the recommendations made due to the results of the survey.

4.5 If it has been determined that a vendor's, supplier's, or subcontractor's specific process contains inadequacies, nonconformances, or discrepancies that can not be resolved during the evaluation and/or survey, and further corrective action must be accomplished before a process can be certified, a Corrective Action Request, Form 3.5.1-1, will be filled in and submitted to the quality assurance department. This form and the method in which it is to be filled in is found in QCP 3.5.1. All inadequacies and nonconformances must be corrected before the specific process will be considered for certification.

4.6 A Vendor Corrective Action Request (see QCP 3.5.2) will be initiated by the quality engineering function of the quality assurance department and after the necessary approvals, will be forwarded to the supplier, vendor, subcontractor for action an response.

4.7 If all inadequacies, nonconformances or discrepancies have been acted upon by the supplier, vendor, or subcontractor and the quality assurance departments approval has been acquired, or there were no inadequacies in the vendors, suppliers or subcontractors special process, a Certification of Compliance will be issued to the party involved. Form 5.1.4-1 will be filled out as follows:

1. The name and address of the vendor, supplier or subcontractor.
2. The process that is being certified.
3. The applicable specification numbers.
4. The certification number.
5. The date of certification.

QUALITY CONTROL PUBLICATION	QCP NO. 5.1.4
	PAGE NO. 3 OF 3
	ISSUE DATE:
TITLE: SUPPLIER/VENDOR PROCESS CERTIFICATION	APPROVED BY:
	REVISION NO: 0
	REVISION DATE:

6. The expiration date of the certification.
7. The name of the person in Quality Engineering that initiated the certification. The date signed.
8. The name of the person approving the certification (Quality Assurance Director). The date signed.
9. Comments applicable to certification and limitations established.

4.8 The approved certification is to be forwarded to the purchasing department, where a master record of certifications is to be maintained. A copy of the certification is to be maintained. A copy of the certification is to be forwarded to the vendor, supplier or subcontractor for their records.

4.9 A copy of the approved certification is to be forwarded to the requestor of the certification for record and information purposes.

4.10 A copy of the certification is to be filed by expiration date in a tickler file in the quality assurance department. If a computerized system is in place, this information will be entered into the appropriate blocks in the date base.

4.11 The certification tickler file or the computer record is to be continually reviewed by the quality assurance department for the purpose of establishing a certification and recertification review of all suppliers, vendors and subcontractors.

PROCESS CERTIFICATION OF COMPLIANCE

SUPPLIER NAME AND ADDRESS (1)	PROCESS CERTIFIED (2) APPLICABLE SPECIFICATIONS (3)
CERTIFICATION NUMBER (4)	DATE OF CERTIFICATION (5)
EXPIRATION DATE OF CERTIFICATION (6)	
NAME OF INITIATOR (7) DATE	NAME OF QUALITY DIRECTOR (8) DATE

THE SUPPLIER NAME ABOVE HAS BEEN
CERTIFIED IN THE PROCESS SO NAMED
IN BLOCK NUMBER 2 OF CERTIFICATE
AS OF THIS DAY OF ________ MONTH OF ______
YEAR ________

COMMENTS OR LIMITATIONS OF CERTIFICATION:

(9)

FORM 5.1.4-1	SIGNATURE OF QUALITY DIRECTOR

QUALITY CONTROL PUBLICATION	QCP NO. 5.1.5
	PAGE NO. 1 OF 3
	ISSUE DATE:
TITLE: QUALITY ASSURANCE REVIEWS OF CONTRACTS/ PURCHASE ORDERS	APPROVED BY:
	REVISION NO: 0
	REVISION DATE:

1.0 PURPOSE

This quality control publication establishes the method and procedures for the review of all purchase orders by the Quality Assurance Department prior to their release to suppliers, vendors, or subcontractors.

2.0 INTENT

This QCP applies to purchases of all material, supplies, parts, subassemblies, assemblies that are to be incorporated into a finished product or the completed product itself, and is to be offered to the government for acceptance.

3.0 APPLICABLE FORMS, PROCEDURES AND PUBLICATIONS

3.1 Purchase Orders.

3.2 Purchase Order Change Notices.

3.3 Subcontracts.

3.4 Inspection And Test Instructions, QCP 3.3.1 and 3.3.3.

3.5 Quality Specifications Transmittal Document, QSTP001, Appendix III.

3.6 GSI At Subcontractor Or Vendor Facilities, QCP 7.1.1.

4.0 PROCEDURE

4.1 Prior to the issuance of all purchase orders, the Purchasing Department is to submit all purchase orders to the quality assurance department for review.

4.2 The quality assurance department will submit copies of the reviews to the government quality assurance representative for possible inclusion of Government Source Inspection (GSI) into the purchase order (see QCP 7.1.1).

QUALITY CONTROL PUBLICATION	QCP NO. 5.1.5
	PAGE NO. 2 OF 3
	ISSUE DATE:
TITLE: QUALITY ASSURANCE REVIEWS OF CONTRACTS/ PURCHASE ORDERS	APPROVED BY:
	REVISION NO: 0
	REVISION DATE:

4.3 The quality assurance department is responsible for reviewing all purchase orders in order to have inserted into the purchase orders, the applicable quality requirements as specified by the government contract or purchase order, and any requirements or specifications that will control the quality of the purchased material/goods. This requirement is to assure that areas of quality control that can not be performed at this facility, due to the nature of the purchased goods, are in fact, controlled by the supplier, vendor, subcontractor at their facilities.

4.4 Applicable references to special controls, not specified in the Quality Specification Transmittal Document, are to be inserted into the purchasing document. Those controls and specifications that are contained in this document are to referenced by the applicable paragraph number of this document in the purchase order.

4.5 The Quality Specification Transmittal Document is to be forwarded to all vendors, suppliers and subcontractors together with the purchase order, with the applicable quality controls referenced on the purchase order. This document is used during the planning cycle of the contract or purchase order in order to determine what quality requirements and specifications are to be included into the purchase order. If further specifications or requirements have to be included into the purchasing documentation, they will be so annotated in the purchasing documentation.

4.5 After the purchase orders have been reviewed by QA, and the quality requirements have been determined for the purchasing document, the purchasing document will be returned to the Purchasing Department for inclusion of the applicable quality requirements and/or specifications into the purchasing documentation.

4.6 After the quality requirements have been inserted into the purchase order, the quality assurance department is to review the purchasing documentation for correctness and completeness of the quality

QUALITY CONTROL PUBLICATION	QCP NO. 5.1.5
	PAGE NO. 3 OF 3
	ISSUE DATE:
TITLE: QUALITY ASSURANCE REVIEWS OF CONTRACTS/ PURCHASE ORDERS	APPROVED BY:
	REVISION NO: 0
	REVISION DATE:

requirements. If the purchasing documentation does not reflect the appropriate quality clauses, the documentation is to be returned to the purchasing department with an explanation of what is missing or inaccurate, or to the additions and/or deletions needed.

4.7 When the quality assurance department has determined that the purchase order meets all of the quality requirements of the contract and/or purchase order, the purchase order is to be stamped with the applicable quality stamp, signed and dated in the appropriate places on the purchase order to indicate quality acceptance of the quality terms and conditions as correct and complete.

4.8 If government source inspection is a requirement of the purchase order, the quality assurance department is to verify that all of the required statements and government stamps have been included in the purchase order.

4.9 The quality assurance department is to maintain records of these purchasing documentation reviews, and the dispositioning of the purchase orders.

QUALITY CONTROL PUBLICATION	QCP NO. 5.1.6
	PAGE NO. 1 OF 3
	ISSUE DATE:
TITLE: SUPPLIER QUALITY RATING	APPROVED BY:
	REVISION NO: 0
	REVISION DATE:

1.0 PURPOSE

This quality control publication establishes the methods and procedures for rating suppliers, vendors, and subcontractors in relation to their ability to produce a product that conforms to the contract or purchase order requirements and specifications.

2.0 INTENT

The rating system is to be used by the quality assurance and purchasing departments in determining if a particular supplier, vendor or subcontractor has the ability to deliver a quality product.

3.0 APPLICABLE FORMS, PROCEDURES AND PUBLICATIONS

3.1 Supplier/Vendor Evaluation Report, Form 5.1.1-2.

3.2 Receiving Inspection, QCP 6.1.1.

3.3 Raw Material Inspection, QCP 6.1.1.

3.4 Supplier, Vendor, Subcontractor Evaluation Reports, QCP 5.1.3.

3.5 Top Ten Recommended Supplier-Vendor-Subcontractor Report, Form 5.1.6-1.

4.0 PROCEDURE

4.1 The rating system consists of reports compiled by the quality assurance department and listed in a Top Ten Recommended Supplier, Vendor, Subcontractor Report, Form 5.1.6-1. This report is updated monthly by the quality assurance department.

4.2 The purchasing department is provided with a monthly updated copy of the report. This report will be used by the purchasing department when selecting suppliers who are to deliver the purchased material, parts, subassemblies or completed assemblies.

QUALITY CONTROL PUBLICATION	QCP NO. 5.1.6
	PAGE NO. 2 OF 3
	ISSUE DATE:
TITLE: SUPPLIER QUALITY RATING	APPROVED BY:
	REVISION NO: 0
	REVISION DATE:

4.3 The Study as pictured in Form 5.1.6-1 is to filled out as follows:

1. Date (year/month) of report.
2. Part or assembly number.
3. Part of assembly description.
4. Supplier, vendor or subcontractor's name and address.
5. Supplier, vendor or subcontractor's identification number (as assigned).
6. Material supplied under contract or purchase no. ________ .
7. Project or program no. ________.
8. Total number of nonconformances cited against this supplier.
9. Failure code (as assigned).
10. Corrective action code (as assigned).
11. Written description of corrective action taken.
12. Corrective action was complete and approved. Yes ______ No. _____.
13. Listed rating - 1 to 10 for this part, material, subassembly.
14. Listed rating - 1 to 10 for this supplier.
15. Percentage of quality.
16. Percentage of delivery. (Two formulas that could be used to figure these percentages are:

Quality: $\dfrac{\text{Items Accepted ( )}}{\text{Items Rejected ( )}} \times 100 = \text{AOQL} \_\_\_\_ \%$

QUALITY CONTROL PUBLICATION	QCP NO. 5.1.6
	PAGE NO. 3 OF 3
	ISSUE DATE:
TITLE: SUPPLIER QUALITY RATING	APPROVED BY:
	REVISION NO: 0
	REVISION DATE:

Delivery: $\dfrac{\text{Items Accepted ( )}}{\text{Items Rejected ( )}} \times 100 =$ ____ %

17. Report prepared by (name, title). (QA department)

18. Report approved by (name, title). (QA department Director)

4.4 This report is formatted in this book so that with minor changes it could be inserted into a computer database.

TOP TEN RECOMMENDED SUPPLIER-VENDOR-SUBCONTRACTOR REPORT

DATE ____________ (1)
(Y/M)

SUPPLIER NAME AND ADDRESS ______________________ (17) REPORT PREPARED BY ____________ DATE ________
(4) ______________________ REPORT APPROVED BY ____________ DATE ________
______________________ (18)

TELEPHONE NUMBER: ______________________

PART NUMBER	PART DESCRIPTION	SUPPLIER ID. NO.	CONTRACT/P.O. NO.	PROJECT NO.
(2)	(3)	(5)	(6)	(7)

TOTAL NONCONF.	FAILURE CODE	C/A CODE	WRITTEN DESCRIPTION OF CORRE. ACTIONS TAKEN	CORR. ACTION COMP./APPR.	PART RATING	SUPPLIER RATING	QUAL. AOQL	DEL. %
(8)	(9)	(10)	(11)	YES NO (12)	(13)	(14)	(15)	(16)

FORM 5.1.6-1

QUALITY CONTROL PUBLICATION	QCP NO. 5.1.7
	PAGE NO. 1 OF 3
	ISSUE DATE:
TITLE: SUPPLIER/VENDOR PART QUALIFICATION	APPROVED BY:
	REVISION NO: 0
	REVISION DATE:

1.0 PURPOSE

This quality control publication establishes the methods and procedures to evaluate and qualify all purchased parts and material at the earliest stages of the planning and production cycle and to establish their reliability prior to their incorporation into any product to be delivered under a contract or purchase order.

2.0 INTENT

This QCP applies to all parts or material purchased from vendors and suppliers, and the role of the quality engineering, reliability engineering, design engineering, production/manufacturing engineering departments' responsibility for verifying the quality of purchased parts and material. This includes the purchasing of parts and material that are listed in the applicable, Qualified Product Lists, or parts and material that are listed in the specifications of a contract or purchase orders as approved material and/or parts to be used by definition.

3.0 APPLICABLE FORMS, PROCEDURES AND PUBLICATIONS

3.1 Supplier/Vendor Quality Evaluation Report, QCP 5.1.3.

3.2 Contract Quality Requirement Analysis, QCP 3.2.1.

3.3 Reliability Engineering's Contribution to the Planning Cycle, QCP 3.2.3.

3.4 Design Review Participation, QCP 3.2.4.

4.0 PROCEDURE

4.1 During the planning cycle (see Chapter 6) it was determined that parts and material to be purchased for suppliers, vendors and subcontractors would be subjected to a qualification process to verify that all

QUALITY CONTROL PUBLICATION	QCP NO. 5.1.7
	PAGE NO. 2 OF 3
	ISSUE DATE:
TITLE: SUPPLIER/VENDOR PART QUALIFICATION	APPROVED BY:
	REVISION NO: 0
	REVISION DATE:

purchased parts, material thus ordered will meet the requirements and specifications of the contract or purchase order.

4.2 Included in the purchase orders to vendors, suppliers, subcontractors will be the requirements for the qualification of material and parts as applicable. These requirements will be transmitted by the quality assurance department to the purchasing departments and will become part of the purchase order. The forms in which the qualification requests of parts and material will take will be as follows:

1. Parts and material certifications - These certifications will as a minimum include the applicable physical/chemical analysis of the material, and will include as applicable, documented results of the inspections and tests as provided for by the specification.
2. Source inspection at the suppliers, vendor or subcontractors facility. (If due to the criticality of the parts or material, or due to material, parts, vendor history).

4.3 All parts, material, subassemblies, assemblies received for the first time, or due to prior parts, material, or supplier history, will be subjected to a first article approval prior to acceptance by the receiving inspection department and stocking of these items. First Article Testing, will also be required of all incoming parts, material, subassemblies, assemblies if there has been any:

1. Change in the location of the supplier location.
2. Changes in the suppliers/vendors/subcontractors critical personnel or methods of manufacturing, inspection or testing.

4.4 The results of qualification inspection/testing or analysis and the impact of these results will be recorded on the form as pictured in Form 5.1.1-1.

QUALITY CONTROL PUBLICATION	QCP NO. 5.1.7
	PAGE NO. 3 OF 3
	ISSUE DATE:
TITLE: SUPPLIER/VENDOR PART QUALIFICATION	APPROVED BY:
	REVISION NO: 0
	REVISION DATE:

4.5 Receiving inspection upon receipt of parts, material or subassemblies will either inspect the parts, material or subassemblies to their respective inspection procedures (see QCP 6.1.1), or if required, will forward the parts or material to the materials laboratory for the applicable inspection, testing and/or analysis.

4.6 The materials laboratory will perform the required inspection, testing, analysis report will be made out (see QCP 6.1.1 and 6.1.2) documenting the results, conclusions and recommendations and forwarded to the receiving inspection department for the appropriate action.

4.7 Upon receiving the above report, receiving inspection will prepare Forms 5.1.1-1 and -2, and distribute the report as follows:

1. A copy will be kept in the receiving inspection department for action and records.
2. If nonconformances were found, a copy of the report and the applicable parts, material or subassemblies will be forwarded to the MRB holding area for disposition, with a copy of the report forwarded to the purchasing department for action.
3. A copy will be forwarded to quality engineering and quality assurance management for notification and action.
4. A copy will be forwarded to the project engineer for information purposes and possible action.

QUALITY CONTROL PUBLICATION	QCP NO. 5.1.8
	PAGE NO. 1 OF 6
	ISSUE DATE:
TITLE: SOURCE INSPECTION AT VENDOR/SUPPLIER FACILITY	APPROVED BY:
	REVISION NO: 0
	REVISION DATE:

1.0 PURPOSE

This quality control publication establishes the methods and procedures for the accomplishment of the required and planned for source inspection at vendor, suppliers and subcontractors facilities.

2.0 INTENT

This QCP establishes the responsibilities of the quality assurance department in the planning for, and the accomplishment of source inspection of materials and supplies at facilities other than in-house inspection and testing prior to the acceptance of such material and supplies.

3.0 APPLICABLE FORMS, PROCEDURES AND PUBLICATIONS

3.1 Request For Source Inspection at Vendor/Supplier/Subcontractor Facility, Form 5.1.8-1.

3.2 Source Inspection Scheduling Record, Form 5.1.8-2.

3.3 Source Inspection Report, Form 5.1.8-3.

3.4 Source Inspection Tag, Form 5.1.8-4.

3.5 Quality Specification Transmittal Document, QSTP, 001.

4.0 PROCEDURE

4.1 A request for source inspection will be initiated when it has been determined during the planning stage of a contract or purchase order, that due to the unusual, complex, or critical nature of the parts, material, subassemblies that are to be purchased, source inspection is necessary in order to verify, at those facilities, the quality of the product being purchased prior to acceptance of that product.

4.2 The quality assurance department is responsible for the initiating of this request. The Request For Source Inspection, Form 5.1.8-1, will be filled out as follows:

QUALITY CONTROL PUBLICATION	QCP NO. 5.1.8
	PAGE NO. 2 OF 6
	ISSUE DATE:
TITLE: SOURCE INSPECTION AT VENDOR/SUPPLIER FACILITY	APPROVED BY:
	REVISION NO: 0
	REVISION DATE:

1. The date of the request.
2. The companies name, address, telephone number, and the name of the person to be contacted at the vendors, suppliers, subcontractors facility, including that person's title.
3. The name, address, telephone number and title of the person who will accomplish the source inspection.
4. If this is a subcontracted source inspection, the name, address and telephone number of the company who is to perform the source inspection, including, the name and title of the management personnel contacted.
5. The purchase order number, if this request is for subcontracted source inspection.
6. The program or project number that is related to this request.
7. The contract or purchase order number.
8. The material, part, subassembly number of the product to be inspected.
9. The product description.
10. The applicable drawing number.
11. The revision level of the drawing.
12. The applicable specification number to be used for the source inspection.
13. The revision level of the specification.
14. The characteristics to be inspected.
15. The name of the initiator of this request, title, department number.

QUALITY CONTROL PUBLICATION	QCP NO. 5.1.8
	PAGE NO. 3 OF 6
	ISSUE DATE:
TITLE: SOURCE INSPECTION AT VENDOR/SUPPLIER FACILITY	APPROVED BY:
	REVISION NO: 0
	REVISION DATE:

16. The name of the initiator of this request, title, department number.

4.3 After the source inspection has been accomplished, the Source Inspection Report is to be filled out as follows:

1. The name, address and telephone number of the supplier/vendor.
2. The purchase order number, if this report is for subcontracted source inspection.
3. The date of the report.
4. The name of the program or project applicable to this source inspection.
5. The applicable contract or purchase order number.
6. The lot number, or serial number, if applicable.
7. The part/assembly number.
8. The quantity ordered.
9. The quantity inspected.
10. The sample size. The applicable sampling tables or inspection levels will be supplied to the source inspector by the Quality Assurance Department.
11. The quantity accepted.
12. The quantity rejected.
13. The characteristics inspected. As required in the specification and/or drawing. Including any special characteristics specified in the purchase order.
14. The drawings and specifications used.

QUALITY CONTROL PUBLICATION	QCP NO. 5.1.8
	PAGE NO. 4 OF 6
	ISSUE DATE:
TITLE: SOURCE INSPECTION AT VENDOR/SUPPLIER FACILITY	APPROVED BY:
	REVISION NO: 0
	REVISION DATE:

15. Applicable revision level.
16. A description of the nonconformances found, relating to a specific part number, and serial number (if applicable).
17. Acceptance/Rejection Tag-number.
18. Corrective action taken by the contractor.
19. Has the above corrective action(s) been approved by our quality assurance department. Yes ______ No ______.
    Who approved the corrective action(s), Name and Title (Quality Assurance).
20. If the required corrective action will extend beyond the time of the source inspection, what is the projected completion date of the corrective action. Yr ______ , Month ________ , Day ________ .
21. If the required corrective action will extend beyond the time of the source inspection, has conditional approval been given to the vendor to accept conforming material.
    Yes ____ , No____ .
22. If conditional approval has been given, who approved it. Name of approving official __________, Title__________ .
    Date: Yr ____, Month ________ , Date ____ .
23. Required date of completion of corrective action. Yr ______ , Month ________, Day ____ .
24. Supplier Signature, Title, and Date.
25. Source Inspector's Signature, Title, and Date.

4.4 At the completion of source inspection, all reports will be submitted to the quality assurance department for action.

QUALITY CONTROL PUBLICATION	QCP NO. 5.1.8
	PAGE NO. 5 OF 6
	ISSUE DATE:
TITLE: SOURCE INSPECTION AT VENDOR/SUPPLIER FACILITY	APPROVED BY:
	REVISION NO: 0
	REVISION DATE:

4.5 All conformances will be investigated and the appropriate corrective action(s) will be obtained from the vendor, supplier or subcontractor.

4.6 The number of characteristics found and the effectiveness of the corrective actions will be reported in the monthly, Top Ten Recommended Supplier-Vendor-Subcontractor Report, Form 5.1.6-1.

4.7 When the material arrives at our receiving inspection, the source inspection report will be matched up with the material and samples of the lots will be subjected to a receiving inspection and/or test (as required by the inspection instructions for that material) and the material will be dispositioned as required for acceptable or nonconforming material.

4.8 The quality assurance department will maintain a Source Inspection Scheduling Record, Form 5.1.8-2. This record will be used to track the scheduled, completed source inspections so that ample notice and plans can be made to accomplish the source inspections scheduled, and to track the effective accomplishmen t of all corrective actions. This record will be filled out as follows:

1. The request for corrective action number.
2. The person assigned to accomplish the source inspection.
3. The date of the scheduled inspection.
4. Nonconformances noted. Yes _____ , No ___ .
5. Scheduled completion of corrective actions (as applicable).
6. Actual completion date of approved corrective actions.
7. If this was a subcontracted source inspection:
    a. The name, address and telephone number of the subcontractor.
    b. The total number of actual hours spent on source inspection.

QUALITY CONTROL PUBLICATION	QCP NO. 5.1.8
	PAGE NO. 6 OF 6
	ISSUE DATE:
TITLE: SOURCE INSPCTION AT VENDOR/SUPPLIER FACILITY	APPROVED BY:
	REVISION NO: 0
	REVISION DATE:

8. The name of the approving official (Quality Assurance).

4.9 When the source inspection has been completed, a source inspection tag will be attached to and become a part of the shipment of the accepted material. If nonconformances were found, that information will be filled out on the individual parts found nonconforming, and the vendor/supplier/subcontractor will be notified that the tag is to remain with the nonconforming material/parts until proper and authorized dispositioning of the material/parts has been accomplished.

REQUEST FOR SOURCE INSPECTION AT VENDOR/SUPPLIER FACILITY	
DATE OF REQUEST ______ (1)	
VENDOR (NAME, ADDRESS) (2) TEL. NO. ______ CONTACT ______ TITLE ______	SOURCE INSPECTOR (NAME, ADDRESS) (3) TEL. NO. ______ TITLE ______ DEPARTMENT ______
SUBCONTRACTOR (NAME, ADDRESS) (4) TEL. NO. ______ CONTACT ______ TITLE ______	P.O. NUMBER (5) | PROG. NAME/NO. (6) CONTRACT/PURCHASE ORDER NO. (7) PART NUMBER (8) PART DESCRIPTION (9)
APPLICABLE DRAWING NUMBERS (10)	DRAWING REVISION (11)
APPLICABLE SPECIFICATION NUMBERS (12)	REVISION LEVEL (13)
CHARACTERISTICS TO BE INSPECTED (14)	
REQUEST INITATOR TITLE (15)	APPROVING OFFICIAL TITLE DATE (16)
FORM 5.1.8-1	

SOURCE INSPECTION SCHEDULING RECORD

APPROVED BY ______ (8)

RQST FOR C/A NUMBER	NAME OF SOURCE INSPECTOR	DATE OF SCH. INSPECTION	NONCONF. YES	NONCONF. NO	C/A COMP. DATE	ACTUAL C/A COMP. DATE	NAME OF SOURCE SUBCONTRACTOR
(1)	(2)	(3)	(4)		(5)	(6)	(7)

FORM 5.1.8-2

SOURCE INSPECTION REPORT

VENDOR (NAME AND ADDRESS) (1)	P.O. NUMBER (2)	DATE (3)
	PROJECT NAME (4)	
	CONTRACT/P.O. NUMBER (5)	
	LOT NO./SERIAL NO. (6)	

PART NUMBER	QUANTITY		SAMPLE SIZE	QUANTITY		CHARA. INSP.
	ORDERED	INSP.		ACCEPT.	REJ.	
(7)	(8)	(9)	(10)	(11)	(12)	(13)

DRAWINGS AND SPECIFICATIONS USED (14)	REVISION LEVEL (15)

DESCRIPTION OF NONCONFORMANCES FOUND (16)

ACC/REJ. TAG NO. ______________ (17)

CORRECTIVE ACTION TAKEN (18)

C/A APPROVED (19) YES NO	C/A COMP DUE (20) YES NO	COND. APPROVAL (21) YES NO	NAME OF APPROVER DATE (22)	C/A REQ. DATE (23)

SUPPLIER (SIGNATURE-TITLE-DATE) (24)	SOURCE INSPECTORS (SIG.-TITLE-DATE) (25)

FORM 5.1.8-3

SOURCE INSPECTION TAG

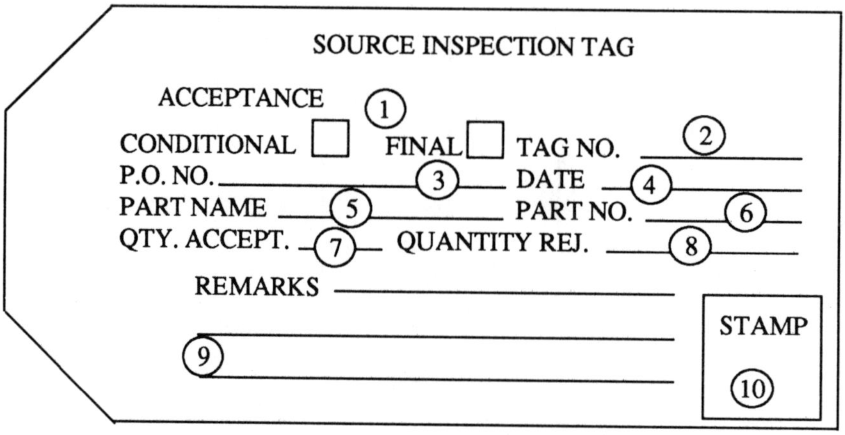

SOURCE INSPECTION TAG

ACCEPTANCE (1)

CONDITIONAL ☐ FINAL ☐ TAG NO. (2)

P.O. NO. (3) DATE (4)

PART NAME (5) PART NO. (6)

QTY. ACCEPT. (7) QUANTITY REJ. (8)

REMARKS (9)

STAMP (10)

FORM 5.1.8-4

CHAPTER TWENTY ONE

Statistical Quality Control

STATISTICAL QUALITY CONTROL

MIL-Q-9858A, MIL-HDBK-H50, paragraph 6.6, Statistical Quality Control and Analysis, describes the required methods under MIL-Q-9858A, by which a contractor is to verify the required control of product quality. MIL-Q-9858A and MIL-HDBK-H50 state the following, "In addition to statistical methods required by the contract, statistical planning, analysis, tests and quality control procedures may be utilized whenever such procedures are suitable to maintain the required control of quality." This statement relates to many of the other requirements (paragraphs) of MIL-Q-9858 (for example, process controls, work instructions, testing, chemical/physical or other types of analysis). "Sampling plans may be used when tests are destructive, or when the records, inherent characteristics of the product (dimensions, parameters, etc.) or the noncritical application of the product, indicate that a reduction in inspection or testing can be achieved without jeopardizing quality. The contractor may employ sampling inspection in accordance with applicable military standards and sampling plans (for example, MIL-STD-105D, MIL-STD-414, or Handbooks H 106, 107 and 108). If the contractor uses other sampling plans, they shall be subject to review by the cognizant government representative. Any sampling plan used shall provide valid confidence and quality levels." Here again is a choice of either using standard military sampling plans or using alternative sampling plans, provided that the alternative plans meet the Governments standards and approval.

Two of the most frequently used types of sampling plans are *attributes sampling* and *variables sampling*. Attributes sampling is used to inspect items on a good/no good basis; how good or how bad is not determined. An example of this type of sampling is the use of go and no-go gauges. The definition of Attributes Sampling is: *Inspection whereby either the unit or characteristics thereof, is classified simply as defective or nondefective, or the number of defects in the unit of product is counted, with respect to a given requirement,* (Source: MIL-STD-105D).

Variables sampling determines how good or bad an item is by making and analyzing actual measurements. This method uses the actual major/minor, critical/noncritical characteristics as specified in the contract/purchase order or those characteristics that have been determined to be the controlling factors in determining the quality of the product. This method is used if the nature of the product warrants it. With variables sampling, fewer observations are necessary for a given degree of assurance.

The definition of Inspection by Variables is: *Inspection wherein certain quality characteristics of sample are evaluated with respect to a continuous numerical scale and expressed as precise points along this scale. Variables inspection records the degree of conformance or nonconformance of the unit with specified requirements for the quality characteristics involved.* This means that specific parameters are either measured, tested or analyzed in order to determine the degree of conformance or nonconformance to the requirements and specifications. Prudent contractors guard against two great dangers to effective sampling: inadequate knowledge and improper use. We have seen circumstances where contractors, due to a lack of knowledge of what statistical sampling by characteristics means, misinterpreted the contract requirements and had decided that all of the characteristics to be controlled would be controlled at final inspection, without taking into regard, that, if nonconformances were found in the finished product, it would have taken a major effort to correct the nonconformances. Some of the characteristics were of such a nature, that they could not have been verified at final inspection. To verify effective control, vendor/supplier controls, incoming inspections, in-process inspections/tests were put into effect in order to validate the required controls.

Statistical process control, or control sampling, is used to determine whether a process is in or out of control (see Chapter 18). Machine control and heat treating control are examples of this method. Statistical process control procedures permit contractors to determine and analyze the causes of significant variations in manufacturing operations. Other processes that can utilize statistical process control are any automatic processes where some type of closed loop system can be employed that will automatically control the operations to be performed, by either automated inspection applications or process information where definite limits have been set.

MIL-I-45208, AQAP-1 and AQAP-4 state similar requirements as to Sampling Inspection. MIL-I-45208A states, "Sampling Inspection procedures used by the contractor to determine quality conformance of supplies shall be as stated in the contract or shall be subject to approval by the Government." In other words, if the contract or purchase order does not specify a specific method of control, the controls established by the contractor is subject to government approval. This approval is usually based on whether or not all characteristics that are controlling the quality of the finished product are taken into consideration prior to the actual start of production.

QUALITY CONTROL PUBLICATION	QCP NO. 6.6.1
	PAGE NO. 1 OF 4
	ISSUE DATE:
TITLE: STATISTICAL QUALITY CONTROL	APPROVED BY:
	REVISION NO: 0
	REVISION DATE:

1.0 PURPOSE

This quality control publication establishes the method and procedures for the using of statistical sampling for the verification of the quality and reliability built into a product.

2.0 INTENT

This QCP applies to the inspection and/or testing of all parts, materials, subassemblies and assemblies where sampling plans are either required by the requirements and specifications of a contract/purchase order, or where controls have been established and approved in order to verify the quality of all product.

3.0 DEFINITIONS

3.1 Sampling Inspection

3.1.1 A determination of the probable quality of all items in a given group of items, or the item itself, on the basis of examining the quality characteristics of a selected segment of that group, or the item itself.

3.2 Acceptable Quality Level (AQL)

3.2.1 (For lot acceptance sampling) - The maximum defect rate at which a lot of materials will be accepted.

3.3 Critical Defects

3.3.1 Those type of defects that will prevent the use or operation of an end item or which could pose a hazard and loss of life to the users.

QUALITY CONTROL PUBLICATION	QCP NO. 6.6.1
	PAGE NO. 2 OF 4
	ISSUE DATE:
TITLE: STATISTICAL QUALITY CONTROL	APPROVED BY:
	REVISION NO: 0
	REVISION DATE:

3.4 Major Defects

3.4.1 Those type of defects that could result in an item's failure or which would reduce or limit an item's usability.

3.5 Minor Defects

3.5.1 Those type of defects that do not significantly reduce an item's usability and/or will not affect form, fit or function. This type of defect must still be, if a Government contract or purchase order is involved or the company has an approved Single Standard System, subject to acceptance by the government assurance representative (QAR).

3.6 Statistical Quality Control

3.6.2 The process of maintaining an acceptable level of product quality by means of statistical methods.

4.0 APPLICABLE FORMS, PROCEDURES AND PUBLICATIONS

4.1 Sampling Procedures and Tables of Inspection by Attributes, MIL-STD-105D.

4.2 Sampling Procedures and Tables for Inspection by Variables for Percent Defective, MIL-STD-414.

4.3 Multi-level Continuous Sampling Procedures and Tables for Inspection by Attributes, DOD-HDBK-H106.

4.4 Single-Level Continuous Sampling Procedures and Table for Inspection by Attributes, DOD-HDBK-H107.

4.5 Inspection/Test Instructions, QCP 3.3.1.

QUALITY CONTROL PUBLICATION	QCP NO. 6.6.1
	PAGE NO. 3 OF 4
	ISSUE DATE:
TITLE: STATISTICAL QUALITY CONTROL	APPROVED BY:
	REVISION NO: 0
	REVISION DATE:

5.0 PROCEDURE

5.1 Inspection by statistical sampling can be applied, as appropriate and when specified, in receiving inspection and test, in-process inspection and test, final inspection and test and the materials laboratory.

5.2 The quality assurance department is responsible for developing and examining sampling plans, alternative sampling plans, testing them, specifying their application and analyzing the results of their use.

5.3 Only sampling plans approved by quality assurance and specified for designated applications can be used.

5.4 Authorized sampling plans, unless otherwise stated, will conform to the military and government standards identified in the contract or purchase order requirements and specifications.

5.5 The specified sampling plan for a designated application is to be provided to the quality assurance inspection and test functions for inclusion into the applicable inspection and testing instructions. (see QCP 3.3.1).

5.6 When applying a sampling plan, inspectors and testing personnel are to carefully select samples from a given lot randomly or the use of random tables will be used as directed. There can be no commingling of like items from different lots.

5.7 When the inspection and/or test is complete, and unless otherwise specified, only items in the sample will be accepted. The inspectors stamp and employee number as applicable is to be recorded on the lot's accompanying paper work to indicate that the inspection and/or test has been completed.

5.8 The statistical sampling plan will be tightened when defects or nonconformances are found in a particular lot and type of material and when quality control records indicates that such action is needed. All

QUALITY CONTROL PUBLICATION	QCP NO. 6.6.1
	PAGE NO. 4 OF 4
	ISSUE DATE:
TITLE:	APPROVED BY:
	REVISION NO: 0
	REVISION DATE:

tightening of inspections or loosening of inspections is under the control of the quality assurance department. No actions of this type are to be taken independently by any inspector.

CHAPTER TWENTY TWO

Work Instructions

WORK INSTRUCTIONS

The topic of work instructions as presented by MIL-Q-9858A and MIL-HDBK-H50 starts with a discussion of what is meant by *Work Instructions*. First, we consider the statement "The quality program shall assure that all work affecting quality (including such things as purchasing, handling, machining, assembling, fabrication, processing, inspection, testing, modification, installation, and any other treatment of product, facilities, standards or equipment from the ordering of materials to dispatch of shipment) shall be prescribed in clear and complete documented instructions of a type appropriate to the circumstances. Such instructions shall provide the criteria for performing the work functions and they shall be compatible with acceptance criteria for workmanship. The instructions are intended also to serve for supervising, inspecting and managing work. The preparation and maintenance of and compliance with work instructions shall be monitored as a function of the quality program." The requirements above have been discussed in previous chapters such as: the control of purchases, handling storage and delivery, planning, completed item inspection and test, drawings, documentation and change, process control, etc. To continue, MIL-HDBK-H50 also states, "Documented work instructions are necessary for work which affects product quality. Instructions must be clear, concise and appropriate to the nature of the work and the circumstances under which the work is to be done. The instructions also must establish quantitative or qualitative means for determining that each work operation has been done satisfactorily." Here again, is a reference to statistical quality and process control, as was discussed in the previous chapter. "Work instructions have different names in different plants and sometimes even in different departments of the same plant. Among the names used are *Production Control Books, Production Control Releases, Job Tickets, Manufacturing Control Sheets* and *Work Tickets.* Regardless of name, each job operation is usually identified with a number that is one of a sequence indicating previous and subsequent work operations. The instructions ordinarily tell how a job will be done, the order in which actions are accomplished, set-up information, speeds and feeds, associated drawings and specifications, and other pertinent information...It is of prime importance that the events that make possible the fabrication of a product follow a systematic, unvarying sequence of work operations. For this reason, work instructions are necessary, regardless of whether a contractor's facilities and organization are considered "small" or "large." Work instructions must be kept current and complete...Just as drawings are used by designers, engineers, customers, machine operators and many others, so work instructions are used by inspectors, supervisors and managers, as well as by production personnel. Supervisors or others responsible for quality improvements often find in the work instructions manufacturing details that need to be changed. Whenever a drawing is changed, a work instruction change is likely; on the other hand, many work instruction changes do not require drawing changes." Here again is the need for sequential operations on a work instruction, or as it will be called in QCP 3.3.1, a *Process and Routing Form.*

MIL-I-45208A takes a slightly different position than the preceding MIL-HDBK-H50, it states, "Inspection and Testing Documentation. Inspection and testing shall be prescribed by clear, complete and current instructions. The instructions shall assure inspection and test of materials, work in process and completed articles as required by the item specification and the contract."

AQAP-1 states, "The contractor shall develop and maintain adequate documented instructions appropriate to the circumstances for work affecting the quality of materiel and services. Work instructions shall be of a type appropriate to the contract and shall be compatible with technical requirements and include, where applicable, acceptable criteria for workmanship...The contractor shall develop and maintain instructions for the conduct of inspections and tests of materials, work in progress, and the finished product to ensure that the specified quality is achieved."

AQAP-4 states, "Clear, complete and current written inspection and test procedures shall be prepared for each inspection operation, including those relating to the assessment of the adequacy of process controls. Exceptions will be allowed when such procedures form an integral part of the detailed fabrication or process control documents, or when lack of written procedures will not adversely affect product quality. The contractor shall identify to the Quality Assurance Representative on request those inspection operations for which no written procedures are provided...Criteria for approval or rejection shall be included in all written procedures. Inspection equipment to be used shall be identified and its uncertainty of measurement stated."

QUALITY CONTROL PUBLICATION	QCP NO. 3.3.1
	PAGE NO. 1 OF 5
	ISSUE DATE:
TITLE: WORK INSTRUCTIONS - INSPECTION/TESTING DOCUMENTATION	APPROVED BY:
	REVISION NO: 0
	REVISION DATE:

1.0 PURPOSE

This quality control publication establishes the method and procedures for the initiation of process and routing forms, inspection and testing instructions and the documentation thereof, and all other work instructions that are to be used to produce parts, subassemblies and completed assemblies.

2.0 INTENT

This QCP is applicable to the quality assurance and manufacturing production planning departments.

3.0 APPLICABLE FORMS, PROCEDURES AND PUBLICATIONS

3.1 Inspection Planning, QCP 3.2.2.

3.2 Test Procedures (provided by the Production Engineering Department in conjunction with the Design Engineering and Quality Engineering functions).

3.3 Process and Routing, Form 3.3.1-1.

3.4 Inspection and Test Instructions, Form 3.3.1-2.

3.5 Receiving Inspection and Testing, QCP 6.1.1.

3.6 Statistical Sampling, QCP 6.6.1.

3.7 In-Process Inspection and Testing, QCP 3.3.4.

3.8 Materials Laboratory Testing/Analysis, QCP 6.1.2.

4.0 PROCEDURE

4.1 During the planning stages of a contract, a review will be held by the planning functions involved to determine the process and production methods that will be used and to plan the initiation of the process and

QUALITY CONTROL PUBLICATION	QCP NO. 3.3.1
	PAGE NO. 2 OF 5
TITLE: WORK INSTRUCTIONS - INSPECTION/TESTING DOCUMENTATION	ISSUE DATE:
	APPROVED BY:
	REVISION NO: 0
	REVISION DATE:

routing form, inspection and test instructions (for incoming, in-process, final inspection), the statistical sampling methods and all other process, manufacturing operations.

4.2 The process and routing form will be made out utilizing the results of the planning stage. The operations will be sequentialized in this form, in the order that has been predetermined by production planning, in order to present a step by step method for the production, inspection, test and/or analysis of a particular product. The format of this form is pictured in Form 3.3.1-1. The flow of information in this form is as follows:

1. The work order/form number.
2. The item, part or assembly number.
3. The item, part of assembly description.
4. The drawing number.
5. The drawing revision (alphanumeric) ex: 1A.
6. The applicable contract or purchase order number.
7. The name of the person who approved this work order.
8. The date of such approval.
9. The operation number (in sequential order by operation).
10. A brief operation description.
11. The tools, gauges, test equipment required.
12. The number of the specifications or procedures required to accomplish the particular operation.
13. The amount of items, parts, subassemblies, assemblies required to be completed.

QUALITY CONTROL PUBLICATION	QCP NO. 3.3.1
	PAGE NO. 3 OF 5
TITLE: WORK INSTRUCTIONS - INSPECTION/TESTING DOCUMENTATION	ISSUE DATE:
	APPROVED BY:
	REVISION NO: 0
	REVISION DATE:

All of the above information is inserted into the form by production planning in coordination with quality and design engineering. The way in which this form is laid out is conducive to computer operation. The following blocks on this form are filled in by the personnel who are accomplishing the work. These blocks are filled in as follows:

14. The quantity of items, parts, subassemblies inspected and/or tested.
15. The quantity accepted.
16. The quantity rejected.
17. The completion date.
18. The total time it took to accomplish the work.
19. The employee number of the operator.

4.3 The inspection and test instructions will be initiated by the quality engineering function in conjunction with the design engineering, production/manufacturing, and production planning departments.

4.4 Form 3.3.1-2 will be used to initiate all inspection and test instructions. This form is to be filled out as follows:

1. Procedure number (as assigned by quality engineering).
2. Date of the procedure.
3. Work order number (the same as the Process & Routing Form No.).
4. The operation number.
5. The applicable specifications (as listed).
6. The specification revision level. (alphanumeric).

<table>
<tr><td rowspan="6">QUALITY CONTROL PUBLICATION
TITLE: WORK INSTRUCTIONS - INSPECTION/TESTING DOCUMENTATION</td><td>QCP NO. 3.3.1</td></tr>
<tr><td>PAGE NO. 4 OF 5</td></tr>
<tr><td>ISSUE DATE:</td></tr>
<tr><td>APPROVED BY:</td></tr>
<tr><td>REVISION NO: 0</td></tr>
<tr><td>REVISION DATE:</td></tr>
</table>

7. The contract or purchase order number.
8. The project name or number.
9. The item, part, subassembly or finished assembly number.
10. The item, etc…name (description).
11. The supplier's, vendor's, subcontractor's name and number.
12. Drawing number.
13. Drawing revision level.
14. Date of Revision.
15. Serial numbers (if applicable).
16. Inspection and/or testing point. (as assigned by QAE and plant facilities engineering).
17. The visual inspection characteristics.
18. The operating characteristics.
19. The dimensional characteristics.
20. The inspection and/or test equipment to be utilized.
21. The AQL to be used for the inspection/test.
22. Name of the person who prepared this instruction and date.
23. Names of the personnel who approved this instruction and date.
    1. Design engineering.
    2. Production/manufacturing engineering.
    3. Quality engineering.

QUALITY CONTROL PUBLICATION	QCP NO. 3.3.1
	PAGE NO. 5 OF 5
	ISSUE DATE:
TITLE: WORK INSTRUCTIONS - INSPECTION/TESTING DOCUMENTATION	APPROVED BY:
	REVISION NO: 0
	REVISION DATE:

4.5 All inspection and testing procedures are to be referenced in the applicable work orders by drawing number and revision level. Whether the next operation is to be accomplished by incoming inspection/test, in-process inspection/test, materials or environmental labs, or by final inspection/test, the referenced specifications or drawings described within each operation number on the Process and Routing Form is to be utilized. If there are questions as to the validity of the referenced drawings or specifications, the operator is to notify department supervision. The department supervisor will notify quality and production/ manufacturing engineering that a potential problem exists.

4.6 All handling and storage of material will be accomplished using the directions as established in QCP 6.4.1.

4.7 The quality assurance department is responsible for maintaining a comprehensive cross-referenced file of all inspection and test instructions, and for the periodic auditing of them in respect to revision changes, effectiveness (quality history), correctness and completeness.

PROCESS AND ROUTING FORM/WORK ORDER

WORK ORDER NO. ___(1)___ PAGE NO. ___ OF ___

ITEM/PART NO.	PART/ASS'Y DESCRIPTION	DRAWING NO.	DWG REV.	CONTRACT/PO NO.	APPROVAL	DATE
(2)	(3)	(4)	(5)	(6)	(7)	(8)

OPN. NO.	OPERATION DESCR.	TOOLS-GAUGES TEST EQUIP.	SPEC/ PROC.	AMT. REQ.	QTY INSP/TEST	QTY ACCPT	QTY. REJ.	COMP. DATE	TIME COMP.	OPERATOR NUMBER
(9)	(10)	(11)	(12)	(13)	(14)	(15)	(16)	(17)	(18)	(19)

FORM 3.3.1-1

INSPECTION AND TEST INSTRUCTIONS

PROCEDURE NUMBER ___(1)___ REVISION ___ DATE ______ PAGE NO.___ OF___

WORK ORDER NO. ___(3)___ OPERATION NO. (4) APPLICABLE SPECIFICATIONS ___(5)___ REV. (6)

CONTRACT/P.O. NO. ___(7)___ PROJECT NAME NO ___(8)___ ______ REV. ___

______ REV. ___

ITEM/PART NO. ___(9)___ ITEM/PART DESCRIPTION ___(10)___ VENDOR'S NAME/NO. ___(11)___

DRAWING NO. ___(12)___ DWG. REV. ___(13)___ DATE REV. ___(14)___ SERIAL NOS. ___(15)___

INSP/TEST POINT NO.	VISUAL INSP. CHARACTERISTICS	OPERATING CHARACTERISTICS	DIMENSIONAL CHARACTERISTICS	INSPECT/TEST EQUIP. TO BE USED	AQL
(16)	(17)	(18)	(19)	(20)	(21)

INITIATOR'S NAME DATE

(22)

APPROVING OFFICIALS	TITLE	DATE
1. DE: ______	______	______
2. PE: ______	(23) ______	______
3. QE: ______	______	______

FORM 3.3.1-2

QUALITY CONTROL PUBLICATION	QCP NO. 3.3.2
	PAGE NO. 1 OF 3
	ISSUE DATE:
TITLE: AUTOMATED TEST EQUIPMENT	APPROVED BY:
	REVISION NO: 0
	REVISION DATE:

1.0 PURPOSE

This quality control publication establishes the procedures for the control and validation of all automatic test equipment that is used in the testing of a deliverable product, to assure that the product meets the requirements and specifications of a contract and/or purchase order. This includes all numerically controlled production machinery.

2.0 INTENT

This QCP provides for a method of both, validating and Automatic Test Equipment used for inspection and testing, and for the validation of programs and tapes that control numerically controlled production equipment.

3.0 APPLICABLE FORMS, PROCEDURES AND PUBLICATIONS

3.1 Chapter 16 - Measuring and Test Equipment.

3.2 Quality Audits - QCP 2.3.1, Chapter 5.

4.0 PROCEDURE

4.1 The following eight steps will be used in determining if the required controls have been established for all automatic test equipment that is used to verify the quality of all deliverable product. This includes numerically controlled machines. These steps are:

1. The actual control of all ATE and NCM's.
2. Repeatability of tests utilizing the ATE.
3. The adequacy and completeness of the calibration of the ATE and all associated equipment.
4. The adequacy of the programming. Validation of the programs.
5. The adequacy of the instructions for using the ATE.

QUALITY CONTROL PUBLICATION	QCP NO. 3.3.2
	PAGE NO. 2 OF 3
	ISSUE DATE:
TITLE: AUTOMATED TEST EQUIPMENT	APPROVED BY:
	REVISION NO: 0
	REVISION DATE:

6. The adequacy of self-tests and checksums.
7. The adequacy and completeness of records, including the protection of the library copies of the program itself.
8. The adequacy of all corrective actions taken due to nonconformances found.

4.2 The quality assurance department is responsible for the method of either verifying the above due to a contract or purchase order or for the auditing of the controls at intervals consistent with the quality program.

4.3 The manner in which ATE is validated will determine whether or not an item/product conforms or does not conform to a stated requirement or specification is a function of the program itself. The program also determines the manner in which a printout of the results, if desired or required, will be accomplished.

4.4 The validity of the program must be determined in order to prove the adequacy and accuracy of the inspections, tests or production results.

4.5 The next step in proving the validity of the program is to check an item and/or product using the ATE. This can usually be accomplished in one of two ways.

4.5.1 To take an actual faulty item with known defects and run trial checks on all variables and/or characteristics.

4.5.2 Use a self test program designed to verify the accuracy of the original program to detect known errors. A checksum is usually programmed into the program to detect differences in the results of a test being performed. A checksum is the sum of every byte contained in an input/output (I/O) record used for assuring the integrity of the programmed entry.

QUALITY CONTROL PUBLICATION	QCP NO. 3.3.2
	PAGE NO. 3 OF 3
	ISSUE DATE:
TITLE: AUTOMATED TEST EQUIPMENT	APPROVED BY:
	REVISION NO: 0
	REVISION DATE:

4.6 In the self test program, a test or a series of tests are performed by the computer upon itself which shows whether or not it is operating within designed limits.

4.7 Calibration of the inspection and/or test equipment and the complete ATE system is mandatory. All inspection/test equipment and ATE must be included in the calibration recall system for certification and recertification.

4.8 Written instructions for the inspection and/or testing of product for the required characteristics must be available and used at each inspection and/or test location. The testers and inspectors must use the written instructions to verify product conformance or nonconformance with the contract/purchase requirements, specifications and drawings.

4.9 When using a ATE system that prints out the inspection/test results utilizing a tape printout program, a black printout means the characteristic checked is conforming. A red readout indicates a nonconforming condition has been found.

4.10 Another check of the program is to verify that the alphanumeric characters are being printed as required by the program, and are correct and legible.

4.11 A first piece run of all characteristics to be checked/tested will be accomplished each shift to verity the continuing validity of the ATE. If the ATE has a selfcheck program, this program is to be run every shift to validate the inspection/test program, or if a different program is used, the selfcheck program must be run again.

4.12 The quality assurance software engineer will in the cases of deliverable test software, validate the software and software controls as required by the contract or purchase order. All nondeliverable ATE software will be at a minimum, be subject to periodic audits to determine the completeness and correctness of the software, and to verify its ability to correctly test deliverable product.

SAMPLE TEST PROGRAM PREPARATION

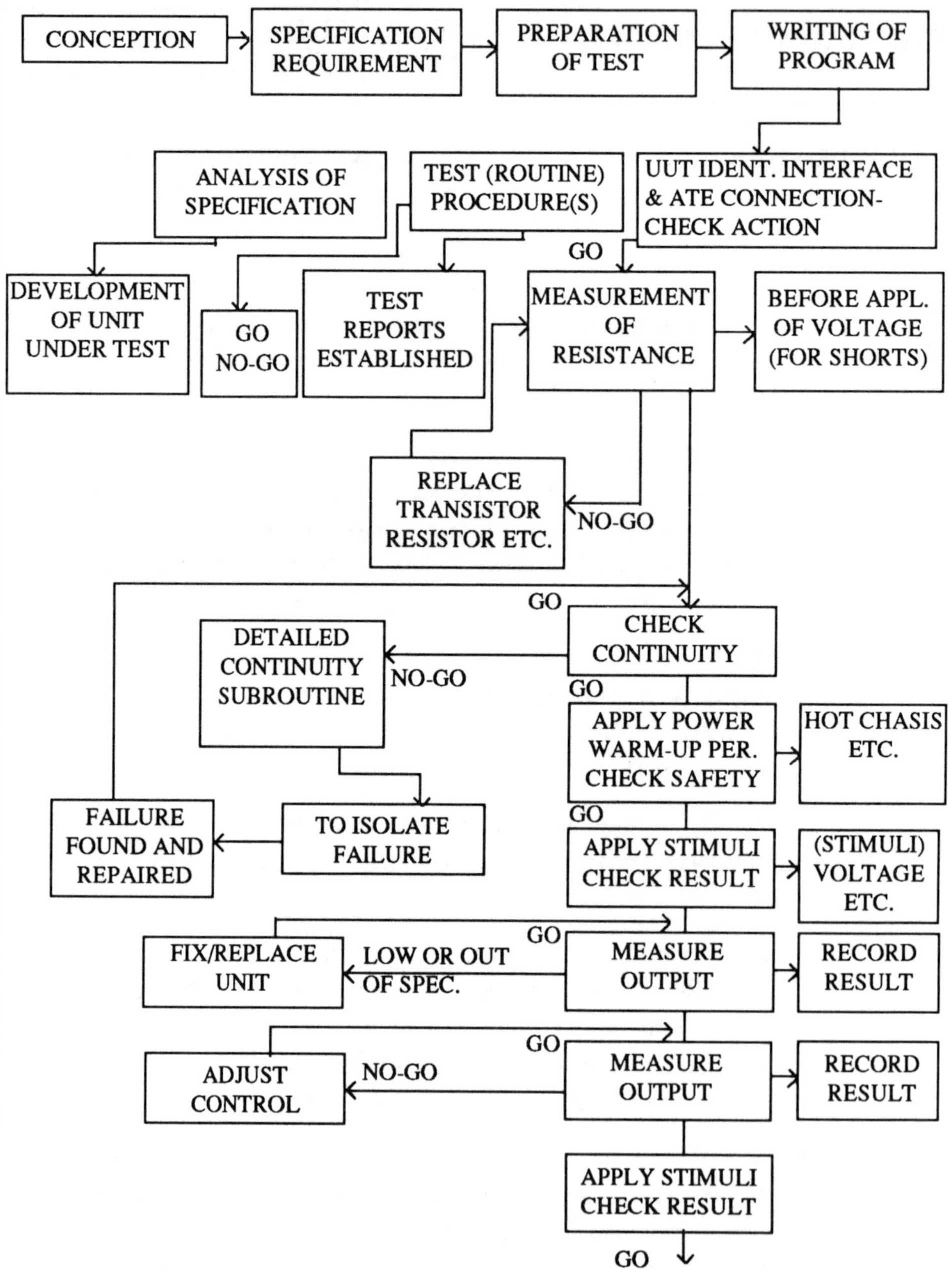

FORM 3.3.2-1

QUALITY CONTROL PUBLICATION	QCP NO. 3.3.3
	PAGE NO. 1 OF 6
	ISSUE DATE:
TITLE: INSPECTION AND TEST REPORTING	APPROVED BY:
	REVISION NO: 0
	REVISION DATE:

1.0 PURPOSE

This quality control publication establishes the procedures for the reporting and documentation of all inspections and tests that are accomplished at receiving, in-process and final inspection/testing, and all other tests and analyses that are accomplished during the complete production cycle.

2.0 INTENT

The QCP defines the quality engineering and production engineering departments' responsibility for the planning and accomplishment of all inspections, tests and analyses that will occur throughout the complete production cycle.

3.0 APPLICABLE FORMS, PROCEDURES AND PUBLICATIONS

3.1 Inspection/test instructions, Form 3.3.1-2.

3.2 Laboratory analysis/test request, Form 3.3.3-1.

3.3 Inspection/test report, Form 3.3.3-2.

3.4 Accepted tag, Form 6.7.1-2.

3.5 Rejection and disposition tag, Form 6.7.1-1.

3.6 Reliability materials laboratory, inspection/test/analysis, Forms 3.2.3-1A and -1B.

4.0 PROCEDURE

4.1 All materials, parts, subassemblies, completed assemblies and complete systems are to be inspected, tested and/or analyzed at the appropriate stages of work and/or completion as specified by the applicable routing form/work order and as specified in the applicable inspection/test instructions or laboratory analysis/test requests that are part of the operation to be accomplished that is specified on all routing forms/work orders.

QUALITY CONTROL PUBLICATION	QCP NO. 3.3.3
	PAGE NO. 2 OF 6
	ISSUE DATE:
TITLE: INSPECTION AND TEST REPORTING	APPROVED BY:
	REVISION NO: 0
	REVISION DATE:

4.2 All requests for analyses/tests relating to material that requires these types of analyses/tests is to be routed to the materials laboratory using the Laboratory Analysis/Test Request as shown in Form 3.3.3-1. This request will be filled out as follows:

1. The assigned request number.
2. The item, part or assembly number.
3. The item, part or assembly name/description.
4. The quantity of items to be tested/analyzed.
5. The operation number (this relates to the operation number that appears on the work order).
6. Operation description (a brief description of the type of test or analysis required).
7. The name/number of the department requesting the test/analysis.
8. The department where the material/item is to be delivered to. Or as specified, the name of the company that is to accomplish the test/analysis.
9. The location/area where the material is located. Or as specified the address of the company that is to accomplish the test/analysis.
10. The name of the person that will accomplish the test/analysis.
11. A description of the tests or analysis.
12. The applicable documents, specifications, requirements required in order to accomplish the test/analysis.
13. A summary of the results of the tests. The actual test reports, Forms 3.2.3-1A and -1B will be attached to a copy of this request and forwarded to the initiator at the completion of the tests/analysis.

QUALITY CONTROL PUBLICATION	QCP NO. 3.3.3
	PAGE NO. 3 OF 6
	ISSUE DATE:
TITLE: INSPECTION AND TEST REPORTING	APPROVED BY:
	REVISION NO: 0
	REVISION DATE:

14. Who to return the results of the tests/analysis.
15. The person that the results of the tests/analysis is to be returned to.
16. The name of the initiator of the request and date of request.
17. The signature of the person who performed the tests/analysis and the date of completion.

4.3 All incoming, in-process, first article (unless the format that is required by the contract or purchase order is different), and final inspections and tests are to be recorded on Form 3.3.3-2. This form will be initiated upon the start of the inspection and/or test, with the following information filled out on the form:

1. The number of pages in the report (e.g., Page No. ______ of ______).
2. The report number (as assigned - concurrent, daily reports).
3. The date of the report.
4. The operation number (the operation number on the work order that coincides with the operation being performed).
5. The part/assembly number.
6. The part/assembly name/description.
7. The revision level of the part/assembly.
8. The employee number of the test operator.
9. The contract or purchase order number.
10. The specification reference number and revision level.
11. The employee number of the inspector accomplishing inspection.

QUALITY CONTROL PUBLICATION	QCP NO. 3.3.3
	PAGE NO. 4 OF 6
	ISSUE DATE:
TITLE: INSPECTION AND TEST REPORTING	APPROVED BY:
	REVISION NO: 0
	REVISION DATE:

12. A brief description of the inspection/test to be performed.

13. The program this inspection/test is applicable to.

14. These blocks are to be checked indicating where in the production cycle the applicable inspection/test is being performed.

14. Is this inspection/test being accomplished in Receiving Inspection? Check if yes.

15. Is this inspection/test being accomplished in one of the in-process inspection/test areas? Check if yes.

16. Is this inspection/test being accomplished as a final inspection/test before final acceptance of product? Check if yes.

17. Is this inspection/test for a piece part or subassembly? Check if yes.

18. Is this inspection/test for a completed system? Check if yes.

19. The specification paragraph number for this characteristic being inspected/tested.

20. What is the required value (by specification/drawing).

21. The applicable tolerance.

22. The actual reading taken by the inspector/tester.

23. What is the specific characteristic being inspected?

24. What is the AQL level for this inspection/test?

25. The lot size for this inspection/test.

26. What is the sample size to be taken if the lot contains two or more pieces?

27. How many parts have been rejected?

QUALITY CONTROL PUBLICATION	QCP NO. 3.3.3
	PAGE NO. 5 OF 6
	ISSUE DATE:
TITLE: INSPECTION AND TEST REPORTING	APPROVED BY:
	REVISION NO: 0
	REVISION DATE:

28. What is the quantity accepted?

29. Comments as to findings of inspections/tests.

30. What is the recommended disposition of the preliminary review board (if one has been established)?

All actions other that scrap must have the approval of the MRB.

4.4 All parts, subassemblies, assemblies or completed systems found to be acceptable and in conformance with the contract or purchase order requirements/specifications are to be either marked or tagged as per inspection/test instructions and/or contract/purchase order requirements/specifications. If the parts are to be tagged, use Form 6.7.1-2. The routing form/work order and inspection records are to be stamped and the inspector/tester's employee number is to be inserted into the applicable blocks on these forms before the parts, material are moved to the next operation.

4.5 Part(s), material, subassemblies, assemblies that are to be reworked are to be routed to the appropriate department together with the approved and documented rework instructions. The Material Review Board is to review these actions to determine if corrective actions have been taken to eliminate the causes of the nonconformances. All rework and repair actions on product that is being manufactured under a government contract or purchase order is subject to the QAR's approval.

4.6 It is standard policy of this company that no standard repair procedures are really standard. The objective of this company is to eliminate the causes for nonconformances and discrepancies so that a standard repair is no longer considered *standard,* it is really a defect in the system, which will not be tolerated.

QUALITY CONTROL PUBLICATION	QCP NO. 3.3.3
	PAGE NO. 6 OF 6
	ISSUE DATE:
TITLE: INSPECTION AND TEST REPORTING	APPROVED BY:
	REVISION NO: 0
	REVISION DATE:

4.7 All material, parts, etc. found to be nonconforming/discrepant will be routed to the MRB for dispositioning and corrective action. This material will be tagged with the Rejection and Disposition Tag, Form 6.7.101. For MRB actions see QCP's 6.5.1 through 6.5.5.

4.8 The quality assurance department will establish an audit system to verify that the topics in these QCP's are being adhered to.

LABORATORY ANALYSIS/TEST REQUEST

______________ (REQUEST NO.) (1)

ITEM/PART NO. (2)	PART DESCRIPTION (3)	QUANTITY (4)
OPERATION NO. (5)	OPERATION DESCRIPTION (6)	REQ. DEPT. (7)

THIS MATERIAL IS TO GO TO THE FOLLOWING:

DEPARTMENT: ____________ (8) ____________

LOCATION: ____________ (9) ____________

____

ATTENTION: ____________ (10) ____________

LABORATORY ANALYSIS OR TESTS REQUIRED:

DESCRIPTION: ____________ (11) ____________

____

____

____

____

DOCUMENTS/SPECIFICATIONS REQUIRED: ______ (12) ______

____

____

SUMMARY OF RESULTS (ATTACH REPORT)

(13) ________________________________

____

____

____

____

____

(14) ____________ WHEN COMPLETE RETURN TO DEPT. (15) ____________ ATTENTION

NAME OF INITIATOR OF REQUEST DATE (16)	SIGNATURE OF PERSON ACCOM. TEST (17)

FORM 3.3.3-1

INSPECTION AND TEST REPORT (1) PAGE NO. ___ OF _____

REPORT NO. (2)	DATE (3)	OPER. NO. (4)	ART/ASSEMBLY NO. (5)	PART/ASS'Y. DESC. (6)	REV. LEVEL (7)
TEST OPERATOR (8)	CONTRACT/P.O. NO. (9)	SPEC. REF. NO. (10)	INSPECTOR (11)	TYPE INSP/TEST (12)	PROGRAM (13)

RECEIVING INSPECTION/ TEST (14) ☐ IN-PROCESS INSPECTION /TEST (15) ☐ FINAL INSPECTION/ TEST (16) ☐ PARTS/SUB. SYS. INSPECTION/ TEST (17) ☐ SYSTEM INSPECTION/ TEST (18) ☐

SPEC. PARA. NO.	REQUIRED VALUE	TOL.	ACTUAL READING	CHARA. INSP.	AQL	LOT SIZE	SAMP. SIZE	QTY. REJ.	QTY. ACCEPT.	COMMENTS
(19)	(20)	(21)	(22)	(23)	(24)	(25)	(26)	(27)	(28)	(29)
										DISPOSITION (30) SCRAP ☐ MRB ☐

FORM 3.3.3-2

CHAPTER TWENTY THREE

Receiving Inspection

RECEIVING INSPECTION

Receiving inspection and materials and materials control has been discussed in previous chapters to the extent that these topics are part of a total quality control system. This chapter contains specific information that applies to paragraph 6.1 of MIL-Q-9858A, paragraph 3.12 of MIL-I-45208A, paragraph 210(c) of AQAP-1, paragraph 205(c) of AQAP-4 and their applicable military handbooks.

MIL-Q-9858A and MIL-HDBK-H50 states the requirement for control of purchased materials, raw material controls, and receiving inspection controls as follows, "Supplier's materials and products shall be subjected to inspection upon receipt to the extent necessary to assure conformance to technical requirements." The wording, *to the extent necessary,* may be misleading to the readers of this paragraph in MIL-Q-9858A. The *extent necessary* statement has a much broader meaning, as it actually incorporates most of the requirements of a quality or inspection system. To go further into this paragraph, "Receiving inspection may be adjusted upon the basis of the quality assurance program exercised by suppliers. Evidence of the suppliers' satisfactory control of quality may be used to adjust the amount and kind of receiving inspection." The following statements in this paragraph can be related to Chapter 20, Control of Purchases, where specific Quality Control Publications were developed to address this requirement. "The quality program shall assure that raw materials to be used in fabrication or processing of products conform to the applicable physical, chemical, and other technical requirements. Laboratory testing shall be employed as necessary. Suppliers shall be required (see Chapter 20) by the contractors' quality program to exercise equivalent control of the raw materials utilized in the production of the parts and items which they supply to the contractor. Raw material awaiting testing must be separately identified or segregated from already tested and approved material but can be released for initial production, providing that identification and control is maintained." Here again, is a reference to the *Handling and Storage* of material requirements as discussed in a previous chapter. "Material tested and approved must be kept identified until such time as its identity is necessarily obliterated by processing. Controls will be established to prevent the inadvertent use of material failing to pass tests." This goes back to *The Control of Nonconforming Material* as discussed previously, and other QCPs addressing these required controls. Contractor receiving inspection is considered essential for effective control of the quality of purchased supplies. (See how there is an interweaving of the requirements in a quality or inspection system). However, the amount and extent of receiving inspection varies. If a supplier has effective quality control, the contractor can safely reduce his receiving inspection. (Substantial verification will be needed for this statement. And in some contracts and purchase orders, the requirements for effective controls are specified in the contract/purchase order itself. Are there critical, major or minor characteristics specified in the contract or purchase order, and are the AQLs required for each contract or purchase order part of the specification?) It should be apparent, however, that a contractor's knowledge of supplier quality stems primarily from proven performance and the records the supplier furnishes. Other controls as specified in the MIL-Q-9858A program were discussed in Chapter 20. Supplier inspection and test results accompanying each shipment can permit contractors to substitute sample testing for (instead of) 100% testing of inspection.

MIL-I-45208A and MIL-HDBK-H51, state, "Subcontracted or purchased supplies shall be subjected to inspection after receipt, as necessary, to assure conformance to contract requirements. The contractor shall report to the government representative any nonconformances found on government source-inspected supplies and shall require his supplier to coordinate with his government representative on corrective action." Meanwhile, the government representative will be coordinating government actions with the contractors' quality assurance department and the supplier's government representative. This is an example of the independent actions taken by the government, and required of government quality personnel.

AQAP-1, states, "Incoming material shall not be used or processed unless and until inspected or otherwise found to conform to contract requirements. In determining the amount and nature of receiving inspection, consideration shall be given to the controls exercised at source and the objective evidence shall be given to the controls exercised at source and the objective evidence provided." Again, these controls were discussed in Chapters 13 and 20. "Incoming material shall be withheld pending completion of required tests or receipt of necessary test reports. Exceptionally as prescribed by contractor procedures, material may be released for immediate manufacturing purposes providing such material does not lose its identity in processing and is identified in a positive manner that permits its immediate recall and replacement in the event that it is found unsatisfactory. (This is at the contractor's risk and could be at considerable expense if the nonconforming material is imbedded into upper level subassemblies, assemblies or completed systems). Upon receipt of nonconforming material from a subcontractor, the contractor shall comply with the provisions of paragraph 215 (discussed earlier) and take the necessary action to obtain appropriate corrective action. The contractor shall notify the QAR of nonconforming material received from a subcontractor that has been subject to government quality assurance."

AQAP-4, states, "Incoming articles shall not be used or processed unless inspected or otherwise ascertained to conform with contract requirements.

QUALITY CONTROL PUBLICATION	QCP NO. 6.1.1
	PAGE NO. 1 OF 3
	ISSUE DATE:
TITLE: RECEIVING AND RAW MATERIAL INSPECTION	APPROVED BY:
	REVISION NO: 0
	REVISION DATE:

1.0 PURPOSE

This quality control publication establishes the method and procedures for the control of purchased materials, parts, subassemblies, assembly(ies) in the receiving inspection department and the testing/analyses of raw material in the materials laboratory.

2.0 INTENT

This QCP applies to the inspection, testing, analyses of all purchased materials, parts, subassemblies, assemblies.

3.0 APPLICABLE FORMS, PROCEDURES AND PUBLICATIONS

3.1 Inspection Planning, QCP 3.2.2.

3.2 Supplier/Vendor Corrective Action, QCP 3.5.2.

3.3 Government Inspection at Subcontractor/Vendor Facility, QCP 7.1.1.

3.4 Handling, Storage and Delivery, QCP 6.4.1.

3.5 Indication Of Inspection Status, QCP 6.7.1.

3.6 Material Review Board, QCP 6.5.3.

3.7 Source Inspection At Vendor/Supplier Facility, QCP 5.1.9.

3.8 Work Instructions & Inspection and Testing Documentation, QCP 3.3.1.

3.9 Inspection and Testing Reporting, QCP 3.3.3.

4.0 PROCEDURE

4.1 All purchased goods, supplies and services are to be inspected, tested by the receiving inspection department and tested/analyzed as required by the materials laboratory.

<table>
<tr><td rowspan="6">QUALITY CONTROL PUBLICATION

TITLE: RECEIVING AND RAW MATERIAL INSPECTION</td><td>QCP NO. 6.1.1</td></tr>
<tr><td>PAGE NO. 2 OF 3</td></tr>
<tr><td>ISSUE DATE:</td></tr>
<tr><td>APPROVED BY:</td></tr>
<tr><td>REVISION NO: 0</td></tr>
<tr><td>REVISION DATE:</td></tr>
</table>

4.2 The receiving inspection department and the materials laboratory operate under the general management of the quality engineering section of the quality assurance department.

4.3 When materials are received by the receiving department that require analyzing and testing, samples will be forwarded to the materials laboratory as required by the work order. The materials laboratory upon receipt of the material or material samples will initiate a quality plan/reliability analysis, Forms 3.2.2-1A and -1B.

4.4 After the tests/analyses have been completed, the Form 3.2.3-1A, will be filled out and returned to the receiving inspection department with the determinations as to the status of the material due to the analyses/tests.

4.5 The receiving department will then forward the material in accordance with the established procedures for storage, MRB, corrective action, processing, etc.

4.6 When measuring and test equipment, inspection and testing devices, calibration standards and subcontracted repairs are received, they will be forwarded to the calibration laboratory for inspection, verification of the accuracy, logging into the calibration system and verification of the certifications received as to the traceability of all equipment to the National Bureau of Standards.

4.7 All parts, material, subassemblies, assemblies received from vendors, suppliers or subcontractors will be inspected and/or tested to the requirements of the purchase order, specification, drawing and the Inspection and Test Instructions, Form 3.3.1-2.

4.8 All acceptable material, parts, etc. will be routed to the next location as required on the Process And Routing/Work Order Form.

4.9 An Accepted Tag, Form 6.7.1-2 will be attached to all accepted materials, parts, etc.

QUALITY CONTROL PUBLICATION	QCP NO. 6.1.1
	PAGE NO. 3 OF 3
	ISSUE DATE:
TITLE: RECEIVING AND RAW MATERIAL INSPECTION	APPROVED BY:
	REVISION NO: 0
	REVISION DATE:

4.10 All nonconforming material will be routed to the MRB-HOLD AREA, for dispositioning. A Rejection Tag, Form 6.7.1-1 will be filled out and attached to the nonconforming material.

QUALITY CONTROL PUBLICATION	QCP NO. 6.1.2
	PAGE NO. 1 OF 1
	ISSUE DATE:
TITLE: MATERIAL PURGE	APPROVED BY:
	REVISION NO: 0
	REVISION DATE:

1.0 PURPOSE

This quality control publication establishes the method and procedure for the disposition of materials, parts, subassemblies, assemblies, that are found to be nonconforming, can not be repaired or reworked to an acceptable condition and will serve no useful purpose due to the nonacceptable condition.

2.0 INTENT

The purpose of this QCP to provide the means for the purging of scrap in order to prevent the scrap from getting back into the production cycle.

3.0 APPLICABLE FORMS, PROCEDURES AND PUBLICATIONS

3.1 Scrap Control, QCP 6.5.5.

4.0 PROCEDURE

4.1 If due to any material review board decisions to purge or scrap any materials, parts, assemblies, etc., has been made, and the proper approvals have been obtained, the procedure in QCP 6.5.5 is to be followed, in order to dispose of this type of material.

4.2 If the scrap material is to be purchased by a scrap and/or carting company, all records of the transactions will be documented and the documentation is to be forwarded to the accounting department for further processing.

4.3 The accounting department will furnish this information to the quality assurance department for inclusion into the Cost of Quality reporting system.

APPENDIX I

How to Prepare the Material Inspection and Receiving Report (DD Form 250)

The Material Inspection And Receiving Report (MIRR) is a document contractors have to know in order to obtain payment for goods and services. This multi-purpose document is used for: Evidence of inspection and acceptance of goods and services by the government, shipping document, packing list, shipping notice, receiving document, contractor invoice support document, contractor release or contractor invoice. This appendix provides information to avoid delays in payment for goods and services rendered. Most delays in payment from the government occur because of improper or incomplete preparation of DD Form 250. The FAR clauses in the contract are the final authority for the preparation of this form. The following abbreviations appear in the instructions on how to fill out this form:

1.	ACO	Administrative Contracting Officer.
2.	ADP	Automatic Data Processing.
3.	BL	Commercial or Government Bill of Lading.
4.	CAO	Contract Administration Office.
5.	CLIN	Contract Line Item Number.
6.	CoC	Certificate of Conformance.
7.	FAR	Federal Acquisition Regulation.
8.	DoDAAD	Department of Defense Activity Address Directory.
9.	DS&M	Directorate of Systems and Financial Management.
10.	FMS	Foreign Military Sales.
11.	FSCM	Federal Supply Codes for Manufacturers. This is the code that will appear on the face of the contract beside the company name and address under code.
12.	FSCNM	Federal Supply Codes for Non-Manufacturers.
13.	GFP	Government Furnished Property.
14.	GS	General Schedule.
15.	GSA	General Services Administration.
16.	MAP	Military Assistance Program.
17.	MILSTRIP	Military Standard Requisitioning and Issue Procedures.
18.	NSN	National Stock Number (formerly FSN-Federal Stock No.)
19.	PCO	Principal Contracting Officer. Formerly, Procuring Contract Officer. This person is usually at the buying activity of the government.
20.	PIIN	Procurement Instrument Identification Number. This is the contract number under which goods and services will be purchased.
21.	QA	Quality Assurance.

22. QAR — This is the government quality assurance representative assigned to the company.

23. SPIIN — Supplemental Procurement Instrument Identification Number. This is the number that appears after the PIIN, and is usually used as an order placed on the PIIN.

24. TCN — Transportation Control Number. This is the code for the mode of shipment and is inserted into the lower right hand corner of Block 4 of the DD Form 250. A listing of these codes and their meaning will be presented next.

LIST OF MODE OF SHIPMENT CODES

Code	Description
A	Motor, truckload
B	Motor, less truckload
C	Van (unpacked, uncrated personal and/or Government property)
D	Driveaway, truckaway, towaway
E	Busline
F	Military Airlift Command (MAC)
G	Regular Mail, parcel post
H	Air Mail, parcel post
I	Government truck, including common service
J	REA express
K	Rail, carload
L	Rail, less carload
M	Freight forwarder
N	Contract air (LOGAIR/QUICKTRANS)
O	Organic military air, Flyaway
P	Through bill of lading
Q	Air Freight
R	Air express
S	Air charter
T	Air freight forwarder
U	Air van
V	Sea-van service
W	Water, river, lake, coastal (Commercial)
X	Sealift Express Service (SEA-EX)
Y	Intratheater Aiflift System
Z	MSC (controlled/contract/arranged space)
2	Government Watercraft, Barge/Lighter
3	Roll-on/Roll-off service
4	Armed Forces Courier Service (ARFCOS)
5	United Parcel Service
6	Military Ordinary Mail (MOM)
7	Weapons System Pouch
8	Pipeline
9	Local delivery, including deliveries to ports from adjacent supply activities, handcarry
*	No Physical Movement
%	Unassigned

BLOCK BY BLOCK INSTRUCTIONS FOR THE FILLING OUT (DD FORM 250)

Block 1 - Instrument Identification (Contract/Order Number):

1. The contract number called PIIN/SPIIN (Purchasing Instrument Identification Number/Supplemental PIIN) is a very important number. It serves to identify shipment to the paying office and the receiving activity. This 13-position alphanumeric contract number must be entered in Block 1 of all DD Forms 250.

2. When delivery orders under indefinite delivery type contracts are involved, enter the four digit alphanumeric call/order serial number and two additional positions for amended orders which are supplementary to the 13-position basic PIIN. (These were usually called BOA's - Basic Ordering Agreements).

3. Do not enter supplementary numbers used in conjunction with basic PIIN to identify modification of contracts. Do not confuse the two.

4. Shipping Instructions. When shipping instructions are furnished by telephone or message, it should be confirmed by a modification to the contract stamped "Confirmation" within five days. If shipment is made prior to receipt of confirmation of modification, the six-digit modification serial number or the two digits call/order modification indicator will be entered immediately following the PIIN or call/order four-digit SPIIN. These numbers will be provided by the contracting officer by telephone call or message.

   REMEMBER! You only show the modification number in Block 1 when you are shipping on the the basis of shipping instructions provided by telephone or message and the shipment is made prior to receipt of the modification.

   Example 1: In the contract number below, an (A) in place of the (C) indicates a BOA. The alphanumeric number before the slash is the PIIN. The combination of alpha and/or numeric symbols after the slash indicate the SPIIN.

1. PROC INSTRUMENT IDEN (CONTRACT) | (ORDER) NO.
(PIIN) (SPIIN)
(Contract No.-PIIN/SPIIN) DAG301-87-C-0028/0001
or -A- as above

The usual placement of PIIN and SPIIN designations relative to (1.) above, is as follows:

DAGE01-87-C-0028/0001 (D lines up with PROC above)

Example 2:

1. PROC INSTRUMENT IDEN (CONTRACT) | (ORDER) NO.
DAG301-87-C-0028/PV0001 (MOD. SERIAL NO.)

In this example the SPIIN is a six position number. It represents a modification (MOD) written by the buying activity and the last five positions are a modification serial number. This modification serial number is only added when shipping instructions have been issued by telephone, message or otherwise, but no formal MOD has been issued.

Example 3:

1. PROC INSTRUMENT IDENT (CONTRACT) | (ORDER) NO.
DAGE01-87-A-0028/0001B1 (MOD. SERIAL NO.)

In this example the last position indicates modification has been issued against a contract. For DoD delivery orders on non DoD contracts, enter the nonDoD contract number immediately below the PII number.

Example 4:

1. PROC INSTRUMENT IDENT (CONTRACT) | (ORDER) NO.
DAGE01-87-F-0028
GS-000S-54811

In this example we have a contract which was written against a General Schedule (GS) established by the General Services Administration (GSA). The 13 position alphanumeric number is very important.

Block 2 - Shipment Number:

2. SHIPMENT NUMBER
KYY 0001

1. The shipment number identifies the activity the shipment is being made from and the number of shipments from that activity (contractor). It is

composed of a *three digit alpha character prefix* and *four digit numeric shipment number* (it must be comprised of four numeric digits) and the complete alphanumeric number can be considered a shipment serial number. *The three digit alpha prefix is controlled and assigned by the prime contractor.* For example, KYY. The *shipment number prefix should different for each "shipped from" address*, (the same as FSCM numbers are assigned — to identify the location of the manufacturing point), and should remain constant throughout the life of the contract/ purchase order. That is, the three alpha digits are to remain the same, and the three numeric digits should run consecutively according to shipment.

2. Again, the first shipment against a contract/order must be 0001 with subsequent partial shipments being numbered consecutively. When multiple tank care or tank truck loads are consolidated on a single DD Form 250, all loads covered by the single DD Form 250 will be considered as one shipment. Only one shipment number should be shown on the DD Form 250.

3. Final Deliveries: A "Z" immediately following the shipment number indicates the last shipment against the contract/order has been made. For example, KYY0004Z. Always reassign the shipment number of the initial shipment where a *replacement shipment* is involved.

Block 3 - Date Shipped:

3. DATE SHIPPED
87Oct20

1. The date shipped identifies the date the shipment is released to the carrier or the date of completion of a service. The date shipped is usually - if inspection (PQA) is at source as specified in the contract (Block 21 of DD 250), when the government QAR signs Block 21 of the DD 250. If the actual shipment date is not known, enter the estimated date of release with an E after the date. This is usually done if the QAR can not be there to sign the DD 250 in Block 21 on the date GSI (Government Source Inspection) is requested. Non-resident government quality assurance personnel have 72 hours to respond to a request like this. The date must consist of seven positions: the first two positions being the last two positions of the year, the third, fourth and fifth being the alphabetic abbreviation of the month, and the last two digits being the day. For example, 87OCT20.

Block 4 - BL/TCN:

4. B/L F-1678962
   TCN AT2020 7650 2367xxx

   1. Three entries may be required as follows:

      a. After B/L enter the commercial or government bill of lading number. If the shipment is to be on a GBL call your local government office for this number.
      b. After the Transportation Control Number (TNC) must be entered when a TCN has been assigned. When more than one TCN applies, enter "See Block 16" and follow the FAR instructions.
      c. Enter the mode of shipment code in the lower right corner of block.

Block 5 - Discount Terms:

5. DISCOUNT TERMS
   3% 12 Days

   1. If the contractor offers a discount it should be shown in this block. Although it is optional, there is a mutual advantage and you will be encouraged to give one. When applicable fill in this block. Example: 2% - 10 days or .5% - 30 days.

Block 6 - Invoice Number/Date:

6. INVOICE
   NO. 4208
   DATE 87 OCT 20

   1. The invoice number/date identifies the date a specific invoice was submitted to the government activity. This block may be left blank except when the DD Form 250 is used as an invoice. When the DD Form 250 is used as an invoice, four copies in addition to regular distribution must be made and forwarded to the payment office. The first copy must be marked, *Original Invoice*, in letters approximately one inch high, the three remaining invoice copies must be marked, *Invoice Copy*. The DD Form 250 should not be corrected to reflect the actual date of invoice submission, except for the copies being used as the invoice.

Block 7 - Page/Of:

7. PAGE | OF
 1 1

 1. The Page/Of identifies the page number and the total number of pages the DD Form 250 consist of. Each page should be numbered consecutively with the total number of pages included in the DD Form 250. Example: 1 of 3, 2 of 3, 3 of 3.

Block 8 - Acceptance Point:

8. ACCEPTANCE POINT
 S or D

 1. The acceptance point is a very important item. It appears on the face of the contract or may be included in the schedule attached to the contract. If a schedule is attached it will be indicated on the face of the contract. The acceptance point is to identify the point where the goods/services are accepted by the government. Enter an "S" for acceptance at origin or "D" for acceptance at destination. If Accept-is at Origin, the government representative who services the plant will have to be called in to sign Block 21 of the DD Form 250 prior to the shipment of goods and services. If the DD Form 250 is sent to the payment office without the government representative's signature and stamp, the government payment office will return the DD Form 250 until the government representative signs the form. This definitely will hold up payment for goods and services rendered.

Blocks 9 & 11 - Prime Contractor name, Address and H8 Code (FSCM):

9. PRIME CONTRACTOR CODE | 20144
 XYC Company |
 Main Street
 Anywhere, U.S.A.
11. SHIPPED FROM (If other than 9) CODE | FOB: D
 "See Block 9"

 1. The prime contractor code also known as contractor name and address code is used to identify the contractor and location of the facility with whom the government is doing business. It appears on the face of the contract, next to the contractor's name and address under |Code. This

five digit alphanumeric code is to be entered on all DD Form 250's along with the company's name and address and zip code 5 + 4.

Block 10 - Administered By and CODE:

1. The name, address and code of the government activity administering a specific contract appears on the face (first page) of the contract. If this code is missing, it is suggested that you call the government ACO office to obtain this code. This information must be entered in Block 10 of the DD Form 250.

Block 11 - Shipped From and Code:

1. This code may be the same as the code in Block 9. It serves to identify the activity from which shipment is made. It may be shown in the contract as plant location or on an attached schedule. This block will differ from Block 9 when performances of service/items do not require delivery of items upon completion of services or DD Form 250 covers performance at multiple locations. If it is the same as Block 9 enter "See Block 9." On the same line to the right of "FOB" enter "S" for origin or "D" for destination as specified in the contract. Enter the name, address, and code cited on the face page of the contract.

Block 12 - Payment will be Made By and Code:

1. The name and address and code of the government payment office that appears on the face of the contract will be inserted into this block. Unless the contract specifies otherwise, this code is the place to which you will mail your invoices for payment. Blocks 10, 12, and 13 must have "in the clear" addresses and DoDAAD codes which should be in the shipping instructions of the contract. Contact your plant's CAO if these codes are missing in the contract. Remember: all mistakes and deletions on this form will delay payment.

Block 13 - Shipped To and Code:

1. The shipped to name, address and code is shown on the front page or on an attached schedule of the contract. It serves to identify the activity to which the shipment is to be made. If more than one location is involved, they will be in a schedule beside the applicable item number or as required in another schedule location in the contract. Enter the name, address and code as contained in the applicable shipping

instructions. The address and code is important. They are used to identify where material is being shipped. If omitted, delays in payment could result.

Block 14 - Mark For and Code:

1. This code may be the same as the shipped to code in Block 13. It is

   shown in the contract on the face page or may be on an attached schedule as part of the contract. This code identifies the activity to which the shipment was marked for but shipment was made to another activity. Enter the *"Mark For"* name, address and code contained in the shipping instructions. This *"Mark For,"* like the *Ship To*, is a very vital part of the DD Form 250. Its absence could also delay payment and cause the receiving activity to have problems identifying the shipment. There may be special entries required in this block by the contract as listed in the FAR.

Block 15 - Item Number:

1. The item number is called a contract line item number (CLIN) or sub-

   line item number. The CLIN may have special requirements called out on the 1423's and Data Item Descriptions in the contract. It serves to identify the item that is being shipped. Enter the line item or subline item number as shown in the contract (exactly). The line item must contain four digits and be placed to the left of the dashed line.

Block 16 - Stock/Part Number and Description

1. The stock/part number, called National Stock Number (NSN), or noncatalog number, appears in the contract either on the face page or as part of a schedule that is part of the contract. It identifies the item/service contained in the shipment. If applicable, enter for each line item the NSN and the descriptive noun of the item nomenclature, using single space when less than four line items and double space when more than four line items, when provided in the shipping instructions. When a TCN is assigned for each line item, enter the transportation control number prefix by "TCN." On the last line enter the requisition number or terminal release order number, when provided in the shipping instructions. When the NSN is required but not cited in a contract and has not been furnished by the government, shipment can be made

without such NSN at the direction of the contracting officer. Enter the authority for such shipment.

NATIONAL STOCK NUMBER (NSN). When an NSN is not provided or it is necessary to supplement the number, include other identification, e.g., manufacturers name or federal supply code and number. Additional part numbers may be shown in parenthesis or slashes. Include the description or item.

GROSS WEIGHT. The gross weight of the shipment is to be put into Block 16 in (lbs.) pounds.

MILSTRIP. The MILSTRIP (Military Standard Requisitioning and Issue Procedure) is used by you if authorized by the terms of the contract to requisition or move government material to supply control cognizance. This is a number that describes where items are to be sent, used or stored at the using facility. Enter the MILSTRIP number on the DD Form 250 when provided in the contract or shipping instructions. When more than one requisition is used enter the unit of measure and the quantity shipped against each requisition on the same line. The MILSTRIP number is of great importance to the receiving activity and ADP efforts and is used to route shipments properly. When the full 22 position MILSTRIP Requisition Number is not provided, the 14 number MILSTRIP should be used.

FMS. When a contract involves FMS (Foreign Military Sales) it will be identified on the face page of the contract or in the item description. Enter in Block 16 the special FMS marking, the applicable FMS country and case identifier as provided in the contract, and the gross weight. Following the words FMS Case No., a two digit Country Code followed by a three digit case code is entered in Block 16. If these codes are not shown on the DD Form 250, both the payment office and the receiving activity will have problems.

Block 17 - Quantity Shipped/Received:

1. The quantity shipped/received identifies the total number of items the shipment contains. Enter the quantity shipped, using the unit of measure indicated in the contract (this is for payment purposes also). When a second unit of measure is used for purposes other than payment, enter the appropriate quantity directly below in parentheses. On the final shipment of a line item of a contract containing a clause permitting a variation of quantity and when an underrun exists, you

should enter a Z below the last digit of the quantity. If a replacement shipment is involved, enter below the last digit of the quantity the letter "A" to designate first replacement, "B" for second, etc. The final shipment "Z" on underrun should not be used when a final line item shipment is replaced. Insert a "Z" only if this completes an authorized underrun, and a "A" for replacement shipments.

Block 18 - Unit:

1. The unit identifies the unit of measure. It appears as a line item in the contract schedule. Enter the abbreviation of the unit measure as indicated in the contract for payment. When a second unit of measure is used for shipping purposes, enter it directly below in parentheses. This unit of measure is another important item, it should be the same as that shown in the contract. Failure to put the correct unit of measure will hold up payments until corrected.

Block 19 - Unit Price:

1. Unit price identifies the price of each unit of measure. This price may be entered at your option except: on Navy procurements, the two copies of the DD Form 250 addressed to the consignee via mail should be priced using actual price or, if not available, estimated prices. If the price is estimated, enter an "E" after the price when the DD Form 250 is used as an invoice. For clothing and textile contracts containing a bailment clause, enter the cited government furnished property unit value opposite "GFP unit value" entry in Block 16. Copies of all DD Form 250 related to a Foreign Military Sales Representative must contain unit price, either actual or estimated. Refer to the FAR, Block 19 instructions.

Block 20 - Amount:

1. The amount in this block serves to identify the total dollar amount of the shipment. It is the extended amount of Block 17 times Block 19. This block should be blank when Block 19 is blank. Remember: Blocks 19 and 20 must be completed if the DD Form 250 is to be used as an invoice. A total invoice dollar value must also be included when the DD Form 250 is used as an invoice.

Block 21 - Procurement Quality Assurance:

1. This block is used by the government representative to indicate that the quality and quantity of items on the report is within the contract terms. The words *"conform to contract"* contained in the printed statement in Blocks A and B relate to contract obligations pertaining to quality and quantity of the items on the report. The statement shall not be modified. Under "Signature of Auth Govt Rep," the government representative's name should be typewritten along with the CAO code as defined in Block 10 of the DD Form 250 in parenthesis. When a shipment is authorized under Alternative Release Procedure (approved for release by the contractor with subsequent signature by the QAR), the appropriate contractor signed certificate should be attached to or included on the top copy of the DD Form 250 copies distributed to the payment office/CAO. Payments may be delayed if this certificate is not included.

2. CERTIFICATE OF CONFORMANCE (CoC). When contract terms provide for use of CoC and shipment is made under these terms, the contractor shall enter "Certificate of Conformance" in Block 21A on the next line following the PQA and acceptance statements. The appropriate contractor signed certificate should be attached to or included on the top copy of the DD Form 250 copies distributed to the payment office/CAO. A copy of the certificate should also be attached or on copies of the DD Form 250 sent with shipment.

3. ALTERNATIVE RELEASE PROCEDURE. When alternative release procedures apply (approved for release by the contractor with subsequent signature by the QAR), the contractor or subcontractor should complete the entries required and enter in capital letters "ALTERNATIVE RELEASE PROCEDURE" on the next line following the printed PQA/acceptance statement. When acceptance is at origin, you should furnish the payment office copies of the DD Form 250 to the authorized government representative for signing and dating and forwarding to the payment office/CAO.

4. FAST PAY. When Fast Pay procedures apply, and a DD Form 25 is prepared, you should enter in capital letters "FAST PAY" on the next line following the printed PQA/acceptance statement. When under the provisions of Fast Pay you elect not to use a DD Form 250, follow the special instructions of the Fast Pay clause related to entries required on your invoice.

Block 22 - Receiver's Use:

1. This block identifies the quantity received and the condition of the shipment. It is to be used by the receiving activity (government or contractor). The date the supplies arrived is the date to be entered.

Block 23 - Contractor Use Only:

1. This block is reserved for your use. It may be used for entries such as the CoC statement or any other information that may be of use to you in keeping tract of shipments, methods of shipment, accounting use, etc.

DD FORM 250 CORRECTION INSTRUCTIONS:

1. Because of errors or omissions, it may be necessary to correct the DD Form 250 after distribution. Corrections can be made to the original DD Form 250 master or on a new DD Form 250. In either case, the corrected document must be redistributed. Corrections should be made as follows:

   a. Circle the error and place the corrected information in the same block. If the space is limited, enter the corrected information in Block 16 reference page and block. Enter omissions in Block 16 referencing omissions page and block.

   b. When corrections have been made to entries for line items (Block 15) or quantity (Block 17) enter "Corrections Have Been Verified" on page 1 of the corrected copy of the DD Form 250. The authorized Government representative will sign and date immediately below the statement. This verification statement and signature are not required for other corrections.

   c. Pages of the DD Form 250 requiring corrections should be clearly marked "Corrected Copy." Avoid obliteration of any other entries. When corrections are only made on continuation sheets, page 1 should also be marked "Corrected Copy."

   d. The only copies that should be distributed to the initial distribution recipients are page 1 and those continuation pages marked "Corrected Copy." A complete DD Form 250 with corrections should be distributed to the new address(es) created by error correction.

CHECK LIST FOR THE PREPARATION OF DD FORM 250

	YES	NO
1. Have you sent the invoice to the proper office? Read your contract to determine the proper office.	___	___
2. Does the name of the company and the address on the invoice match the contract? The check will be mailed to the contract address unless *the contract* specifies a separate remittance address.	___	___
3. Is the contract number correct? An example is DAAE07-87-C-2043. If the contract is a Basic Ordering Agreement, the order number (SPIIN) is also necessary. An example is DLA600-87-A-0001-0001. The contract number is used to trace all actions on a contract.	___	___
4. Is the Contract Line Item Number (CLIN) or Exhibit Line Item Number (ELIN) correct and does it match the contract? Examples are 0001, 0001AA or A001.	___	___
5. Is the shipment number on the invoice, and is it correct? It should be a seven position alphanumeric number, such as ABC0001. If the shipment is final, a Z must appear after the seventh position, such as ABC0001Z.	___	___
6. Is the unit price correct? Same as in the contract?	___	___
7. Are the extensions correct?	___	___
8. Is the invoice total correct?	___	___
9. Is the description of the material shown on the invoice and is the national stock number included?	___	___
10. Are shipped quantities for each item shown on the invoice?	___	___
11. Are the ship to/mark for locations shown on the invoice?	___	___
12. Is the unit of measure shown for each item? Same as in the contract?	___	___
13. Are invoice number and date shown on the invoice?	___	___

	YES	NO
14. Are discount rates and terms on the invoice?	___	___
15. Have you offered a small discount to speed payment? Only discounts earning an annual 9% return will be considered.	___	___
16. Does the contract call for Certificate of Conformance (CoC)? Be sure the certificate is signed by a contractor's representative and the Quality Assurance Representative signs the Material Inspection and Receiving Report DD Form 250. The CoC must be attached to or included on the DD Form 250, or payment will be delayed.	___	___
17. Is a DD Form 250 required? If so, be sure it is sent to the Contract Administration Office, not the Finance Office. In case the CAO is also the Regional DCASR, the invoice and the DDForm 250 should be sent in separately.	___	___
18. Is First Article approval required? If so, this means the First Article must be approved before any further shipment can be placed.	___	___
19. Is ACO approval required? If yes, the invoice should be sent directly to the ACO's office.	___	___
20. Is PCO approval required? If yes, the invoice should be sent directly to the PCO's office.	___	___
21. FAST PAY. If FAR Clause for (Fast Pay) is specified by your contract you may elect not to prepare a DD Form 250. If so, then you must mark all copies of your invoice with the words FAST PAY and no DD 250 is prepared. Further, the invoice must contain all the information normally required on the DD Form 250.	___	___
22. FAST PAY. If you ship by Post Office or Common Carrier, you must include evidence of shipment such as shipment documents (e.g., Post Office receipt) or show date of shipment, name and address of carrier, bill of lading or other shipment identification number. If you	___	___

	YES	NO
ship by other means, e.g., your truck, provide a receipted copy of your delivery document.		
23. Are "Fast Payment" invoices stamped "Fast Pay"? If they are not, this will delay payment.	___	___
24. Are there enough copies of the invoice? An original and three copies are required.	___	___
25. Is the original invoice marked Original Invoice and are the copies marked Copy?	___	___
26. Do you wish to use the DD Form 250 as an Invoice? If so, the same information, distribution and marking, are required as for a commercial invoice.	___	___
27. If the invoice is for subsistence items (DLA13H), is DPSC Form 300M attached to the Invoice? DPSC Form 300M should cite only the items shipped and billed on the invoice.	___	___
28. Is evidence of shipment required? If contractual terms call for inspection and acceptance at source and F.O.B. DESTINATION, a copy of evidence of shipment should be attached to the invoice.	___	___
29. If you prepare and submit your invoices by complying with the above provisions, there should be no problems with the processing and payment of your invoices. However, if problems should develop and you need assistance, you should contact your nearest CAO office of DCAS.	___	___

MATERIAL INSPECTION AND RECEIVING REPORT

1. PROC. INSTRUMENT IDEN (CONTRACT)

ORDER NO.

6. INVOICE NO.

DATE

7. PAGE OF

8. ACCEPTANCE POINT

2. SHIPMENT NO.

3. DATE SHIPPED

4. B/L

TCN

5. DISCOUNT TERMS

9. PRIME CONTRACTOR *CODE*

10. ADMINISTERED BY *CODE*

11. SHIPPED FROM *If other than 9) *CODE* F.O.B.

12. PAYMENT WILL BE MADE BY *CODE*

13. SHIPPED TO *CODE*

14. MARKED FOR *CODE*

15. ITEM NO.	16. STOCK PART NO. DESCRIPTION *(Indicate number of shipping containers - type of container-container number)*	17. QUANTITY SHIP-D/REC'D	18. UNIT	19. UNIT PRICE	20. AMOUNT

21. PROCUREMENT QUALITY ASSURANCE

☐ POA ☐ A. ORIGIN

ACCEPTANCE of listed items has been made by me or under my supervision and they conform to contract, accept as noted herein or on supporting documents.

DATE SIGNATURE OF AUTH GOVT REP

TYPED NAME AND OFFICE

☐ POA ☐ B. DESTINATION

ACCEPTANCE of listed items has been made by me or under my supervision and they conform to contract, accept as noted herein or on supporting documents.

DATE SIGNATURE OF AUTH GOVT REP

TYPED NAME AND OFFICE

22. RECEIVER'S USE

Quantities show in column 17 were received in apparent good condition except as noted.

DATE RECEIVED SIGNATURE OF AUTH GOVT REP

TYPED NAME AND OFFICE

* If quantity received by the Government is the same as quantity shipped, indicate by (*) mark, if different, enter actual quantity received below quantity shipped and encircle.

23. CONTRACTOR USE ONLY

DD FORM 1 NOV 68 250

REPLACES EDITION OF 1 AUG 67 WHICH MAY BE USED

APPENDIX II

Automatic Test Equipment (ATE)

QUALITY CONTROL PUBLICATION	QCP NO. APPENDIX II
	PAGE NO. 1 OF 19
	ISSUE DATE:
TITLE: AUTOMATIC TEST EQUIPMENT	APPROVED BY:
	REVISION NO: 0
	REVISION DATE:

This review of the Department of Defense requirements for the control of Automatic Test Equipment (ATE) will enable contractors to understand the section of DLAM 8200.1 that addresses this requirement and its applicability to MIL-Q-9858A, MIL-I-45208A, the NATO AQAP, and the NASA quality programs.

Following is a table of contents that formats the ATE discussion that follows.

TABLE OF CONTENTS

DISCUSSION:

1. Testing Philosophy And Introduction To Test Systems

   The following definitions and descriptions show the variety of items or functions to be found in any measuring system, manual or automatic.

   a. Device to be tested.

   b. A stimulus (source of signal to the device/unit under test UUT).

QUALITY CONTROL PUBLICATION	QCP NO. APPENDIX II
	PAGE NO. 2 OF 19
	ISSUE DATE:
TITLE: AUTOMATIC TEST EQUIPMENT	APPROVED BY:
	REVISION NO: 0
	REVISION DATE:

c. A measurement instrument to quantify the response.

d. An operator to make the whole process work.

e. Other functions that can be added to ease the operator's task and the automating of the test function.

The operator acts less as a mechanical part of the measurement process and can devote his/her attention to the results rather than the details of the applicable measurement. If the results are used for automatic control of other equipment operating on the device under test, a process-control system can be achieved.

A. Measurement Systems

Depicted below are various definitions and descriptions of the items and/or functions to be found in a measuring system, manual or automatic. These are:

1. Device under test

A component is made out of materials, a network is made out of components, a circuit is made out of networks, and so on. The categories can be further subdivided.

a. Components and networks can be linear, active or passive.
b. Circuits can be analog or digital, discrete or integrated. The hierarchy of electronic devices can be shown to be imperfect, such as: Is a transformer, component, network, a circuit? In general, any electronic device can be fitted into one of these categories.

2. Adaptor

The adaptor block is used to define items that interface the device under test into the measurement system. This category includes test boards, fixtures, or sockets that contact the leads or terminals

QUALITY CONTROL PUBLICATION	QCP NO. APPENDIX II
	PAGE NO. 3 OF 19
	ISSUE DATE:
TITLE: AUTOMATIC TEST EQUIPMENT	APPROVED BY:
	REVISION NO: 0
	REVISION DATE:

of a component or network, or a multipoint prober that contacts the nodes/trace of a microcircuit.

3. Input

   Input equipment facilitates the insertion of the device under test into the adaptor. Examples are:

   a. Vibratory-bowl component feeders
   b. Rotary and linear transports
   c. Other mechanical devices

4. Condition

   Conditioning equipment applies to the device under test as a secondary stimulus, such as:

   a. Power
   b. Bias
   c. Heat
   d. Cold
   e. Shock
   f. Set up terminal load conditions

5. Switching

   Switching equipment is used to connect the device or device adaptor to the test system and vary the connections of the device terminals.

   a. Solid-state scanners (multi-plexors)
   b. Relay trees
   c. Crossbar scanners
   d. Reed-relay scanners

QUALITY CONTROL PUBLICATION	QCP NO. APPENDIX II
	PAGE NO. 4 OF 19
	ISSUE DATE:
TITLE: AUTOMATIC TEST EQUIPMENT	APPROVED BY:
	REVISION NO: 0
	REVISION DATE:

6. Stimulus

Stimulus sources for measurement systems are many and include:

a. DC supplies
b. Oscillators
c. Synthesizers
d. Function generators
e. Ramp, pulse, burst, word generators
f. D/A and A/D converters
g. And others

7. Measure

There are many types of measuring devices. Examples of such devices are:

a. Voltmeters
b. Current meters
c. Phase meters
d. Impedance bridges
e. Frequency counters
f. A/D and D/A converters
g. Optical comparators
h. Video measuring devices
i. Laser measuring devices
j. And other types

These instruments should also be programmable. Data output in digital form is useful but not always a necessary characteristic of such instruments. The signal measurement functions are often combined in a single instrument, as in:

k. Automatic capacitance bridges
l. Digital ohmeters

QUALITY CONTROL PUBLICATION	QCP NO. APPENDIX II
	PAGE NO. 5 OF 19
	ISSUE DATE:
TITLE: AUTOMATIC TEST EQUIPMENT	APPROVED BY:
	REVISION NO: 0
	REVISION DATE:

8. Control

The control function can be accomplished by a variety of equipment in a variety of ways. Card readers and tape readers are often used to program and sequence automatic equipment with the actual program determined by the holes in the cards or tape. Patchboards, plugboards, and switches can be used as "memories" to set up test conditions and sequences. Cam-operated, motor-driven switches and relay networks are used also. Specialized digital logic circuits are often applied to this function. The most versatile programmer/controller of all, the computer, many of which are in the workplace today, will be discussed in a later section.

9. Process

Data from the measurement instruments must often be processed in some way. One example of processing is limit comparison. The comparator may be an analog or digital circuit. It compares the measured data with preset or programmed limits and determines whether the data is above, below, or within the limits and provides appropriate output signals such as: lamp illumination, contact closures, digital logic signals, etc. Another form of processing is coupling. The coupler may store and convert parallel data (all digits at once) to serial data (one digit at a time) to operate card punches, storage tape, disks, tape punches or strip printers, or it may perform the opposite function (serial to parallel conversion) to operate gang punches or line printers or displays. Yet another form of processing is computation or data processing. The processor may perform arithmetic computations on the data to provide corrections or conversions or to somehow convert the data to a more useful form.

10. Output

The output function of an automatic test system is also performed by a variety of equipment and appears in a variety of equipment and appears in a variety of ways. One typical output function is that of display. Measurement results or test conditions may be displayed by means of oscilloscopes, panel meters, indicator lamps, digital indicators (visual display), or by ringing a bell or buzzer (auditory display). Hard-copy output can be provided in the form of graphs, printed lists, or typed reports by means of recorders, printers, or typewriters. Output can also consist of signals for on-line processing by local or remote equipment. Finally, output signals can be used to close the loop on the test process by activating sorters, automatic handlers, lasers, or other devices that affect the device under test.

11. Interface

An interface can be considered a miscellaneous category used to dignify any function that cannot be conveniently forced into one of the other categories. In general, it defines any item that is used to tie together some of the other items. This function becomes one of extreme importance in computer controlled systems, as will be discussed later. It should be noted that the above descriptions are functional rather than hardware. The hardware may be similar, but often it is not. Since many hardware items combine several of the above functions.

B. The Computer

The largest single factor contributing to the revolution in the art of automatic testing has been the emergence of the computer. In particular, the mini-computer, and the micro-computer, as an available and reliable item of hardware with immense capability. It appears everywhere in automatic test systems, for programming, controlling,

QUALITY CONTROL PUBLICATION TITLE: AUTOMATIC TEST EQUIPMENT	QCP NO. APPENDIX II
	PAGE NO. 7 OF 19
	ISSUE DATE:
	APPROVED BY:
	REVISION NO: 0
	REVISION DATE:

and for data processing. Due to the relatively low cost of today's microcomputers, they are being used more extensively in all aspects of the production/test cycle. The following subsections of this topic discuss some of the considerations to be given in the choice of what type of ATE will be utilized.

1. Operational flexibility

   If the job of the test system is fixed and well defined, for example: the sorting of resistors into prescribed categories, and the test system will be used for that one specific task forever, a computer may or may not be required. It will not take much, however, to warrant a computer. When the number of possible controls and settings becomes large (nominal values, upper and lower limits, bias voltage, test voltage, test frequency, advance, dwell and soak times, etc., the sheer number of knobs, dials, and switches to adjust can get out of hand and some form of sophisticated programming will be required. For this reason alone, the computer could represent an economical solution.

2. Changing requirements

   When the test system must be rapidly converted from one job to another and enough hardware can be combined in one system to do all the jobs, the computer will most often be the economical way to provide this rapid conversion.

3. Data manipulation and output

   Due to today's mass manipulation and output of data required in the work environment, the computer presents the most efficient and cost effective method of accomplishing such tasks, due to its relatively low cost. If the data must be adjusted or corrected and a complicated output format provided, the computer may offer the only solution. The computer also provides some side benefits:

QUALITY CONTROL PUBLICATION	QCP NO. APPENDIX II
	PAGE NO. 8 OF 19
	ISSUE DATE:
TITLE: AUTOMATIC TEST EQUIPMENT	APPROVED BY:
	REVISION NO: 0
	REVISION DATE:

a. The ability to correct measurement data for fixed or systematic errors, and thus improving the accuracy of the basic measurement system.
b. The possibility of providing data analysis in the desired form and eliminating the need for further off-line processing.

4. Computer functions

The computer can perform two basic functions:

a. The control function
The computer performs the control function by means of a program stored in its memory.
b. The process function
The computer performs the process function by means of its central processor.

To make use of these capabilities, two other elements are required:

1. An interface system

The interface system is required to tie various external pieces of equipment to the computer, since neither the computer or the test instruments may be directly compatible. Cost considerations in the design of general purpose test instruments do not allow the inclusion of expensive interface circuits. Today, however, test instruments are available that make the interfacing task, if not unnecessary, at least easier. The design of computers cannot anticipate all of the possible interface requirements. The interface circuits perform the functions of I/O (input/output) bus expansion, level conversion, decoding, storage, transfer, and control. By storing data signals, both from and to the computer, the interface system allows the (fast) computer to keep busy while the (slow) test instruments are doing their job. When the test instruments are ready, either to receive instructions or to give up their data, their

QUALITY CONTROL PUBLICATION	QCP NO. APPENDIX II
	PAGE NO. 9 OF 19
	ISSUE DATE:
TITLE: AUTOMATIC TEST EQUIPMENT	APPROVED BY:
	REVISION NO: 0
	REVISION DATE:

interface control circuits can provide an "interrupt" signal (flag) to the computer to request its attention. Some micro and mini computers make provision for plug-in interface circuit cards within their housings/packages while others require an external unit (external to the main housing/package of the computer itself).

2. The computer software (program)

   To make the most efficient use of the memory of the computer, operating programs are often written in assembly language. This language is easily linked to the computer's core but is difficult and lengthy to write. This approach works fine if the test set will be used with few infrequently changed programs. If not, more memory and perhaps the use of a higher level test-set language may be needed.

   a. Computer languages

      Looking into a local bookstore, it will be noted that much has been and is being written on the topic of computer language. Computer language, and the various levels of this language, is the terminology of communication between the programmer and the computer. There are no strict definitions of language level. In general, high-level languages allow the programmer to write program statements (commands) in terms that are familiar, such as English words or mathematical equations, and has few rules of order or format, so the particular characteristics of the computer can be ignored when running the program. Low-level languages force the programmer to adapt his particular problem to the characteristics of the machine to be used. The programer may use mnemonics or octal numbers which are related to the operation of the computer and its subsections (hardware/firmware, bus

QUALITY CONTROL PUBLICATION	QCP NO. APPENDIX II
	PAGE NO. 10 OF 19
	ISSUE DATE:
TITLE: AUTOMATIC TEST EQUIPMENT	APPROVED BY:
	REVISION NO: 0
	REVISION DATE:

operations, memory locations etc.) The use of higher-level languages may require several intermediate steps before a final operating program is prepared and run, that is, editing, debugging, punching tapes, loading tapes, preparing and running floppy disks or hard disks, etc. Given sufficient computer capability, the steps can be handled automatically (with little programmer action) by the use of a sophisticated operating-system program. Programs can be prepared and run at essentially the same time.

b. Test-set languages

There are also programming and operating languages for automatic test systems. Test-set languages can be high-level or low-level depending on their application (problem) or to the test-set (equipment). When the function knob of a digital counter is set to "Frequency," you are using a high-level language related to the application, but of little flexibility. Setting the power switch to "OFF" uses a lower-level language. This concept has given rise to a host of test-set languages such as: POL (Problem Oriented Language), TOOL (Test Oriented Operator Language), ATLAS (Abbreviated Test Language for All Systems), the UNIX operating language, and many others that have no names but do their jobs well. If the test-set is dedicated to a specific application (capacitor testing, transformer testing, logic circuit testing), the language can be made high-level and use terms relating to the device under test (nominal value, transformer terminals, logic drive pattern). If the test is for more universal use, its language should be lower-level and use terms relating to the instruments within the set (function, range, connection). The program of a dedicated test can provide two levels of language for the users of the set: A low-

QUALITY CONTROL PUBLICATION	QCP NO. APPENDIX II
	PAGE NO. 11 OF 19
	ISSUE DATE:
TITLE: AUTOMATIC TEST EQUIPMENT	APPROVED BY:
	REVISION NO: 0
	REVISION DATE:

level language for the programmer, which will enable the user to change certain operating constants or test sequences, and a higher-level language for the operator, which will enable the operator to control the set for a specific test. A particularly useful mode of operation with such languages is an interactive or conversational mode, wherein programming questions are automatically displayed, printed, or typed by the operator. The main resident program, "The Operating System" interprets the operator's instructions and runs the test.

II. Test Systems

A. ATE Self Test

ATE self-test programs are critical to the success or failure of any large-scale programming effort. The prime function of ATE self-test programs are to establish confidence in ATE performance and to provide programmed procedures for isolation and repair of ATE operational failures. The extremely high testing speed possible on ATE contributes strongly to maintenance efficiency. Whereas a single ATE system can replace many conventional test stands, the impact of ATE failure is correspondingly more severe. For example, the loss of a multimeter in one of many conventional stands is much less severe than a similar loss in the ATE that replaced them. The backlog of units waiting for test will increase rapidly while the ATE system is down for repair. Self-test for ATE systems generally falls into one of two categories:

1. System self-test

System self-test programs (functionally called "Confidence and Maintenance Programs") provide an overall performance isolation to a level determined by the spares complement at the ATE installation. It is recommended that these programs be developed

QUALITY CONTROL PUBLICATION	QCP NO. APPENDIX II
	PAGE NO. 12 OF 19
	ISSUE DATE:
TITLE: AUTOMATIC TEST EQUIPMENT	APPROVED BY:
	REVISION NO: 0
	REVISION DATE:

by the ATE system contractor concurrent with ATE hardware development to assure complete compatibility. A successful ATE system is a fully integrated software-hardware complex. System software includes the on-line operating system and off-line operating system and off-line support programs such as compilers. System self-test programs which are developed concurrent with ATE hardware also provide a valuable system integration tool for debugging the hardware-software.

2. Survey self-test

   This is a short test on each ATE building block used in a given test program which is run each time that items are tested.

B. Fault Isolation Level

The level of fault isolation in system self-test is generally based on the spares complement for the ATE installation, the mean-time-to-repair (MTTR) goals, and the ATE system test-point availability. Isolation of a system fault to single removable subassembly is the preferred approach, but it is very dependent on system test points. One practical alternative is isolation to a small number of sub-assemblies. In this approach, if extensive testing or time-consuming manual procedures are required to identify one of a set of subassemblies, repair is expedited by replacement of the entire set. Another alternative is to identify only the faulty function. Identification of the specific fault can then be accomplished by manual procedures.

C. Self-test Accuracy

Accuracy is defined as a function of the allowable deviation from nominal value after specified response time. The self-test program must allow no more than this specified time when evaluating system performance. Accuracy should be tested under worst-case conditions at the UUT (Unit under test) interface connector panel. For example,

QUALITY CONTROL PUBLICATION	QCP NO. APPENDIX II
	PAGE NO. 13 OF 19
	ISSUE DATE:
TITLE: AUTOMATIC TEST EQUIPMENT	APPROVED BY:
	REVISION NO: 0
	REVISION DATE:

the accuracy of a digital multimeter, measuring near positive full-scale should be verified immediately after having measured a full-scale negative value, allowing no more than the specified settling time. Limits are determined by the same rules used for UUT testing. All ATE stimulus and measurement accuracies which cannot be tested within the minimum accuracy-ratio constraint must be recalibrated at periodic interval. Ideally, the self-test reference standard will be the only device requiring calibration.

1. Testing time

   Testing time is often increased by performance tests configured to simplify fault isolation. The trade-off, however, should favor time because self-test is one of the most frequently used programs in the ATE program library. Attention to the following rules will help decrease testing time:

   a. ATE validation

      Self-test is essential to an adequate ATE system. By self-test the system validates itself. The self-test can be extended to all components of the ATE system.

   b. ATE calibration

      With adequate reference standards and measurement accuracies, the complete ATE system can be maintenance calibrated to the reference standards. Accuracy requirements, however, will sometimes preclude the incorporation of all the devices over the entire spectrum. When this happens, calibration of ATE functions in addition to the reference standards must be performed on a periodic basis. Calibration of ATE functions can be expedited by a test program designed to control the calibration process. The program is an integrated group of independent tests and procedures to

<table>
<tr><td rowspan="3">QUALITY CONTROL PUBLICATION</td><td>QCP NO. APPENDIX II</td></tr>
<tr><td>PAGE NO. 14 OF 19</td></tr>
<tr><td>ISSUE DATE:</td></tr>
<tr><td rowspan="3">TITLE: AUTOMATIC TEST EQUIPMENT</td><td>APPROVED BY:</td></tr>
<tr><td>REVISION NO: 0</td></tr>
<tr><td>REVISION DATE:</td></tr>
</table>

control the ATE in a step-by-step calibration sequence. In advanced computer controlled ATE systems, it is possible to measure and store system offsets each time the system self-test is run. These stored offsets can be used to automatically adjust stimulus programming and measured values to compensate for system offsets, thus eliminating the necessity of frequency calibration adjustments.

c. Reference standards for self-test

The effectiveness of ATE self-test programs is greatly influenced by ATE standards. Preferred standards are ones that provide all requirements for system calibration as well as system maintenance. To provide this capability, ATE standards should have an accuracy ratio, with respect to the ATE measurement subsystem of 10:1.

3. The Contractor's ATE Quality Program

A. Quality Assurance

Quality is a product characteristic which can be designed into a test program by means of deliberate control efforts in all phases of conception, design, production, validation, and field usage. A satisfactory level of quality can be achieved only by a planned effort with specifically defined tasks and objectives. The role of quality control is to establish a plan that assures compliance with requirements of the contract. A good quality program will detect promptly and correct design practices which could result in defective program sets. Technical data, design policy, or other elements of contract performance which could create system support problems must be identified and changed as the result of the quality program plan. Personnel performing the quality functions should have sufficiently well-defined responsibility, authority, and organizational stature to:

QUALITY CONTROL PUBLICATION	QCP NO. APPENDIX II
	PAGE NO. 15 OF 19
	ISSUE DATE:
TITLE: AUTOMATIC TEST EQUIPMENT	APPROVED BY:
	REVISION NO: 0
	REVISION DATE:

1. Identify and act on quality problems.
2. Maintain design policy to current levels.
3. To accumulate all the necessary design review results, inspection reports, quality conformance data, and shipping dates as evidence of meeting contractual requirements.

B. Quality Program Plan

The development of a "Quality Program Plan" is the first step in the quality assurance process. It is a general description of the tasks required to assure that the procurement software will satisfy the support requirements of the prime equipment and the ATE. It indicates the planning, organization, direction, and control necessary to carry out each task. An optimal plan will make maximum use of the techniques and procedures discussed in this section and will be kept current by revisions, supplements, and bulletins (alerts), as necessary, throughout the life of the project.

C. Quality Program Outline

Following is a suggested ATE quality program outline that could be used in the formatting and writing procedures for the control of ATE.

1. Quality program plan

The quality program plan provides effective requirements and procedures for implementing a quality program plan for ATE. As stated previously in this book, quality is not the province of any one department within a company's structure. All disciplines and personnel within a company should be encouraged to participate in total quality program, including top management. Without this participation "Quality" will work ineffectively or not at all. All the necessary disciplines including quality engineering should participate in the initial planning, design reviews, production planning, and the implementation of an audit system to check whether or not the plan is being implemented.

QUALITY CONTROL PUBLICATION	QCP NO. APPENDIX II
	PAGE NO. 16 OF 19
	ISSUE DATE:
TITLE: AUTOMATIC TEST EQUIPMENT	APPROVED BY:
	REVISION NO: 0
	REVISION DATE:

2. Quality instructions

   Quality instructions are detailed instructions covering all tasks described in the quality program plan and constitute quality requirements imposed on applicable design, production, quality, and configuration control groups for their particular efforts.

3. Concept review

   The concept review provides a qualitative design review of the test plan to assure a uniform design approach consistent with conventional design practices and the application of optimum and standard techniques.

4. Design reviews

   The design review provides a qualitative review of the completed ELP and a quantitative design review of the fault-isolation logic.

5. Production procedures

   The production procedures ensure against loss of data, destruction of magnetic tape, floppy disks, or other information/program storage devices, library files, and unnecessary computer runs during the production and validation phases.

6. Quality demonstration plan

   The quality demonstration plan provides statistical and procedural means of demonstrating program set quality at the time of software release.

7. Failure reporting, analysis, and feedback system

   Failure reporting, analysis, and feedback provide data to correct program set deficiencies identified by shakedown in an operational environment.

QUALITY CONTROL PUBLICATION	QCP NO. APPENDIX II
	PAGE NO. 17 OF 19
	ISSUE DATE:
TITLE: AUTOMATIC TEST EQUIPMENT	APPROVED BY:
	REVISION NO: 0
	REVISION DATE:

8. Human factors engineering

   Human factors engineering analyzes the man-machine interface associated with software items to evaluate critical factors.

9. Configuration management team

   The configuration management of ATE establishes a baseline for the production item, and controls all changes to it thereafter.

IV. Government Requirements for ATE

DLAM 8200.1, Part 8, Automated Inspection and Part 9, Test Procedures and Reports, are the guidelines established by the Defense Logistics Agency in verifying and approving or disapproving a contractor's ATE program. Paragraph 9-804, Quality Assurance Representative (QAR) Responsibilities states, "In PQA now CQA (Contract Quality Assurance) planning, the QAR shall determine if the contractor plans to use automated inspection. Where ATE is used, the QAR should request technical specialist assistance to assure that the system being utilized by the contractor provides for the required assurance of product quality. The specialist and/or QAR will identify the tasks to be performed by the Government to assure that the contractor complies with contract requirements. The QAR will review the contractor's system for assuring the accuracy of the ATE and the adequacy and completeness of the ATE programming. The AQR will plan and conduct his PQA program as required by this manual."

A. Control and Review of ATE

"When the contract does not invoke a specific requirement for a documented ATE validation system, the contractor's method for control and maintenance of ATE and its programming will be reviewed and evaluated based on the characteristics essential to control of product quality. The QAR will include calibration procedures and frequencies for the test equipment for adequacy and for contractor compliance to the contract. Where computerized or tape driven equipment is used for

QUALITY CONTROL PUBLICATION	QCP NO. APPENDIX II
	PAGE NO. 18 OF 19
	ISSUE DATE:
TITLE: AUTOMATIC TEST EQUIPMENT	APPROVED BY:
	REVISION NO: 0
	REVISION DATE:

automated inspection, the QAR through procedures evaluation (Audits) shall determine the contractor's compliance to his procedures designed to control the repeatability of the test. This may involve the running of a self-test program prior to the testing of an individual item of equipment or for the periodic insertion of an item or product containing known defective characteristics to assure that the testing equipment is properly detecting the known defect. Where a printout is provided, the QAR should include a review of the printout against the requirement to assure that the contractor has properly identified the defective characteristics ... When witnessing automated inspection, the QAR should verify operator compliance with written instructions particularly where the operator inputs instructions to the ATE to supplement the stored program."

B. Elements Of Quality Assurance Of A Contractor's Automatic Inspection Program

QA of automatic inspection has the following elements which a contractor must control, and the government QAR must verify that the contractor is controlling:

1. Control of the ATE
2. Configuration management controls
3. Library controls
4. Repeatability of the ATE
5. Adequacy and completeness of calibration of the ATE
6. Adequate programming
7. Adequacy of instruction to the ATE
8. Adequacy of self-test
9. Adequacy and completeness of records
10. Necessary corrective action taken

Prior to the start of regular production and testing, contractors must have in place a complete quality program. This includes input from

QUALITY CONTROL PUBLICATION	QCP NO. APPENDIX II
	PAGE NO. 19 OF 19
	ISSUE DATE:
TITLE: AUTOMATIC TEST EQUIPMENT	APPROVED BY:
	REVISION NO: 0
	REVISION DATE:

various disciplines and management personnel within the organization. The QAR or other government personnel can request to participate in any planning stage, design review, etc., of a contract.

APPENDIX III

Quality Specifications Transmittal Document (QSTP 001)

COVER PAGE

FOR

QUALITY SPECIFICATIONS TRANSMITTAL DOCUMENT

THIS DOCUMENT IS APPROVED FOR DISTRIBUTION BY:

NAME ______________________ TITLE ____________________

NAME ______________________ TITLE ____________________

NAME ______________________ TITLE ____________________

DATE OF FINAL APPROVAL ____________

REVISION NUMBER ____________
REVISION DATE ____________

NOTE: This document is to be reviewed during the planning stages of each contract to determine if new, additional or clarification of existing quality requirements are to be transmitted to vendors, suppliers, subcontractors.

This document is to be transmitted with all purchase orders to vendors, suppliers, and subcontractors as the means of transmitting quality requirements that are required by a contract or to fulfill the specifications of the company. The alphabetical prefix to each requirement in this document is to be noted on each purchase order as it pertains to that supplier, vendor, or subcontractor.

NAME AND ADDRESS OF ORIGINATING COMPANY	QCP NO. QSTP 001
	PAGE NO. 1 OF 5
	ISSUE DATE:
TITLE: QUALITY SPECIFICATIONS TRANSMITTAL DOCUMENT	APPROVED BY:
	REVISION NO: 0
	REVISION DATE:

The requirements in this document are referenced on the face of the Purchase Order and form a part of the purchase order, in addition to other provisions of the purchase order as applicable.

AA. Certification of Conformance:

Supplier, vendor, subcontractor shipments under this Purchase Order shall constitute supplier/vendor/subcontractor Certification of Conformance to all purchase order requirements, specifications.

AB. Material Certification:

The seller shall supply a Certification of Conformance, identified to the purchase order. The C of C shall be signed by an official of the organization, preferably quality assurance, attesting that the materials, parts supplied fulfill all the requirements/specifications of the purchase order and that all inspection and test records of the company and its suppliers are on file and will be made available to the purchaser and the Government upon request, for a period of at least ten years.

AC. A Certification of Conformance shall be supplied, attesting that all processes were in accordance with the specifications referenced on the purchase order and supplied drawings, specifications. The certification shall be identified to the purchase order and enclosed in an envelope marked "ATTENTION RECEIVING DEPARTMENT." Any lack of responsiveness to this certification requirement will constitute a non-conformance to specification/drawing and will be considered as cause to return supplies or withhold acceptance until CoC is received. These actions are due to the nature of the contract. This request is also extended to Material Certifications.

AD. Inspection by (name of purchaser) is required prior to shipment of parts, material from the facility (source inspection). Evidence of source inspection will be by stamp/signature of (name of purchaser) representative affixed on

NAME AND ADDRESS OF ORIGINATING COMPANY	QCP NO. QSTP 001
	PAGE NO. 2 OF 5
	ISSUE DATE:
TITLE: QUALITY SPECIFICATIONS TRANSMITTAL DOCUMENTS	APPROVED BY:
	REVISION NO: 0
	REVISION DATE:

the shipping documents, and inspection/test reports, if applicable, will accompany the shipment. It is requested that you notify (name of purchaser) 10 days prior to the start of applicable inspections/tests to assure participation by the Government Representative.

AE. Government Source Inspection is required prior to shipment from your facility. Upon receipt of the purchase order and this document, promptly notify the Government Representative who normally services your facility, so that appropriate planning for Government inspection can be accomplished.

On receipt of this requirement in the purchase order, promptly furnish a copy of the purchase order to the Government Representative who normally services your plant, or, if none, to the nearest Army, Navy, Air Force, or Defense Supply Agency inspection office. In the event the representative or office cannot be located, notify (name of purchaser) purchasing office immediately.

AF. The supplier/vendor/subcontractor shall forward to (name of purchaser) a test report containing the physical properties and/or chemical composition of all new materials supplied under the purchase order. The report must identify the material to the drawing, specification, and referenced to the melt, cast, heat, drop, lot, or other similar designation, and must indicate the applicable specification revision. Test reports shall be enclosed in an envelope marked "ATTENTION RECEIVING DEPARTMENT" and be enclosed with the shipping documents that are to be delivered to (name of purchaser).

AG. The supplier/vendor/subcontractor, will furnish a copy, as applicable, of electrical/mechanical test data that verifies compliance of the materials to (name of purchaser) and/or Government drawings/specifications.

NAME AND ADDRESS OF ORIGINATING COMPANY	QCP NO. QSTP 001
	PAGE NO. 3 OF 5
	ISSUE DATE:
TITLE: QUALITY SPECIFICATIONS TRANSMITTAL DOCUMENT	APPROVED BY:
	REVISION NO: 0
	REVISION DATE:

AH. Reservation of Inspection Rights

Items being purchased may be inspected by representatives of (name of purchaser) the U.S. Government and other customers at all times and places, including the place and time of manufacture. If any inspection or test is made by the above mentioned representatives on the premises of the seller, the seller shall without additional charge, provide all reasonable facilities and assistance for the safety and convenience of the inspectors in the performance of their duty. All inspections and tests shall be performed in such a manner as not to unduly delay work in progress. No inspection or test made prior to final inspection/test acceptance shall relieve the seller of the responsibility for defects or other failures to meet the requirements of the purchase order.

AI. The seller shall have in place, an inspection system that complies to the requirements of MIL-I-45208A. The system is subject to audit by the purchaser, U.S. Government Representatives at the suppliers/sellers facility.

AJ. The seller shall have in place, a quality program that complies to the requirements of MIL-Q-9858A. The program is subject to audit by the purchaser, U.S. Government Representatives at the suppliers/sellers facility.

AK. The seller shall have a Quality Assurance Program that meets the requirements of NASA NHB 5300.4 (2B). The program is subject to audit by the purchaser, U.S. Government Representatives at the suppliers/sellers facility.

AL. The seller shall maintain a system for the calibration of all measuring and test equipment used in the fulfillment of the purchase order and in accordance with MIL-STD-45662A.

AM. Materials shipped against this purchase order shall have not less than three quarter (3/4) of the shelf life remaining at the time of shipment. Materials and containers shall be marked with the date of manufacture. Where storage at

NAME AND ADDRESS OF ORIGINATING COMPANY	QCP NO. QSTP 001
	PAGE NO. 4 OF 5
	ISSUE DATE:
TITLE: QUALITY SPECIFICATIONS TRANSMITTAL DOCUMENTS	APPROVED BY:
	REVISION NO: 0
	REVISION DATE:

other than room temperature is needed, the recommended storage conditions shall be marked on the material and/or container.

AN. This order is for MOS or CMOS devices. These items must be packaged in conductive material, or must be packaged in material which is inherently anti-static or which has been coated or treated with an anti-static material to prevent buildup of static charges. If anti-static material is used, the seller shall furnish certification with the delivery that states that the packing material is or has been treated to prevent buildup of static charges.

AO. Marking of items shall conform to requirement 67 of MIL-STD-454. Seller will identify the items with the number of the source control drawing. Seller's part number shall not appear on the items.

AP. Parts and material requirements shall conform to MIL-E-16400.

AQ. Conformal coating when used/specified, shall conform to MIL-E-16400.

AR. Micro-electronic devices shall conform to MIL-M-38510, JAN parts, Class B. When MIL-M-38510 parts are not available, micro-electronics shall be screened in accordance with MIL-STD-883, Methods 5004 and 5005, Class B.

AS. Semiconductors shall be JANTXV devices. Where JANTXV devices are not available, the following order shall take precedence:

1. JANTX.
2. JAN screened to TX level.
3. Non-standard screened to TXV level.

AT. Items adversely affected by electrostatic field forces shall be wrapped in material conforming to MIL-B-81705, Type I or II, cushioned in material conforming to PPP-C-1842, Type III, Style A or B, and unit packaged in

NAME AND ADDRESS OF ORIGINATING COMPANY	QCP NO. QSTP 001
	PAGE NO. 5 OF 5
	ISSUE DATE:
TITLE: QUALITY SPECIFICATIONS TRANSMITTAL DOCUMENT	APPROVED BY:
	REVISION NO: 0
	REVISION DATE:

heat-sealed bags conforming to MIL-B-117, Type I, Class A, Style 2 or Type I, Class F, Style I. Alternatively, reclosable cushioned pouches conforming to MIL-P-81997, Type I or II, may be used in lieu of the initial wrap or cushioning. Non-corrosive conductive materials shall be applied to all exposed leads and connector pins to maintain a common potential. Protective packaging must contain warning labels indicating parts are sensitive to electrostatic discharge. MIL-STD-129, Markings For Sensitive Electronic Items, shall apply.

LIST OF FORMS

INDEX